Developing Effective
User Documentation

D0170847

List of Trademarks

CLICK ART is a registered trademark/product of T/Maker Graphics.

DA VINCI LANDSCAPES is a registered trademark/product of Hayden Publishing Co.

EINSTEINWRITER is a registered trademark/product of Perceptronics, Inc.

FACT CRUNCHER is a registered trademark/product of Infostructures.

FRAMEWORK is a registered trademark/product of Ashton-Tate Co.

FREESTYLE is a registered trademark/product of Select Information Systems.

FULLPAINT is a registered trademark/product of Ann Arbor Softworks.

HARVARD TOTAL PROJECT MANAGER is a registered trademark/product of Software Publishing Corp.

MACDRAFT is a registered trademark/product of Innovative Data Design.

MACINTOSH, MACDRAW, MACPAINT, MACWRITE, and MACPROJECT are registered trademarks/products of Apple Computer Corp.

MACLIGHTNING is a registered trademark/product of Target Software.

MACPUBLISHER (version 1.25) is a registered trademark/product of Boston Publishing Systems.

MAXTHINK is a registered trademark/product of MaxThink, Inc.

MICROPLANNER PLUS is a registered trademark/product of Micro Planning Software.

MICROSOFT FILE, MICROSOFT CHART, MICROSOFT EXCEL, MICROSOFT MULTIPLAN, and MICROSOFT WORD are registered trademarks/products of Microsoft Corp.

PAGEMAKER is a registered trademark/product of Aldus Corp.

PFS:FILE and PFS:WRITE are registered trademarks/products of PFS Corp.

PMS-II is a registered trademark/product of North American MICA Inc.

POST SCRIPT is a registered trademark/product of Adobe Systems.

PRODESIGN II is a registered trademark/product of American Small Business Computers.

PROJECT MANAGER WORKBENCH is a registered trademark/product of Applied Business Technology Corp.

READY is a registered trademark/product of Living Videotext.

READYSETGO is a registered trademark/product of Letraset USA.

SEMANTIC'S Q & A is a registered trademark/product of Semantic Corp.

SOUND PRESENTATIONS is a registered trademark/product of Communication Dynamics, Inc.

SPELLSWELL is a registered trademark/product of Green, Johnson, Inc.

SUPERPAINT is a registered trademark/product of Silicon Beach Software.

THINKTANK is a registered trademark/product of Living Videotext Co.

TIMELINE is a registered trademark/product of Breakthrough Software Corp.

UNIX is a registered trademark/product of Bell Telephone Laboratories, Inc.

VISICALC is a registered trademark/product of Personal Software Inc.

WEBSTER'S NEW WORLD SPELLING CHECKER and WEBSTER'S NEW WORLD ON-LINE THESAURUS are registered trademarks/products of Simon & Schuster.

WINDOWS PAINT is a registered trademark/product of Microsoft Corp.

WORDFINDER is a registered trademark/product of Writing Consultants.

WORDPERFECT is a registered trademark/product of SSI Software.

WORDSTAR is a registered trademark/product of Micro Pro Inc.

XEROX STAR is a registered trademark/product of Xerox.

Developing Effective User Documentation

A Human Factors Approach

Henry Simpson

Steven M. Casey

McGraw-Hill Book Company

New York   St. Louis   San Francisco   Auckland
Bogotá   Hamburg   London   Madrid   Mexico
Milan   Montreal   New Delhi   Panama
Paris   São Paulo   Singapore
Sydney   Tokyo   Toronto

Library of Congress Cataloging-in-Publication Data

Simpson, Henry.
  Developing effective user documentation.

  Bibliography: p.
  Includes index.
  1. Electronic data processing documentation.
  2. Computer software—Development.   I. Casey,
  Steven M. (Steven Michael), 1952–   . II. Title.
  QA76.9.D6S56   1988   005.1'5   87-29690
  ISBN 0-07-057336-0

  234567890   DOC/DOC   921

ISBN 0-07-057336-0

nwst

IADJ 2778

*The editors for this book were Theron Shreve and Marlene
Hamerling, the designer was Naomi Auerbach, and the production
supervisor was Richard Ausburn. This book was set in Century
Schoolbook. It was composed by the McGraw-Hill Book Company
Professional and Reference Division Composition unit. Printed and
bound by R. R. Donnelley and Sons Company.*

Contents

Preface

This book was written for people who want to develop effective user documentation for computer programs. It was written for technical writers, editors, documentation managers, programmers, and others involved in documentation development. User documentation is the hard-copy or on-line documentation provided with an application program. It tells the user how to get the program up and running, trains the user in its operation, and provides reference information once the user becomes experienced. It may do additional things as well—such as help build the user's confidence, entertain, or sell the user on the merits of the program—but these are incidental. The main thing is to allow the user to make the program work.

User documentation comes in many different forms. Most people think of it as the manual that comes with a computer program, usually with a title containing the words "user's guide" or "reference manual." The term also applies to quick reference cards and guides, job performance aids, computer-based tutorials and help screens, keyboard overlays, and anything else that will support the user. The various documentation possibilities are complementary rather than competing alternatives. Each has its strengths and weaknesses. Deciding which types to develop to support an application requires thought and analysis. This book is designed, in part, to help you make the right decisions.

A few words about how this book is unique. First, it deals with user documentation from a human factors, rather than a technical writing, viewpoint. It will help you make decisions concerning what type of documentation your program needs, its content, its format, and how it (like the computer program it supports) should be developed, debugged, evaluated, and refined.

Second, it assumes that you already know how to write; it does not dwell on spelling, punctuation, or grammar. These matters are left to texts on expository or technical writing.

Finally, it shows how you can use the tool whose software you are documenting (the computer) to support the documentation effort. A software revolution has occurred in the last few years, and many of its products—word processors, graphics programs, desktop publishing programs—can make life easier for the documentation developer. Ironically, much of the publishing industry still works with the technology of the past—typewriters, tape, scissors, rubber cement, and so on—and is only slowly beginning to make use of the computer.

This book is divided into 12 chapters. Chapter 1 provides an overview of the various types of user documentation. Chapters 2 and 3 focus on the user and show how to make the "user-documentation match." Chapter 4 describes a systematic process for developing documentation. Chapters 5 and 6 describe tools for management and production during a documentation development project. Chapters 7 through 11 focus on documentation, with discussions of design, architecture, graphics, documentation models, and on-line documentation. Chapter 12 tells how to test, evaluate, and validate documentation.

The best strategy for using this book is to start at the beginning and read straight through to the end. Regardless of the role you play in documentation development—manager, editor, writer, or other interested party—all of the material contained in this book is relevant. It is our sincere hope that it will help you develop better user documentation.

The authors gratefully acknowledge the help of the following software companies for answering questions and providing review software: American Small Business Computers, Ashton-Tate, Breakthrough Software, Communication Dynamics, Computer Associates, Greene-Johnson, Hayden Software, InfoStructures, Innovative Data Design, Lifetree Software, Living Videotext, Manhattan Graphics, MaxThink, Microsoft, North American Mica, Perceptronics, Simon & Schuster, SoftCorp, SSI Software, Symantec, T/Maker Graphics, Target Software, and Writing Consultants. Special thanks to SSI Software, Microsoft Corporation, and Perceptronics for permitting the reproduction of several pages of their documentation. We would also like to thank Dick Noffz, documentation editor, for his helpful commentary. Finally, thanks to the many researchers and authors whose research, analyses, and opinions were incorporated into this book.

Henry Simpson
Steven M. Casey

1

Overview of
User Documentation

This chapter defines terms and presents ideas that will be used throughout the book. The first section briefly discusses the evolution of user documentation. The second section describes some common reasons user documentation fails when put to the test in the real world. The third section discusses three different ways of classifying user documentation—system versus user, procedural versus reference, and internal versus external. The fourth and fifth sections provide an overview of the common forms of user documentation. The sixth section discusses documentation systems—the set of documentation components used to support a program. The final section describes the three elements of documentation design. Incidentally, in this and later chapters the terms "user" and "operator" are used interchangeably; they mean the same thing.

Evolution of User Documentation

User documentation is extremely important. It is accurate to say that, for most programs and users, user documentation will make the difference between whether a program can be used effectively or not. In fact, it is reasonable to go a step further and say that, if the program is not documented properly, it may not be usable at all. It follows from this that it is only sound practice to give as much attention to user documentation as to the program itself. Doing otherwise is perilous.

Awareness of the importance of user documentation has undergone a steady evolution over the years. This is due in large part to the increasing growth of the market for software products, particularly microcomputer software. Software publishers have discovered that programs people can use sell more copies. Good user documentation makes programs usable; ergo, there is more interest in making it good, or at least look good. User documentation is increasingly becoming a selling point for software products.

Precedent and history leave much room for improvement. The documentation provided with most computer programs has not been distinguished by its completeness, quality, or ease of use. In fact, much of it to date has been awful. The situation does appear to be changing, however. In the early days of computers, documentation might be written by an engineer or technician who had little writing skill or understanding of the requirements for communicating with the reader. Thankfully, this era of user documentation—its sort of "Dark Ages"—now seems to be passing. The documentation provided with software products is much better today than it was in the past.

Still, the outlook is not particularly bright. The documentation departments of many firms—if such departments exist at all—have little prestige and even less influence on the engineering departments that create software. Technical writers spend a lot of time running after engineers attempting to obtain information needed to create user documentation. One still sees ads for technical writers followed by the words "experience preferred but not essential." Pay scales leave little doubt why few people major in technical writing in college.

One of the authors once became involved with a trade magazine, the management of which had a similar view of its editorial staff. The publisher was literally incapable of constructing a grammatical sentence, but was a terrific ad salesman and made several times the salary of the magazine's editor. The publisher once explained that management justified the disparity on the basis that many people could write, but few could sell. However unfair, this is sound thinking from a business viewpoint, and also shows how little esteem many people have for those who use the English language and their imaginations to explain technical mysteries to readers. It may not represent the prevailing view of the importance of good technical writing, but it does represent a fairly widely held view. We may take some comfort from the fact that the situation seems to be improving.

For all the optimistic signs, it probably remains true that the writing of user documentation is widely considered to be of less importance than the writing of the software that the documentation describes. The attitude is understandable. Think about it the next time you are flying in a jetliner; ask yourself how important manuals are to pilots, navigators, and mechanics. Likewise, as you are being wheeled into the operating room to have your appendix removed, consider the utility of textbooks describing surgical procedures.

Why Documentation Fails

There are several common reasons the creator of a product may develop poor supporting documentation. As you read, see if you have direct experience with any of these problems on the documentation projects on which you have worked.

A Documentation Editor's Perspective

The documentation editor for a major mainframe computer manufacturer identified four major problems with the user documentation developed within his organization. While the problems he identified are not necessarily universal, they are typical.

First, much user documentation is written at the wrong level. The usual case—especially if documentation is prepared by programmers or other technical professionals—is for it to be too technical, too complex, and to assume too much knowledge on the part of the reader. The opposite—writing material at too simple a level—can also occur but is relatively rare. As emphasized elsewhere in this book, the first step in developing effective user documentation is to have a good understanding of the user and, ideally, to conduct function and task analyses that allow definition of user information requirements (see Chapter 3).

Second, many user documents are actually technical documents. That is, instead of helping the user understand the program and how to use it, they tend to focus on the mechanics of software and the methods by which operations are performed. Often, the document is written in the technical language of its author—and not well suited to the end user. The editor said he spent much of his time modifying such material to suit the needs of the users.

Third, many user documents suffer from the "multiple-author syndrome." The authors of different parts of the document may have contrasting styles, use terms differently, discuss the same topics, cover topics at different depths and breadths, and so forth. Often, working these separate contributions into a unified document requires a major editorial effort (as the authors of the present book are well aware, incidentally). In the best of all possible worlds, a given user document has a single author. Since most of us live in one of the other possible worlds, this ideal is seldom achievable. However, negative consequences of multiple authors can be reduced considerably by adequate planning, outlining, and developing documentation standards (see Chapters 3, 4, 5, and 7).

Fourth, many documents suffer from inconsistent terminology—the practice of describing the same thing with different words. Related to this is the use of the same word to mean different things. These problems occur with single authors but are compounded when multiple authors are involved. Prevention is probably impossible, but effects can be minimized by stressing the use of concrete language, minimizing the use of technical terms, and careful outlining. It is absolutely essential that an editor work through such materials to correct the inconsistencies before the document is released to the world.

Resource Allocation

The most inexcusable reason for poor documentation is the belief on the part of its developer that such documentation is of secondary importance and does not justify the expenditure of the monetary, personnel, and time resources necessary to produce a first-rate product. The developer might follow the line of reasoning that computer programs are complex things and the document user must expect to work hard to learn what is necessary to operate the program successfully. Nothing, of course, is further from the truth. In recent years, as software has reached the mass marketplace and come into the hands of many unsophisticated users, there has been an increasing design emphasis on ease of use. Inadequate documentation undercuts this whole philosophy. Indeed, many a good program has been sunk by poor documentation.

The "Myopia Syndrome"

Related to the problem just cited is the software expert's familiarity with his or her product. This might be termed the "myopia syndrome." Software developers become so familiar with their products that they fail to approach the problems of learning and operating a program from the perspective of the new user. When developers are solely responsible for documentation development and that documentation is not evaluated properly by outside users, the chances are good that the resulting documentation will not be adequate. Common problems are the use of unnecessarily complex language, incomplete coverage of topics, and a tendency to assume that the reader knows more than should be expected. The foregoing is not meant as a condemnation of system developers as documentation developers. The real issue is a frame of mind, which in simple terms amounts to an appreciation that the user comes to a new program with much less knowledge than its developer. This gap must be crossed if documentation is to do its job.

Time

Another common reason for poor user documentation is that it is often developed late in the product development cycle, perhaps even after the software itself has been released (Mosier, 1984). Time is short, deadlines are tight, and the documentation is developed under pressures that mitigate against adequate planning, quality control, user field testing, and other factors important in a documentation development project. The earlier documentation is developed, the better. The converse is also true.

Documentation Development Skills

Quite often, documentation is developed by people who lack the requisite skills for a successful product. It is common to point the finger at programmers and engineers who may, in some cases, produce user documentation themselves or provide the source documentation from which technical writers work. There is an old cliché about engineers not being able to write. One of the authors of this book is an engineer and has heard it often enough. There may be some truth in it, as there is in the notion that all psychologists are a little crazy (the other author of this book is a psychologist), but such sweeping statements really miss the point of why engineers do not usually produce good documentation. They tend to consider — and rightly so— that writing is not their primary function. As is widely acknowledged, they have other primary functions—designing things, debugging them, making them work properly—and writing documentation comes second, if at all. If the engineer has the inclination, time, motivation, and writing skills, he or she may be the ideal author of user documentation.

Who, then, writes the documentation? Technical writers, those "poor, harmless drudges" of the computer industry, as Samuel Johnson might have put it. The skills of these writers vary greatly but, as in most things, you get what you pay for. If you hire cheap, you get the kid with the English degree whose novel was unpublishable, the technician who was unable to move up a rung, or the out-of-date engineer who was unable to hack it in the first profession.

If you are willing to pay for talent, you may hope to find a professional who knows how to put the words together, has an appreciation of documentation as a learning and teaching tool, and who understands that adequate analysis of users and the tasks they must perform underlies all good documentation. In fact, it is fair to say that writing skill, though important, is probably not as important as understanding the last two factors just cited: creating learning and teaching tools, and being able to respond to users' needs in developing documentation.

As a sort of footnote and for whatever it's worth, the acquisitions editor for the publisher of this book, upon receiving the authors' book proposal, remarked that he received many such proposals from people who wanted to write books on how to prepare user documentation and that most of them were badly written. The point is not that we had written such a great proposal—it went through three revisions before finally being accepted—but that so many folks who ply the writing trade aren't good writers. If there's a message there, it's a disquieting one.

Obsolescence

Documentation often fails because it becomes outdated. Printed documentation may be difficult to modify or update because of structure or layout, or because of the way it is generated physically. As we all know, no one uses typewriters, editor's scissors, rubber cement, and such any more for creating and editing documents. (Of course not!) These are outdated techniques that make it terribly inefficient and time-consuming to create and edit documentation. Now we have the word-processing program, along with various automated production tools, graphics packages, and other software, to make the developer's life easier. However, not everyone has yet gotten the word.

To give an actual example, one of the authors recently visited a two-year-old computer company that is developing a very advanced minisupercomputer. An outside consultant had determined that at least 20 separate documents would be required to support this new computer. These included installation manuals, hardware manuals, user's guides for various programming languages, and so forth. The company's documentation manager (actually, the marketing director) planned to hire a team of technical writers and to have them produce text on microcomputers using a popular word-processing program, have the copy typeset, have the artwork produced by a consultant, and then have the documents offset-printed by a contractor. (Incidentally, the word-processing program, which shall remain nameless, is one of the most popular ones, also widely acknowledged to be nonintuitive, difficult to use, and to take a long time to master. Like lemmings, a lot of people continue to use it— presumably, because a lot of other people continue to use it. See Chapter 6 for an in-depth discussion of word-processing software.)

The proposed documentation development method is a great improvement over using typewriters and such. Still, it presents problems in terms of updating because so many separate parties are involved in document production. It would make much more sense to use a desktop publishing program and to produce all documentation in house. But that, as they say, is a new idea in the documentation world. The irony of the situation is that the system being documented is one of the most advanced on the drawing board. (Desktop publishing is discussed in detail in Chapter 6.)

Documentation Development Process

Perhaps the most common reason for poor documentation is the failure to spend the necessary time and funds on the documentation development process (Hendricks, Kilduff, Brooks, & Marshak, 1982) (Figure 1.1). Too often a piece of documentation—for example, a user's manual—is thought of in isolation and regarded as the product solely

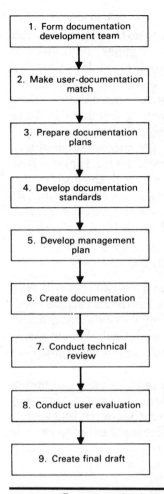

Figure 1.1   Documentation is most effective when developed systematically, according to a well-thought-out documentation development process.

of writing. To develop proper documentation, considerable front-end work is required beforehand; writing should be the last thing done. Documentation objectives must be defined. A documentation plan must be developed. The types of documentation for the project must be chosen. The various user groups must be specified, and documentation must be tailored to satisfy their needs. All of these things should be done before the writing begins, and all too often they are not. In short, the documentation development process entails more than writing. Chapters 3 and 4 discuss the documentation development process in detail; Chapter 2 discusses users.

Documentation developers often fail to assess the needs of users before developing documentation and may fail to do the other front-end analyses required before putting pen squib to paper (or fingers to keyboard). Typically, they are not willing or able to expend the time and funds needed to develop and maintain good documentation. Documentation developers must realize that their task entails more than writing. More importantly, those responsible for allocating resources to documentation development projects must understand the process themselves and allocate the resources necessary for successful products. Without this appreciation, the documentation will be inadequate. Poor documentation influences the user's perception of both the documentation and the software being documented. Write a bad manual, and its user is liable to throw both it and the software out the window or, more likely, send them back to the manufacturer for a refund.

Documentation Systems

The larger and more complex the program, the more likely it will need several separate documentation components to fulfill the various needs of its audience. The documentation developer must decide what components are needed and the function to be fulfilled by each (Hendricks, et al., 1982; Mosier, 1984). Together, the various components comprise a documentation system (Figure 1.2).

A documentation system is a system in the same sense as any other type of system—including a computer system. A system, formally defined, is a set of interdependent components that work together to achieve a goal. (Documentation systems are discussed in detail later in

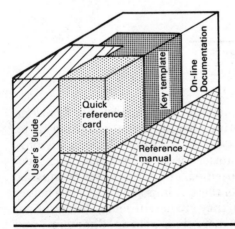

Figure 1.2 A documentation system is a set of interdependent documentation components, each with an assigned role.

this chapter.) Documentation developers frequently fail to recognize the separate roles and interdependent nature of the various document components they develop. For example, they may fail to identify certain components needed for a product or assume that a particular type of document will fulfill the needs of another. For example, it is quite common to open a new software package and discover that the documentation consists of a reference manual—without a tutorial, quick-reference material, or other documentation components needed to learn how to use the program and use it efficiently once the learning phase is over. Obviously, making this mistake can have serious consequences.

Some Ways to Classify User Documentation

This section distinguishes between system and user documentation, procedural and reference documentation, and internal and external documentation.

System Versus User Documentation

There are two classes of program documentation (Figure 1.3). The first is documentation intended for the programmers who create, maintain, troubleshoot, and update an existing program. This documentation consists of such elements as program listings; tables of variables, functions, and procedures; written explanations of parts of the program; and remarks in program code. This documentation is prepared by the program's authors and maintainers and is referred to as "system documentation." Beyond the description just given, this book does not discuss system documentation.

The second type of documentation is "user documentation." This may be in written or other forms. It may be provided outside the program, appear within the program, or be a combination of both. Such documen-

	System documentation	User documentation
For:	Programmers	Users
Purpose:	Design	Operation
	Maintenance	
	Troubleshooting	
	Updating	
Contents:	Program listings	Program explanation
	Tables of variables, functions, procedures	Program operation
	Written explanations	Reference information
	Remarks in code	

Figure 1.3   The audience for, purpose of, and contents of system and user documentation differ.

tation must explain the program, initiate the new user, and provide the reference information the experienced user needs. This type of documentation is the subject of this book.

Procedural Versus Reference Documentation

Psychologists commonly distinguish between procedural and declarative knowledge. Procedural knowledge is knowledge of how to do things —for example, to ride a bicycle. Declarative knowledge is knowledge about things—for example, that bicycles are ridden with the hands on the handlebars, feet on the pedals, and that centrifugal force plays a role. Declarative knowledge is usually a prerequisite to procedural knowledge, but not vice versa. For example, it is important to know about bicycles before attempting to ride one, but such knowledge does not guarantee that one will be able to ride successfully. As we all know, one cannot learn to cook, box, or perform open-heart surgery simply by reading a book; the activity must be practiced until the skills are "in the hands." It is possible for procedural knowledge to exist in the absence of complete declarative knowledge; this is demonstrated by musicians who play by ear, politicians who write legislation on complex issues, and engineering managers who lack detailed technical knowledge.

For all these technicalities, the important point is that a program user must master more than facts to operate a computer program successfully. Facts form the foundation, but procedures tell how actually to do things. User documentation provides the necessary facts in the form of reference information—in reference manuals, guides, or quick reference cards. Procedural information, if provided, usually appears in tutorials or descriptions of procedures in a user's guide.

There is a problem. It is common for user documentation to cover facts adequately but to overlook procedural information. The reasons for this oversight are debatable but probably reduce to ignorance by authors of the importance of procedural information. It is quite understandable that such ignorance should exist. People who learn to do things often forget how they learned them and have difficulty explaining how to do them. (Have you ever seen a description of how to ride a bicycle, pilot an airplane, or play the piano?) Thus, it may seem to the skilled person that the essentials reduce to a set of easily explainable facts. Clearly, there is much more to the matter, and the procedures—however difficult they are to describe—need to be explained. Fortunately, the procedures for operating most computer programs can be laid out in simple step-by-step fashion and don't pose the difficulty of explanation of complex skills. Put another way, how to work *Microsoft Multiplan* isn't as hard to describe as how to play a Beethoven piano sonata.

Internal Versus External Documentation

User documentation comes in two forms: internal and external. Internal (or "on-line") documentation consists of help screens, directions, and other explanatory information that the operator can access within the program. To use this documentation, the program must be up and running. External documentation is outside the program itself. Its most common form is the user's guide, although it comes in several other written forms as well as nonwritten forms, such as audiocassette and videotape.

The common purpose of all documentation. All user documentation has the same purpose: to explain the features of the program and help the operator gain proficiency in using it. While the purpose of internal and external documentation is the same, each has unique strengths and limitations and is more suited to certain things than the other. The two documentation approaches should be considered complementary rather than competing alternatives.

Internal Documentation. Internal documentation is best used to aid the operator's memory concerning procedures (e.g., how to open a new file) and program vocabulary (e.g., the commands required for text formatting with a word processor). The small text window and memory overhead of internal documentation combine to make it a poor candidate for presenting a lot of detail. However, there is no question but that it is useful for the operator to be able to access detailed information concerning procedures and program vocabulary while using the program.

Figures 1.4, 1.5, and 1.6 illustrate three screens containing internal documentation. Each is accessed, at operator request, within the program. Figure 1.4 is a set of directions describing the procedure of creating a new file. Figure 1.5 contains a summary of text-formatting commands for use in a word-processing program. Figure 1.6 contains guidelines for interpreting the results produced by a stock analysis program. These examples illustrate the type of information that internal documentation is best suited to present.

More has been and can be done with internal documentation, but the cost-effectiveness of such efforts must be examined critically. And while we are on the subject of cost, it is important to warn against a total preoccupation with it in creating user documentation. To illustrate one example, many software publishers disseminate user documentation exclusively on floppy disk, without using paper documentation at all. Essentially, they generate the text of their manuals and publish it on disk instead of on paper. The argument is made that doing it this way makes

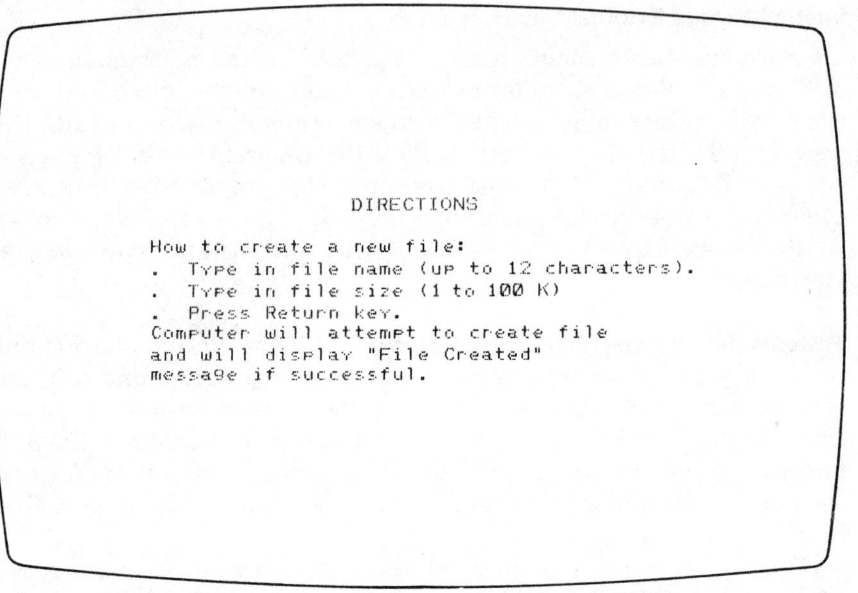

```
                    DIRECTIONS

How to create a new file:
.    Type in file name (up to 12 characters).
.    Type in file size (1 to 100 K)
.    Press Return key.
Computer will attempt to create file
and will display "File Created"
message if successful.
```

Figure 1.4 An example of internal documentation—a help screen. The screen, presented when the operator asks for help, gives the procedure for creating a new file. (*From Simpson*, Design of User-Friendly Programs for Small Computers, *McGraw-Hill, New York, 1985.*)

it easier to circulate corrections and updates, which is certainly true, but one suspects that the real reason for doing things this way is cost. Clearly, a manual on disk is not as easy for the user to work with as one on paper that sits solidly, tangibly on a desk, albeit the disk version is more up to date, accurate, or whatever. The truth is that manuals on disk are an internal form of external documentation (if there is such a thing), and an illegitimate form (to put it kindly) at best.

To justify its existence, internal documentation needs to be something more or do something better than external documentation.

External documentation.   Although some people regard the printed word on paper as outdated and science fiction writers have explored the possibility of a world without writing, we should not anticipate the imminent demise of either. In a short story a few years ago, Isaac Asimov described a new information medium that was compact, portable, required no external power, had impressive storage capability, and was capable of nearly instantaneous random access to any part. Viewed from this perspective, books—which are what Asimov was opening the reader's eyes to—don't seem "low-tech" at all. Nearly all of us could get along more successfully in a world without computers and software than in one without books. By extension it follows that we could sooner get along without internal documentation than without external documentation.

Asimov was right. The fact is that a written manual is an excellent medium for storing and accessing information. True, it is not as fast or as flashy as a computer, but it is a lot easier to turn book pages than to page through computer screens. Moreover, the manual allows you to do such wonders as stick fingers into separate pages and flip back and forth between them.

The internal versus external documentation trade-off.   The relative advantages of internal versus external documentation have been considered in various forums. What follows is a brief discussion based on formal analyses. These analyses suggest that external documentation has the edge.

External documentation has certain inherent advantages over internal documentation. The advantages exist provided the documentation is in hard-copy form and immediately accessible—as opposed to being on some secondary medium, such as microfiche or videotape. Paper manuals can be read at work, on airplanes, at home, or any other place

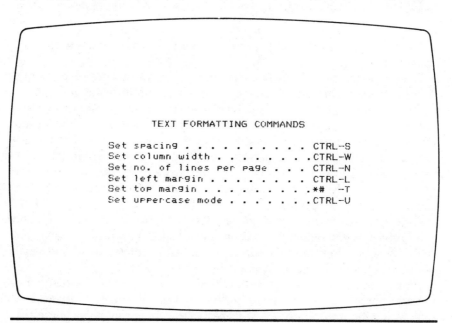

Figure 1.5   Another help screen. This one provides reference information needed for formatting text in a word-processing program. (*From Simpson,* Design of User-Friendly Programs for Small Computers, *McGraw-Hill, New York, 1985.*)

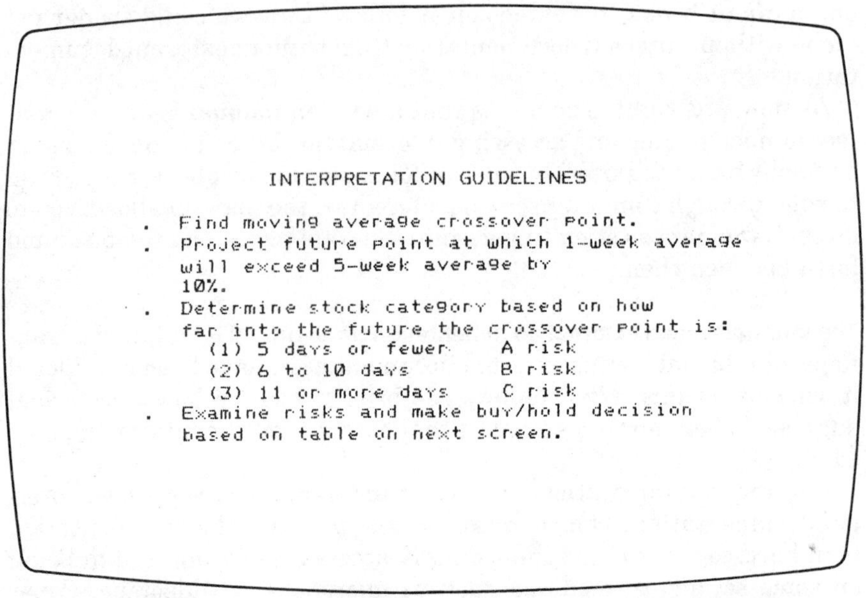

```
INTERPRETATION GUIDELINES

  .  Find moving average crossover point.
  .  Project future point at which 1-week average
     will exceed 5-week average by
     10%.
  .  Determine stock category based on how
     far into the future the crossover point is:
        (1) 5 days or fewer    A risk
        (2) 6 to 10 days       B risk
        (3) 11 or more days    C risk
  .  Examine risks and make buy/hold decision
     based on table on next screen.
```

Figure 1.6   A third example of internal documentation. This screen, accessed when requested, gives guidelines for interpreting the graphs of price moving averages in a stock market analysis program. (*From Simpson*, Design of User-Friendly Programs for Small Computers, *McGraw-Hill Book, New York, 1985.*)

with light, for that matter. It is not necessary to have access to the software, a computer, or electricity.

External documentation is usually superior to internal documentation for quick-reference purposes. Paging through internal documentation or attempting to locate the proper entry point via menus or other means can be a time-consuming process. One can leaf through a manual much more quickly. For the same reason, external documentation is much more suitable for browsing. The reader can acquire much information serendipitously simply by leafing through the manual. A reader can flip through pages and acquire the gist of page and document content with a few glances.

External documentation supports user orientation much more effectively than internal documentation. You can tell how far you have gone and how much remains based on the relative thickness of the pages before and after the current reading point.

Paper documentation can be modified by the user. The user can write margin notes, use bookmarks, highlight items of interest, insert new pages, or even tear pages out. (Interestingly, this property is beginning to find its way into internal documentation, some of which now allows the user to insert the electronic equivalent of stick-on labels within the electronic document.) Finally, external documentation has the weight of history on its side. It is the standard and familiar method for literate people to access information. People have experience with it, feel comfortable with it, and have developed fairly sophisticated skills and shortcuts for using it.

There is another side to this picture, however. If designed properly, internal documentation can provide information very quickly. The user often requires help while on line with the computer. If the information is available within the program, the user does not have to look it up in the manual or, perhaps, get up and go find the manual. On-line documentation, as it is stored magnetically, can be updated very quickly. Thus, the program's manufacturer does not have to print and distribute revisions to existing manuals. It is simply a matter of sending a diskette or other appropriate magnetic storage medium. On-line documentation eliminates the need for distribution and filing. A printed manual weighs considerably more than a diskette, and large manuals may be unwieldy. Finally, preparation, modification, and production of on-line documentation is certainly less expensive than for hard-copy documentation.

The available data indicate that on-line and hard-copy documentation are both superior to optically based documentation, particularly fiche (Judisch, Rupp, & Dassinger, 1981). The authors just cited conducted a study to assess the effectiveness of (a) fiche versus hard copy and (b) standard text presentations and augmented graphics formats in a repair task. Results indicated that the cost savings of fiche (compared to hard copy) were outweighed by the reduction in technician performance associated with fiche. In this particular study, there was a 5.3 percent difference between hard-copy graphic manuals and fiche-based graphic manuals, and a 5.1 percent difference between nongraphic hard copy and nongraphic fiche-based manuals. The conclusions were that both graphics and hard copy improved performance.

"Intelligent" internal documentation.   Do we actually need internal documentation? We probably need it less than external documentation, but it can come in very handy and can do some things that external documentation, because it is passive, cannot. The most basic form of internal documentation—summaries of program procedures and vocabulary—is also passive, but justified because of its low overhead within the program. It does not capitalize on any unique capabilities of the computer as compared to words printed on paper. However, the computer has the potential to show some responsiveness, adaptation, or intelligence to the user, and in that sense it has a capability that the manual does not.

Consider that it is possible, in principle, to build "intelligence" into a program and thereby help the user obtain the type and amount of documentation support needed in a given operating context. The intelligence, as such, may range from marginal to considerable, depending upon the amount of effort the program developer wants to expend.

An example of marginal intelligence is the program's ability to select and present help screens based upon the current state of the program. For example, if the user issues a help command while using the program's text editor, the program has the smarts to note that the editor is being used and to select a help screen on that topic.

At the other end of the intelligence scale is the program's ability to track program state and user inputs, keep track of errors, determine that the operator is having problems, and to offer a specific type of help without being asked. Here the program continuously looks over the operator's shoulder like a kindly, solicitous servant and offers help when it senses the operator getting into trouble. Writing software that can do this sort of thing may require techniques taken from artificial intelligence and be quite costly. Moreover, this degree of helpfulness is probably not necessary in most programs, but it charts the limit. (Actually, a further limit was suggested by Douglas Adams in *The Hitchhiker's Guide to the Galaxy* [1979], a future world in which some androids got on a lot of people's nerves by sounding too much like overly helpful and overwrought parents.)

The basic idea is that software can respond to the user, but printed paper cannot. The test of whether internal documentation is being used properly and is justified is whether or not it is capitalizing on what computers can do that printed pages cannot. It is clear that some forms of "internal" documentation, such as the disk-based manual, fail the test. Moreover, the native "intelligence" of a disk-based manual falls well below "idiot" on the measurement scale.

External Documentation

The most common forms of external documentation probably are the program user's guide, reference manual, quick reference card, quick reference guide, and job performance aid (JPA). These generic types take several different forms, and there is no universal formula for writing one. Moreover, the user's guide and reference manual usually contain more than one type of information, and distinctions are of the loose rather than strict type. Let us ignore these complications and consider the "typical" version of each genre.

User's guides usually contain a mixture of factual and procedural information and are designed to help the user develop both declarative and procedural knowledge. Reference manuals, quick reference cards, and reference guides usually contain factual reference information and not procedures. Job performance aids focus on procedural information.

While these distinctions generally hold, exceptions are common and probably desirable. As noted earlier, user documentation tends to underemphasize procedures; it is desirable to develop reference documentation—manuals, cards, guides—that provides greater coverage of them.

User's Guide

The following is a description of a user's guide (Figure 1.7) that might be prepared for use in a serious, everyday application, such as a word processor, database management system, or budget management and analysis program. The user's guide is often designed to work at two levels: tutorial and reference.

The tutorial guides new users until they gain the basic skills and confidence they need to operate the program effectively. The tutorial is written based on the premise that the reader knows nothing about the program; it may also assume that the reader knows nothing about computers or about the technical area of the program itself. It provides a step-by-step description of the procedure for using the program and tells the user what keys to press and characters to type to make things happen; the magic word is "interactive." The tutorial is seldom comprehensive, but it covers enough of the program's features to enable the user to develop basic operating skills. Once the user has developed these skills, the tutorial is no longer needed.

Reference information is the factual data the user needs to use the

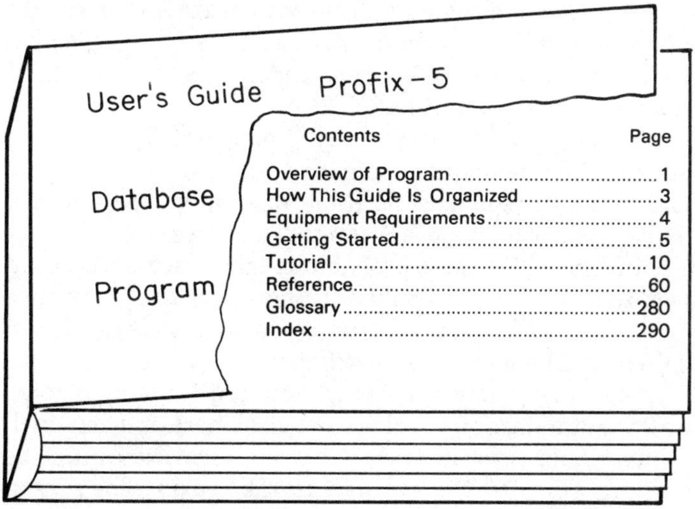

User's Guide   Profix - 5

Database

Program

Contents	Page
Overview of Program	1
How This Guide Is Organized	3
Equipment Requirements	4
Getting Started	5
Tutorial	10
Reference	60
Glossary	280
Index	290

Figure 1.7 A program user's guide usually provides both tutorial and reference information, as well as other introductory information.

program effectively. It concerns every aspect of the program about which the user needs to know. For example, it would include such things as detailed descriptions of the procedures for opening files and using the text editor, function key definitions, and a list of key words and their definitions. Reference information is (or attempts to be) comprehensive. The user should be able to go to it to obtain the answer to any technical question about the program. Unlike the tutorial, it assumes that the user does know about the program and has basic operating skills.

In addition to these two elements, user's guides often contain additional information and features. It is fairly common to include an introduction that provides an overview of the program and explains how the guide is organized and is to be used. Also common is a section describing equipment requirements and giving directions for setting up the program according the user's particular equipment configuration. (Recommendations concerning the content of user's guides are given in Chapter 7; model guides are presented in Chapter 10.)

Reference Manual

Reference manuals serve much the same purpose as the reference information in a user's guide, as just described. A reference manual is seldom provided with an application program, although it is quite common if the user is expected to perform programming. For example, reference manuals are commonly provided for operating systems such as Microsoft DOS (MS-DOS); programming languages such as BASIC or Pascal; and for application programs with their own special languages, e.g., a word-processing language such as WPL or a database management language, such as that used with *dBASE III.*

The more complex the application, the more important the reference manual. Regrettably, it is common for software publishers to provide a reference manual in the guise of a user's guide, or simply to publish the reference manual alone, without a user's guide. There are several possible reasons for doing this. The most probable is ignorance of the need for a proper user's guide. Too, the publisher may feel that reference information—provided in a reference manual—is all that is needed to use the program. The publisher may be justified in providing a reference manual alone for certain widely used programming languages (e.g., BASIC, C, Pascal) the standards for which exist elsewhere and for which there are many available tutorial texts. This justification cannot be extended to programs aimed at the average user, however. The reason is simple and obvious: reference manuals are not designed to help the user learn, but to provide reference information. To learn, the user needs a tutorial, as well as other introductory documentation.

Quick Reference Card

The quick reference card provides the user with a small amount of key, quick- reference information in convenient form that can be used apart from more comprehensive documentation (Figure 1.8). A common use is to provide a list of key commands or codes for use in a word-processing program. When the publisher does not provide such information, thoughtful users often make up their own quick reference cards containing the required information. (Programmers are notorious for doing this sort of thing and often keep stacks of cards or small pieces of paper beside their computer to keep track of ASCII code conversions, subroutine labels, and other factual information necessary during programming.) The reference information is provided on a single card that may be placed near the computer and referred to as needed.

Another form of quick reference card is the keyboard overlay (Figure 1.9), which provides labels for keys (such as function keys) that work in ways unique to the application.

Quick reference cards are often provided as tearouts within a user's

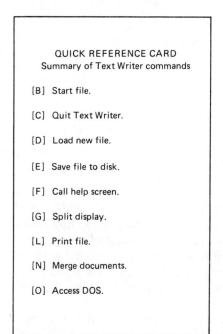

Figure 1.8   An example of a quick reference card. This card contains key reference information important for use during the program. (*From Simpson*, Design of User-Friendly Programs for Small Computers, *McGraw-Hill, New York, 1985.*)

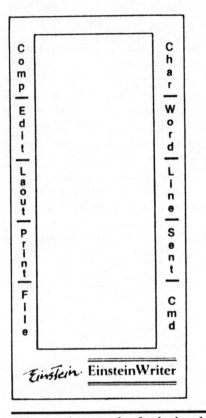

Figure 1.9 An example of a keyboard overlay. This one is for the functions keys on the IBM PC and is provided with the *EinsteinWriter* word processing program. (*Courtesy of Perceptronics, Inc.*)

guide. One or more cards may be provided with a program, although if a large number of cards are used, their purpose—to provide key information in compact form—is defeated. If a large amount of quick-reference information is needed, the sensible alternative to several cards is to prepare a separate quick reference guide (see next section). Ideally, a program uses one or, at the most, a half dozen or so, quick reference cards.

As the quick reference card is compact, it is reasonable to incorporate it as a form of within-program documentation. For example, quick-reference information can usually be provided as a help screen that the user calls from within the program by typing in a standard help call, such as the Control-? key combination. The help information then appears on the screen, temporarily displacing the current display or perhaps appearing in a separate window (Figure 1.10). The advantage is that the user does not have to keep track of a separate card or risk losing it beneath the other debris on the desk. The disadvantage is that display of the quick-reference information will disrupt the current computer display. Of course, there is nothing to preclude providing the information in both forms, and this is probably the best option.

Quick Reference Guide

The quick reference guide is a small booklet containing selected reference information (Figure 1.11). It is like a bound set of quick reference cards. The guide may also be thought of as a cross between a reference manual and a quick reference card. It contains more than a card but less than a manual. An example is the quick reference guide for the MS-DOS version of the *Microsoft Multiplan* spreadsheet program, a guide about 20 pages in length summarizing keyboard commands and describing menu options, formulas, functions, and error conditions.

Why not use a reference manual instead? In most cases, a reference manual could be used in place of either a quick reference card or guide, but would not be as convenient. These three forms of reference information—manual, guide, and card—are all based on the reference manual

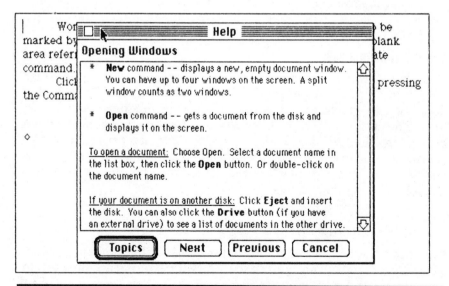

Figure 1.10 Help information provided in a separate window. This example is a help screen provided with the Macintosh version of *Microsoft Word.* (*Courtesy of Microsoft Corporation.*)

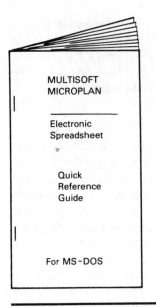

MULTISOFT
MICROPLAN

Electronic
Spreadsheet

Quick
Reference
Guide

For MS-DOS

Figure 1.11 A quick reference guide is a small booklet containing selected quick reference information, and is like a bound set of quick reference cards.

but represent various degrees of information selection and condensation. Most programs need a reference manual and some need cards or guides.

Job Performance Aid

The job performance aid is the procedural equivalent of the quick reference card or guide. An example of a JPA is shown in Figure 1.12. It describes the procedure for performing a task in simple step-by-step form. The user places the JPA beside the computer and refers to it while performing the task. It is both a learning tool and a performance tool. It is used while learning the task and may be referred to later on. Eventually, when the user masters the procedure, the JPA is no longer needed and may be put away.

Internal Documentation

The most common forms of internal documentation probably are the help screen, tutorial, and guided tour. As with external documentation, the generic types of internal documentation take several different forms, and there are no universal formulas for design.

Help screens may contain anything—reference information, procedures, or both—although they are usually brief. Organized groups of help screens, which are sometimes referred to as "help menus," permit the user to access several pages of related help screens in a systematic way. Tutorials attempt to involve the user in hands-on interaction with the program and tend to emphasize procedures. Guided tours are noninteractive and usually attempt to provide overview-type factual information to familiarize the user with the general features of a program. While these distinctions usually hold, exceptions are common and probably desirable.

Internal documentation may be accessed in many possible ways. Perhaps the most common is to type in a universal help command (such as Ctrl-?) through the keyboard. A menu-driven program may offer a help option. These two possibilities make help information available whenever commands can be issued or a menu is on the screen; at other times, help is unavailable.

Alternatively, the dedicated function key or "desk accessory" approach makes help information always available. A dedicated func-

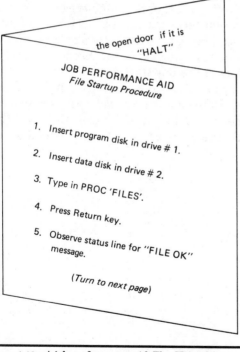

Figure 1.12 A job performance aid. The JPA is like a quick reference card, but it describes the steps in a procedure. (*From Simpson*, Design of User-Friendly Programs for Small Computers, *McGraw-Hill, New York, 1985.*)

tion key may be pressed to access help; this can happen at any time. This is also possible with the desk accessory approach, which is typified by miniapplications such as the Apple Macintosh Apple menu (Figure 1.13) or the options available on programs such as Borland's *Sidekick*. These miniapplications can be activated without terminating the ongoing program and permit the user to access them, perform any function they offer, and then return to the main application where it last left off. It has become standard practice in the case of the Macintosh, at least, to title one of the options on the Apple menu "About [application name]..."; selecting this option causes a series of help screens to be presented.

An additional alternative, already discussed, is to provide an intelligent help feature which, solicited or not, provides help information to the user when difficulties arise.

Help Screens and Help Menus

A help screen is a single screen of information that explains something (see Figures 1.4, 1.5, and 1.6). It may contain the same type of information as a quick reference card or job performance aid. Such redundancy is, in fact, desirable. A help screen may extend to a second or third screen through paging, if necessary, although beyond about three screens it is probably better to rely on external documentation.

Help menus are another way of presenting more help information than will fit onto a single screen. Help menus consist of a network of help screens, accessible through menus, and permit the user to locate the help information desired, much like using a table of contents in a book.

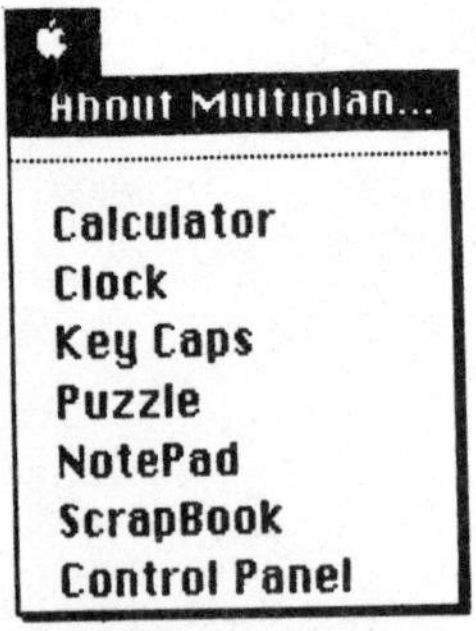

Figure 1.13 The first option on the Apple menu on most Macintosh applications can be used to access help information while using the application. This example, from *Microsoft Multiplan*, is no exception. (*Courtesy of Microsoft Corporation.*)

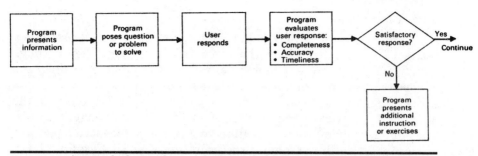

Figure 1.14 A properly designed tutorial presents information, requires the user to respond, evaluates responses, and, when the user responds incorrectly, provides additional instruction and exercises tailored to the individual user.

Interactive Tutorial

A tutorial is an instructional program that forces the user to interact with the computer and thereby learn (Figure 1.14). A proper tutorial presents information, calls for a response from the user, evaluates that response, and then takes the next step based on the completeness and accuracy of the user's response. If the user responds correctly, the instruction proceeds to the next step. If the user makes an error, the tutorial determines the nature of the error and provides appropriate additional instruction or exercises before continuing.

Desirable qualities of tutorials are interactiveness and responsiveness (Figure 1.15). That is, the program must adjust its instruction, testing, and review based on the user's response. A program which does not do these things may be instructional, but is not truly a tutorial. A page-turning exercise, for example, is not a tutorial. Neither is a program that bounces the user back to the question missed repeatedly until the correct answer is finally selected.

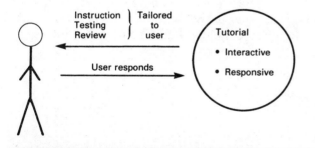

Figure 1.15 A properly tailored tutorial is both interactive and responsive: It adjusts instruction, testing, and review based on the user's responses. It is more than a page-turning exercise, and it does more than simply reroute the user to the beginning of the lesson if an error is made.

Guided Tour

A guided tour is like a movie that tells about a program. It presents a series of screens, paced by the computer or by user signals (e.g., keypresses), that present high-level information about the program. Guided tours are not interactive and are not designed to teach hands-on skills (Figure 1.16). However, they may be very effective in giving the user the "big picture" about a program and for filling in factual details. The similarity to movies is useful to keep in mind, for motion pictures are useful for much the same purposes in education as are guided tours for learning about computer programs.

The most visible guided tours currently are those written for the Macintosh computer. The tours are provided to Macintosh purchasers in the form of audiocassette and diskette. The implementation is an animated computer demonstration of program features, accompanied by a time-synchronized tape narration that explains what is going on. To set things in motion, the user turns on the cassette, inserts the diskette into the computer, and uses an audio cue in the program to start the tape. Tape and computer video then present a series of animated screens which are explained by a narrator; drama is heightened, some believe, by the musical score in the background (although others just find it distracting). Apple's guided tours to the *MacWrite* and *MacPaint* programs are very good, and other software manufacturers have mimicked the approach in their own tours. Each of Apple's tours is fairly short (about 15 minutes), has a fairly slow pace, and limits the presentation to high points.

Guided tours are very good for illustrating program features dynamically, although they seldom permit interaction with the viewer. Moreover, not all guided tours are as good as Apple's. This is probably because not everyone understands the ground rules for creating a good tour. For example, the manufacturer of one Macintosh database program provides a 60-minute tour of the features of its program that presents so much screen activity so rapidly that it is simply bewildering.

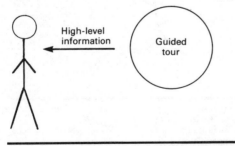

Figure 1.16 A guided tour, though instructional in nature, is noninteractive and not intended to teach hands-on skills. It is most effective for presenting "big picture"–type information.

Windows open on windows, icons move, and screens shrink and expand every few seconds. Meanwhile, the confident voice of the narrator, supported by an insistent, rhythmic musical score, explains what is going on as if it were as simple as walking to the corner. Simpler content and better pacing are necessary to get the message across—also an awareness that the human attention span is limited.

But even if a guided tour can be constructed, it is not usually the best way to educate the user. The main reason is the requirement for everything to proceed by the clock. This mitigates against letting the user try things, get feedback, and learn. In sum, guided tours may be good for giving the user the "big picture," but are not really instructional programs.

Documentation Systems

A system is a set of interdependent elements that work together to achieve a goal (Figure 1.17). For example, in a computer system these

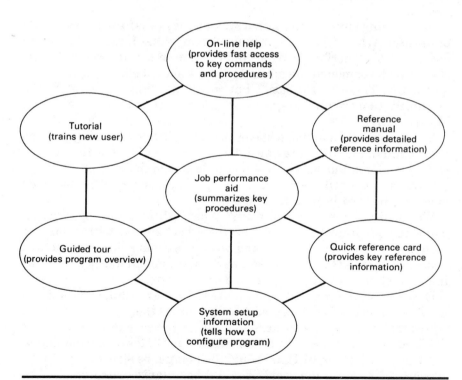

Figure 1.17 A documentation system is a set of interdependent documentation components designed to support the user in learning and using the program. The various components have different purposes and support this goal in different ways, but all, in one way or another, support the ultimate goal.

elements consist of central processing unit, memory, video display, storage media, and so forth. Likewise, a documentation system consists of a set of documentation elements such as program overview, tutorial, procedural descriptions, quick reference guide, and help screens. Various other documentation systems might also be devised, depending upon (1) the particular application, (2) the needs of users, and (3) the operating environment (more on this in Chapter 3).

A system is (or should be) designed to meet the needs of its users. Different computer users often configure their computer systems in different ways by using different amounts of memory, types of peripherals, coprocessors, and so forth. Likewise, it is nonsensical to expect a single type of documentation to be appropriate for every application, user, and operating environment. However obvious this might seem to us, the point is often ignored or simply overlooked. To many, user documentation simply means a program user's guide. We who develop documentation should be thinking in terms of documentation systems, not the components of those systems such as the user's guide, reference manual, help screen, or any other single documentation element.

In designing any documentation system, the key is to define the needs of the user. Who will use the documentation? What functions must the documentation perform? What information must it provide? How should each component be formatted? How should each component be structured? These are the basic—but not all that simple—questions the documentation system designer must address (Hendricks, et al., 1982; Mosier, 1984).

In developing a manual, some of the possibilities are straight reference manual, a source of review information, a self-instructional tutorial, or a manual designed to support classroom instruction. Perhaps several manuals will be required and, perhaps, some of the functions may be combined in a single manual.

Who will use the documentation? What will be their objectives in using the program? What will be their background with computer systems, with other software, and with programs similar to the one being documented? Will they use a particular manual independently or in conjunction with other program documentation?

How should the manual be formatted? How are similar documents used? Are there widely accepted conventions for the documentation as, for example, in the case of the Macintosh? What physical properties of the document are important for its effective use? How is the manual to be updated and revised? How should the manual be structured so as to support the needs of the user? Should it be organized according to the tasks the user will perform, on the basis of program functions, or in some other meaningful way? How can the information be presented in the most direct and simplest way possible?

The foregoing are some of the questions that must be addressed while designing and developing documentation systems. No answers are offered here, for these are subjects covered later in this book. But the questions are important, and the documentation system designer and developer must be aware of them and address them systematically.

Several documentation elements and their characteristics were discussed in this chapter. The list includes both external and internal documentation and procedural and reference information. Included in the list of external documentation are the user's guide, which commonly contains background, procedural, and reference information, and which may contain a tutorial; reference information in the form of the reference manual, reference guide, and quick reference card; and the job performance aid.

Of these elements, the user's guide is the most eclectic and may also include information that would be present in the form of reference information or job performance aids. The three forms of reference information are redundant and overlapping—variant forms of the same source documentation that are refined and condensed to various degrees for more convenient use. Reference information may include procedures, but the job performance aid deals strictly with procedures. Included in the list of internal documentation are the help screen, which contains a single screen of reference or procedural information; help menus, which are organized sets of help screens; and guided tours, which present an animated demonstration of program features.

The Three Elements of Documentation Design

Bailey, an authority on computer operators and the sources of operator errors, estimates that 10 percent of all operator errors are attributable in one way or another to written documentation (Bailey, 1983). This is a rough estimate and does not reflect the costs of wasted time, idle computer equipment, or the resulting frustration of the user. Undoubtedly, the immediate costs of poor documentation are considerable. Most operators have undergone time-consuming and frustrating experiences while using documentation for such tasks as learning how to use a program, attempting to find the answer to a straightforward question, or determining the cause of an error condition.

The problem can be attributable to one or more of several different causes. Among the possibilities are inappropriate physical structure and layout, a mismatch between the user's information requirements and the document's technical content, poor instructional design of tutorials, physical characteristics of type and page design, and the quality of pictorial and written text. These are only a few of the things that may be wrong with the document; the list of possible problems is much longer. But if all these things may be wrong, what does it take to create "good" documentation?

The simple answer is threefold. The most important factors in good document design are (1) orderly development of ideas, (2) technical accuracy and completeness, and (3) logical arrangement of information (Figure 1.18). Ideas and information should not be transformed into a document until user requirements have been identified and the objectives of the documentation have been specified. The user must know where he or she is headed, and ideas must be conveyed in the most direct fashion possible. Documents must be technically accurate and up to date. The physical structure and arrangement of the pages, sections, and the overall structure of the product can have a major impact on both the short- and long-term utility of the document.

Research conducted by Bethke (1983) of IBM illustrates the importance of the three fundamentals of documentation design just described. Bethke evaluated several user documents by gathering follow-up data from users and found a clear relationship among the three factors and users' ratings of document utility. Documentation adhering to the three factors was rated higher in utility than documentation not adhering to the factors.

Second, Bethke found that the factors influenced user's perceptions of the difficulty of the software being used. When software is accompanied by poor documentation, users are more likely to rate the software—as well as its documentation—as being difficult to use. This evidence—as well as common sense—suggests that the software developer should provide the best documentation possible within the resource constraints

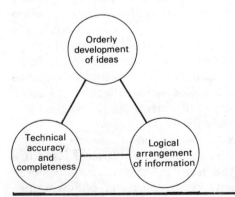

Figure 1.18 The three most important factors in good documentation design.

of the project. Cutting corners in this area is detrimental not only to user effectiveness but may well degrade the user's perception of the software product. The selection and use of these documentation elements is discussed in greater detail in Chapters 3 and 4.

Chapter 2

A Look Inside
the Documentation User

No microscopes, please. And no anatomy lessons. But we do need to check out what goes on inside the audience. Documentation is designed for computer users, and it is extremely important to know about that audience before you design or write anything. Once that audience (or audiences) has been identified, the documentation system can be designed to meet user needs. The present chapter takes a close look at users in terms of their goals, motivations, and the way they are changing as the software industry matures. It also explores some of their key strengths and limitations in terms of human information processing theory. This chapter may tell you more than you ever felt you needed to know about the user. However, knowing the user is the key to producing sound documentation, and the more you know, the more effective will be the documentation you produce.

The Desktop Revolution

The advent of the small desktop computer has brought many people who lack prior computer experience into contact with computers. This has had a significant effect on the machines themselves, the software they use, and what is today regarded as acceptable user documentation. This section explores some of the effects of the desktop revolution.

"Old-Line" and "New-Line" Computer Users

As just mentioned, one of the most important innovations of recent years is the advent of the inexpensive desktop computer. Such machines have produced something of a revolution in the home and office. They have proliferated widely and have brought many people with little or no prior computer experience into contact with a computer for the first time. Before this happened, most computer users were highly specialized systems programmers or members of data-processing departments. Programs were run in batch mode, and the number of users having direct exposure to any particular program was limited. Today, there are still such organizations, but the majority of program users are individuals who use desktop computers to operate programs to increase their personal productivity. The accountant or financial analyst uses a spreadsheet program because it is faster than doing analyses by hand or than waiting for someone else to perform them. The writer uses a word-processing program because it increases the speed at which a draft can be produced and considerably simplifies editing. The artist or illustrator uses a drawing program or set of stored images to produce pictures, diagrams, or charts. The publisher of a newsletter—or software documentation—uses a desktop publishing program to compose pages. The list, as they say, goes on.

Changes in Computers and Software

Many of the early desktop computers were difficult to program, and the available software was limited and often quite poor. As the microcomputer market matured, so did the quality of the machines and available software. Software is being designed increasingly with the needs of the user in mind. To use the popular label, it is becoming more "user friendly." Users have come to expect that the software package they buy will allow them to accomplish a task simply, effectively, and without crashing and dropping their database into the ether. Users have, in other words, come to expect more than they once did of the hardware and software products they use. To a certain extent, this reflects a change not just in the software industry, but in the users themselves.

One of the most significant changes of recent years is the advent of computers with "friendly" or "intuitive" user interfaces. The prime example is Apple's Macintosh computer. This was not the first computer to use a mouse, provide a "desktop metaphor," and to display most program objects and functions in graphic form (Figures 2.1a, b, and c). That credit belongs to the Xerox Star. However, the Macintosh was the first machine of this kind to provide the essential features at a reasonable price. Almost everyone who works around people who use microcomputers knows at least one former computerphobe who has fallen in love with the Macintosh.The main reason, apparently, is that it is easy to learn and use.

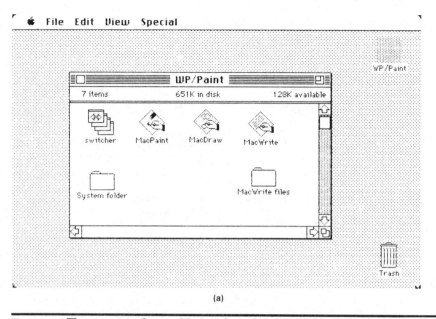

File Edit View Special

(a)

Figure 2.1   Three screens from a Macintosh application illustrating the graphic orientation and highly intuitive nature of the user interface: (*a*) the Macintosh "desktop," which presents the various programs, files, and functions as icons; (*b*) a screen from the *MacWrite* word processing program; and (*c*) a screen from the *MacPaint* drawing program.

Changes in Computer Documentation

It has been suggested that if a computer's software is designed properly, no documentation should be required. The authors of this book know people who use the Macintosh and have never opened a manual. But this is perhaps taking an extreme and somewhat unreasonable position. Not everyone likes the Macintosh, and it seems doubtful that its design approach will ever be adopted universally. But the central point remains valid. That is, people like to be able to learn and use their computers quickly. We need to keep this in mind. More to the point, even if the program we are documenting is not particularly easy to learn and use, we must attempt to make it as easy to learn and use as is humanly possible.

And, just as computers and software have changed, so have user expectations in terms of documentation. The average computer user of today is not a computer expert, although he or she may be an expert at something else—for example, accounting, treating patients, designing building structures. Computer documentation cannot be written as it was 20 years ago—for computer scientists and others with extensive computer experience. Moreover, these changing expectations apply

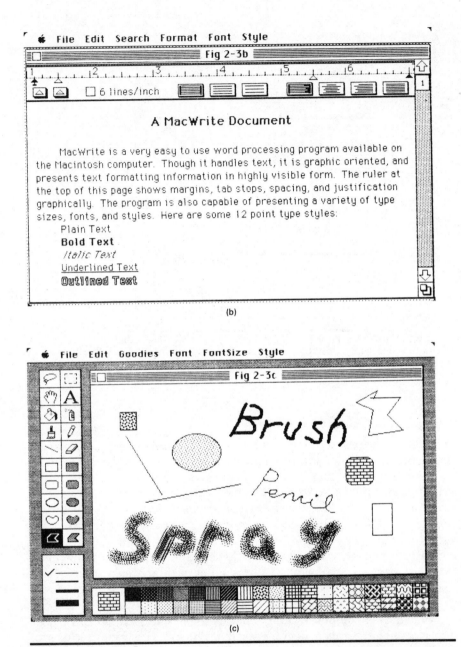

(b)

(c)

Figure 2.1   (*Continued*)

beyond the desktop computer. Even computer experts expect more these days. This is due in part to the increasing overall quality of computer documentation and in part to the very simple fact that many computer experts use desktop computers and have been exposed to good documentation themselves.

User Goals, Attitudes, and Time Constraints

The documentation user is primarily interested in using a program to save time, reduce work, or to perform a task that would otherwise be impractical or impossible. These motivations are reflected in user goals, attitudes, and time constraints.

The Goal-Oriented User

Users differ in several different ways, and we must take these differences into account in writing documentation. Four key differences among users are their goals, levels of expertise, work styles, and preferences (Walker, 1986) (Figure 2.2). What they have in common is the desire to use the program as a productivity tool.

Most users are very goal-oriented. They want to perform a task quickly, efficiently, and easily to improve their productivity. They are not interested in the details of program operation or other arcana unrelated to the practical task at hand (Figure 2.3). To use a road map analogy, if you are interested in getting from point A to point B, the most useful information concerns routes and landmarks. What is not useful is a description of the composition of the streets, local historical sites, or other things unrelated to navigation. There is a place for such information, but it does not belong with routes and landmarks.

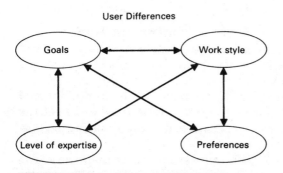

Figure 2.2 Four key differences among computer users are their goals, levels of expertise, work styles, and preferences. (*From Walker, 1986.*)

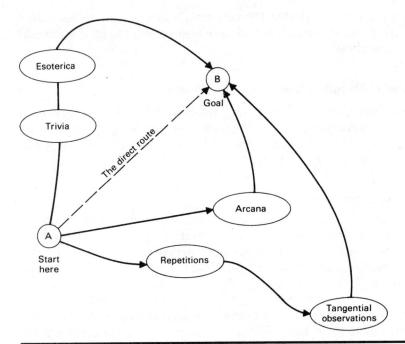

Figure 2.3 Most users are goal-oriented and interested in performing a task quickly, efficiently, and easily to improve their productivity. They want to get from the starting point to the goal without unnecessary detours.

There will always be hackers around who enjoy playing with their software with no particular object other than their own pleasure. But the vast majority of users have more practical motives when they sit down at their computers.

User Time Constraints

Time is an important concern of most computer users. Users want to spend as little of it as possible in using a program to perform a task. You may safely assume that the reader of documentation is impatient and desires to obtain information from documentation quickly. More to the point, for users who employ a program on the job or in professional pursuits, time amounts to money. The more time it takes to get the information, the greater the cost in person-hours, time-sharing expenses, or other very tangible dollar costs.

Most users view programs as tools that assist them in their work. The goal is to complete a task. The means is the tool, i.e., the computer program. To employ the tool, the user must understand how to make it work, and here documentation is the key. If the documentation is inadequate or incomplete, then the tool cannot be operated properly, time is wasted, and the goal is not met.

Many users operate programs and consult user documentation while engaged in another primary task. For example, a marketing director uses his graphics program while preparing a presentation. An engineering consultant sits down at her structural beam analysis program while preparing a design plan. A company comptroller uses a spreadsheet program between meetings while working in his office on the company budget. Very few people use a single program on a continuous, dedicated basis. Thus, the program and its documentation get a small chunk of the user's time and, during that chunk, the user wants to do the job quickly, conveniently, and without unpleasant surprises. Documentation must provide the information needed to do the job in the most concise, convenient form possible.

User Attitudes

At least one researcher believes that most users are already "confused, frustrated, or mad" (Walker, 1986). While this is probably an overgeneralization, the fact remains that it is quite easy to be reduced to these states of mind while attempting to use a computer program when the documentation is not doing its job properly. It is a rather logical progression and may be linked to the various stages at which one refers to documentation while using a program (Figure 2.4). Confusion is the first

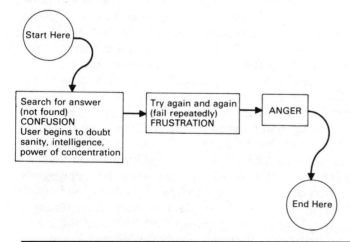

Figure 2.4 Confusion, frustration, and anger are a logical progression of emotional states when the user cannot find what is needed in documentation. The final stage is to discard the program.

stage and results when the answer cannot be found in the documentation or is so incomprehensible that you begin to doubt your intelligence, sanity, or power of concentration. The frustration stage is reached when, after repeated tries, you still cannot figure out what to do. Anger is the final stage, which comes when you stop blaming yourself for the problem and point the finger at the software manufacturer. The final stage—which is not listed—may be the fairly reasoned and unemotional act of discarding the program.

Program user support groups are not the solution to this problem. Neither is the inclusion of soothing words of reassurance within the program or documentation. Users want direct answers to questions. If the documentation is unnecessarily complex, incomplete, poorly organized, or difficult to read, you increase the likelihood that the reader will have difficulty finding the answer and accomplishing the goal. (Jack up confusion, frustration, and anger a notch.) The solution, as to many other documentation problems, is to provide the information in the most concise, convenient form possible.

Human Information Processing Limitations

Many newspaper and magazine articles have suggested that human beings are tapping only a small portion of their intelligence but have almost unlimited potential. For example, someone once estimated that only 10 percent or so of a person's mental capacity is being tapped, and if the other 90 percent could be, then we could all perform intellectual wonders. Left- and right-brain theorists posit that creative capacities lie in one hemisphere and rational capacities in the other. Now, if we could only get the two to work together, then engineers would be writing symphonies in their spare time and artists could fill their leisure hours by theorizing about the properties of multidimensional space. Speed-reading advocates contend that we can learn to read, with comprehension, at several thousand words per minute. And so on.

While there may be some truth in these notions, they are made up more of wishful thinking than hard data. Believing in them is a little like believing in benevolent creatures who ride about in flying saucers, keeping a watchful eye on us. The truth about what humans can do with their gray matter is somewhat more sobering, as research psychologists have discovered. There are many true wonders, though we tend not to notice them. For example, given only amateur instruction (parents), a child masters a spoken language very quickly and, by the age of five or so, is able to communicate very effectively. People appear to have unlimited information storage capacity (i.e., long-term memory). With effort, they can learn to accomplish very complex and difficult cognitive or motor tasks. We have all learned an enormous amount during our lives, much taken for granted, but the fact of where we have gotten from where we started is, as some folks say, mind-boggling. In this section, we'll examine some key properties of human perception, information processing, and memory. While these topics may seem esoteric, they govern how well a user can comprehend and respond to documentation. Just as the programmer must understand something of what goes on inside a computer, the documentation designer—who writes software for the mind—must understand something of what goes on inside the user.

Human Information Processing and Memory

Let us take the viewpoint of cognitive psychologists, who draw an analogy between the human mind and a computer. We'll look at what goes on inside a human while performing the task of operating an interactive computer program. The task may be regarded as a model for many other types of tasks—for example, using a computer manual, driving an automobile, or any of a host of other tasks that require a person to gather information from the environment, process it, and take some action.

A sequence of actions occurs as the operator monitors a display. This sequence is illustrated in Figure 2.5 and described in the following sections.

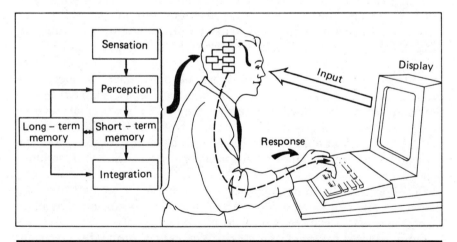

Figure 2.5 Human information processing involves several stages: Incoming information must first be sensed, which is done preconsciously. Next, sensation is integrated into a conscious awareness of the stimulus; perception occurs. Active, deliberate processing begins with short-term memory, and naming is assigned. Eventually, the information becomes fully integrated and the operator responds to it. (*From Simpson*, Design of User-Friendly Programs for Small Computers, *McGraw-Hill, New York, 1985.*)

Sensation. Note that human beings are regarded as single-channel processors. They are able to switch their attention quickly among tasks but are incapable of true parallel processing. When information appears on the display, light waves travel though the air and affect the operator's sensory apparatus—the eyes and the part of the brain that sense light. This is the act of sensation. If the operator is not attending to the display, then sensation does not occur. Sensation is not conscious, but is required before any conscious awareness of the information can exist.

Perception. Following sensation is the act of perception. Perception amounts to the integration of sensation into some meaningful awareness—that light has been seen, sound has been heard, something has been felt—though meaning has not yet been assigned. Perception is influenced by learning and by what has happened to the individual in the past. It is also influenced by the state of arousal and fatigue.

Short-term memory. Active, deliberate processing commences with short-term memory. The term "short-term memory" is something of a misnomer. This "memory" is really much more like a processing buffer. That is, as new information enters, old information is displaced. It does not retain information for long; during normal processing, its content is lost after about 15 seconds. It is a site at which there is an interplay between information coming in from the senses and long-term memory. The information is processed, and the human being makes sense of it.

Short-term memory has been studied extensively, and what is known about it is important to those who design and create user documentation. Here are some of its key properties. First, the contents of short-term memory are what you are currently attending to, not memory for recent events. Second, the contents of short-term memory are constantly updated, as in a buffer. Old information is shifted out as new information enters. Third, the capacity of short-term memory is well defined and surprisingly limited. A review by G.A. Miller (Miller, 1956) puts its capacity at about seven items, plus or minus two, i.e., between five and nine items. More recent studies suggest that it is smaller, perhaps as little as three items.

Consider how the limitations of short-term memory may influence a person's ability to use a component of user documentation. The main things to bear in mind are that short-term memory (a) has a small capacity and (b) loses information quickly. You cannot inundate the reader with a lot of information and expect that information to be retained. There are serious, built-in limitations that make this impossible.

The information coming in through the sensory channel must be decoded and integrated. For example, the symbols on the page must be converted to words and into sentences, syntax must be unraveled, context must be considered, and meaning must be determined—in other words, the reader must go through a series of transformations involving an interplay between short- and long-term memory.

Long-term memory. Long-term memory contains all the information that a person has encoded throughout a lifetime. In practical terms, it seems to have unlimited capacity. If short-term memory is like a processing buffer, then long-term memory is more like permanent disk or hard-copy storage. Many researchers model long-term memory as a network in which each concept is located at a node and accessed through links that correspond to relevant semantic categories. (For example, if somebody asks you to name all the bearded men you personally know, you can access the relevant information via two cues: "bearded" and "men.") The more cues provided and the more concrete the cues, the more likely you are to access the appropriate node, i.e., memory trace.

Information may be encoded in long-term memory to various degrees. The more "deeply" the information is encoded, the more readily accessible it is.

Information may be encoded in more than one form. For example, you may encode a concept in terms of its name, its graphic form, both, or in other ways. The more different ways the concept is encoded, the easier it is to retrieve from memory. For example, you will have better luck recalling information about an historical figure if you know both name and appearance (e.g., tall, gaunt, bearded) than if you simply know a name.

Information retrieval is also influenced by a factor called the "encoding specificity principle." In simple terms, this principle states that you associate certain cues with information when you store it in long-term memory. To retrieve it, you must use some or all of those same cues. (For example, if you see a large, threatening insect crawling up your leg and a knowledgeable friend informs you that it is a "green, wall-eyed spider wasp," you will store this knowledge—if you are not distracted—using the cues "large insect," "green," "wasp," "wall-eyed spider wasp," and perhaps "creepy-crawly" and some other cues. At some later point in time, you may retrieve information about the wasp using any of these cues or their combinations.) But the more cues provided and the more closely they match the encoding cues, the better recognition will be.

The encoding specificity principle has some important implications. Concrete objects, such as wasps, can be defined in terms of fewer cues than abstract ones. You cannot readily define an abstract idea such as Truth—or a computer program's functions—in terms of a few concrete properties. This means that concreteness makes it easier to learn and later to recall a concept.

Consider what lessons this has for people who prepare program documentation. There are a few. For example, use concrete language and examples, if possible. Support the presentation of abstract ideas with illustrative graphics. In presenting procedural information, be very literal-minded; tell the reader precisely what to do, down to what buttons to press and the other specific actions required. The bottom line is that people have a great deal more difficulty dealing with the abstract than with the concrete. You must take this property of readers into account in writing documentation.

In extracting information from long-term memory, the operator may be required either to recall or recognize it. In a recall task, a person is presented with a question to answer. For example, "Name all your friends whose names begin with A." In a recognition task, the person is presented with a set of data and must determine whether or not one or more items is familiar. Recognition tasks are easier than recall tasks because the person does not have to organize and conduct a memory search. This is one of the reasons that menu-driven programs are easier for inexperienced operators to use than are programs that require operators to use commands that they have memorized. It is also one of the reasons that user documents need to be generous in providing reminders and other cues to refresh the reader's memory about information covered previously, and why indexes and glossaries are so important. Readers forget and need to be helped.

Conscious action. Eventually, people deal at the conscious level with information that has worked its way through their processing systems. They may ignore it, maintain it in short-term memory, or make a response. But note that, before a person can act on the information at the conscious level, a good deal of earlier, preconscious processing and filtering must occur. In short, presenting information to someone on a computer display or in a manual does not guarantee that it will eventually work its way up to the conscious level. We need only consider the limitations of the human information processor to see why this is true. Here is a summary of those basic limitations:

- Single-channel processing
- Must be focused on display (or documentation) to sense information
- Perception governed by attention, which in turn depends upon state of arousal and fatigue
- Short-term memory capacity of roughly seven items
- Information lost through decay in about 15 seconds
- Retrieval of information from long-term memory influenced by:
  - Information coding
  - Encoding specificity
  - Concreteness of concept

- Recognition versus recall task

The human information processing model described above is a highly condensed and simplified version of the model used by cognitive psychologists. For more complete descriptions of the model, refer to the books listed in the References by Card, Moran, and Newell (1983) and Lachman, Lachman, and Butterfield (1979).

Pattern Recognition

Human beings are capable of recognizing familiar patterns almost instantaneously. An example of this in everyday experience is the recognition of faces. All of us have learned and know literally thousands of faces—of family members, friends, celebrities, teachers, and so on. At least two things about this are striking. First, recognition occurs almost instantly. Second, we seldom make mistakes.

An enormous amount of research has been done on pattern recognition, and the theory-builders have yet to explain it fully. Aside from theory, however, human performance in recognizing patterns tells us some important things (Figure 2.6). First, patterns do not have to be analyzed to be interpreted. When you turn a corner and see someone's face, you do not go through a deliberate process of noting hair color, shape of nose, distance between eyes, facial coloring, and so forth. The face is apprehended as a whole and instantly interpreted. One theory of pattern recognition—"template matching"—likens recognition to matching a shape with an overlay. The theory has serious limitations—particularly in explaining people's ability to recognize a pattern as the same under different conditions—but is a useful metaphor.

Pattern recognition is interesting in its own right, as well as when contrasted with how people process certain other kinds of information. For example, most people will read a mathematical equation character by character, from left to right. On the other hand, a mathematician who works regularly with common expressions and functions may read the entire equation at once, like a word or pattern. This is also true of reading lines of programming code.

Similarly, when you see the following,

```
dlgehkij
```

each character must be read separately, since the letters together do not form a word.

However, if these characters are presented,

```
dirigible
```

they form a word, which is apprehended as a pattern. The point is that certain familiar entities—faces, letters, words, and so on—may, with experience and skill, be apprehended as patterns. Since pattern recog-

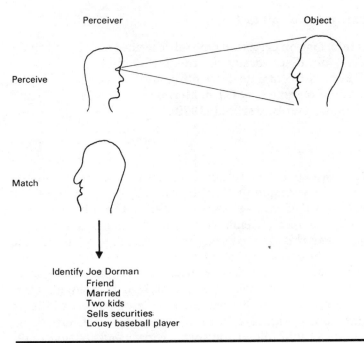

Perceiver

Object

Perceive

Match

Identify Joe Dorman
Friend
Married
Two kids
Sells securities
Lousy baseball player

Figure 2.6   Pattern recognition involves the wholistic apprehension of an object—a face, a word, or other familiar thing. It occurs almost instantaneously and with a high degree of accuracy. One theory of how it works is through "template matching," as illustrated here. The perceiver matches the perceived object with a series of internal templates and identifies the object based on the best match.

nition occurs much more rapidly than serial processing, it enables a person to perform such wonders as reading at 300 to 400 words per minute.

Think about that for a moment. Reading at 300 words per minute requires you to read 5 words per second. If the average word contains 7 letters, that means plowing through 35 letters per second. Skilled readers do not, of course, do this. Instead, they recognize the words. Paradoxically, a reader can recognize words more rapidly than individual letters.

This also tells you something about why it is better not to abbreviate words that you want people to recognize. An abbreviation—unless it is a very familiar one that is itself recognized as a word—requires the reader to interpret its characters serially, instead of relying on the built-in pattern recognizer. This is slower, more work, and more likely to cause errors. It is also a good reason to construct your sentences of commonly used words that the reader has learned to recognize. When you drop a long, unfamiliar word in a sentence, not only does it take longer to interpret, but it also takes longer to recognize.

User Skill and Experience

Here's a hot news flash: No two people are completely alike. They may vary by type (i.e., how closely they fit one or more stereotypes, as discussed in the next chapter), how they process information, what they know, and in various other ways. Not only are they not alike, but any specific person is a moving target. A person may be very sophisticated using one computer program but a complete novice with others. Performance also depends upon the person's knowledge and skill in the particular subject matter area of the program. People change as they learn and gain experience. The novice of today may become the expert of tomorrow.

The Power Law of Practice

Given all of these factors, it is still possible to determine the shape of the user "learning curve," i.e., the graph showing the effect of practice upon performance (Figure 2.7). User performance is usually measured in terms of speed, accuracy, number of tasks accomplished, and similar variables. (As performance improves, errors decrease, and so errors are an inverse measure of performance.) Practice is usually specified in terms of elapsed time, trial number, or related variables. Card, Moran, and Newell (1983) have shown that user learning curves are power functions of this general form:

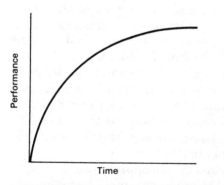

Figure 2.7   The user learning curve takes the form of a power function, with the most rapid growth in skill occurring early.

Performance $= TBN^{-\alpha}$

where T = elapsed time
B = a scaling constant
N = trial number
α = the exponent for the particular task

The factors in the equation vary based on the task and subject, but the shape of the function is fairly universal. The exponent alpha is commonly between 0.2 and 0.4, although it may be smaller or larger. For example, in a research study, Card, English, and Burr (1978) found that the relevant factors for performance in a motor task involving pointing to objects with a mouse pointer are the following:

$B = 3.02$

$\alpha = 0.13$

As you may have guessed, speed in using a mouse is not the important point here. Motor skills are not of any great interest either. Fortunately, the power function applies to many other types of tasks as well and is fairly universal in showing how a person's performance will improve with practice, e.g., practice in using a computer program or using a computer manual. Examine Figure 2.7 and note that most of the improvement occurs early and that performance tends to level out later on. What this curve tells us is that people tend to learn rapidly at first, but that as time goes on, the rate at which they acquire new knowledge tends to slow down considerably.

How does this apply to the design of documentation? Actually, it applies in several different ways, both directly and indirectly. First, you can expect that when someone first starts using a computer program, performance will tend to be fairly slow and error-prone. At this stage of learning, the user will frequently refer to program documentation. As experience and skill are gained, performance will improve and the need to refer to documentation will tend to decline. In other words, the user becomes expert on both the program and its documentation. But even as the user continues to gain knowledge and skill, it will be necessary periodically to check reference documentation. The user's need at that point is quite different than during early learning. At the outset, the learner must take each step slowly. Later, the user knows a good deal more and wants to get quick answers to questions.

The needs of the novice program and documentation user are quite different from those of the expert. This difference must be taken into account during design. How? There are a number of different approaches (Figure 2.8). One is to provide separate tutorial documen-

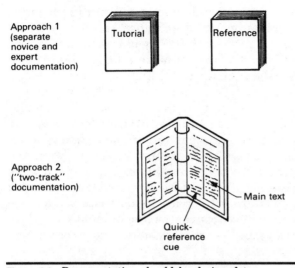

Approach 1
(separate
novice and
expert
documentation)

Tutorial

Reference

Approach 2
("two-track"
documentation)

Main text

Quick-
reference
cue

Figure 2.8 Documentation should be designed to take the separate needs of novice and expert program users into account. One approach is to provide separate documentation for the two user groups. Another approach is to provide "two-track" documentation—documentation that can be used at two different levels—by, for example, offering quick-reference cues within the margins.

tation for use during early learning and concise reference documentation for use later. Another approach is to build "two-track" documentation which allows the user to access information at two different levels. The important point here is to note that users change as they learn, and that documentation should accommodate their changing needs.

Transfer of training.   Transfer of training refers to the degree to which skills developed in one domain can be transferred to another. For example, when you climb into a rental car at an airport, you face the transfer-of-training problem directly. If you have driven similar cars, there is a high degree of transfer, and you can get going and move into traffic without a hitch; your learning curve will be steep. If the car is unfamiliar—if, for example, you have rented a Porsche Turbo Carrera and have never driven one before—then there is less transfer and your learning curve will not rise as rapidly.

Most automobiles work in similar ways, and you can expect a high degree of transfer among them. Complications arise, however, when the usual ways of doing things are changed. For example, suppose you rent the car in London, where the steering wheel is on the right, the gearshift is on the left, and you must drive on the left side of the road. For North

Americans this takes some getting used to and can result in "negative transfer"—a serious degradation of performance resulting from a contradiction in expectations for how things should work.

Like the Power Law of Practice, transfer of training applies to documentation design in several different ways (Figure 2.9). The transfer-of-training principle means that you can expect a certain amount of either positive or negative transfer among different sets of documentation. The more similar the sets, the more positive transfer is possible. Similarity here has nothing to do with what the documentation covers—i.e., their subject matter—but with the manner of presentation and adherence to certain recognized conventions. For example, if you write a manual called a "user's guide" that is in fact a reference manual, you can expect some negative transfer to occur. If you write a reference manual and do not follow recognized conventions for defining the syntax of program commands, you face the same problem. And so on.

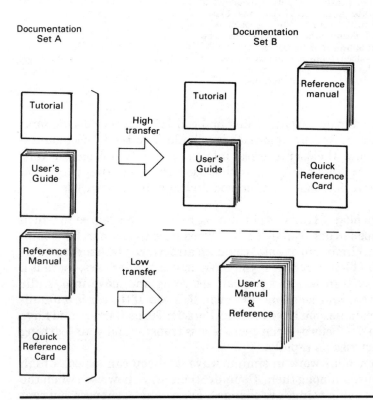

Figure 2.9 Transfer of training among different document sets is influenced by the similarity of the sets. The greater the similarity, the more transfer can be expected; the more dissimiliar, the less transfer.

The key to avoiding problems with negative transfer is to be fully aware of what the documentation design conventions are and to adhere to them—unless there is a very good reason to do otherwise.

Cognitive Models

A cognitive model is a person's representation of something in the external world (Figure 2.10). Since such phenomena are many and varied, people's models of them can take many different forms.

One type of cognitive model is a mental map that helps you find your way around the physical world of your daily life. On this map are the locations of your home, the place you work, the grocery store, and so forth. You built up this map through practice and probably do not think about it. However, you become very conscious of the need for such an internal representation—or an actual, paper map—when you visit an unfamiliar area and get lost.

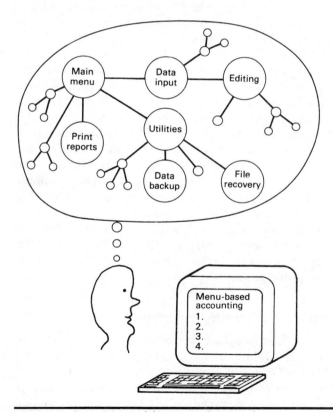

Figure 2.10   A cognitive model is a person's internal representation of the external world. Such models can take many different forms and are often incomplete and inaccurate.

Using a computer program involves many of the same processes as finding your way around unfamiliar geography. A typical program consists of several subprograms which are linked together with a control structure. The subprograms may allow various types of data entry, display, file manipulation, and so forth. Before operators can use such programs effectively, they must know their destination (the subprograms they want to use) and what streets to turn on (control actions) to get there. They will have to check signs (display indications of current subprogram, status, etc.), make decisions, make incorrect turns, and so forth, until they get to their destination. There is an orientation problem in using a computer program, just as in moving about physical geography.

Computer programs can ease orientation considerably by providing the operator with landmarks that provide locational or status cues, such as meaningful window titles and field labels. Alternatively, a program can be written in such a way that the user will often get lost and feel as if he or she had just been blindfolded and dropped into an alien landscape. The important point is that users do not automatically know how to get from point A to point B in a program. This must be learned, and the Power Law of Practice tells us that this takes time.

In addition to mental maps, people seem to possess and use internal models of how things work. The accuracy and completeness of these models varies with the individual and the device. It follows that people form models of how computers and computer programs work, and that these are often incomplete and inaccurate. The Macintosh goes a long way toward easing the user's burden by providing a simple model—the desktop Finder—at the outer edges of most applications. The user can adopt this model and use it instead of inventing one. Other simple models—such as cutting and pasting—work (or should work) within most applications. Again, these reduce the burden on the user.

Cognitive models and mental maps are useful metaphors for describing how people seem to represent the world. Although they should not be taken too literally, they are useful in considering the user's needs when designing a computer program.

Writing for "Dummies" and Other Misconceptions

There is a fairly common misconception that developing documentation that supports the user is equivalent to designing documentation for "dummies." One of the premises of good human factors design is that a particular product—for example, a chair, hair dryer, computer program, or manual—should accommodate the full range of product users. That is why properly designed chairs are adjustable, hair dryers come in different sizes, there is more than one word-processing program, and documentation should be tailored to the user—not (with double exclamation points) the other way around.

The product—in this case the various components of a documentation system (see Chapter 1)—should be usable by both unsophisticated and sophisticated users. In some cases, this means developing different products for different parts of the audience. In others, it means writing for the lowest common denominator. If the resources to develop separate products are not available, then writing for the lowest common denominator is required.

Writing for the novice takes considerable work. Writers must put themselves into the minds of that unknowledgeable reader, attempt to ask the questions the reader would ask, and present the answers in the clearest and simplest language possible. There is an art to this, and if you doubt it, you have only to read the very best technical or scientific prose to prove it to yourself. Of the former, good examples are the documentation provided with most Apple Computer and Microsoft products and, of the latter, *Scientific American* magazine offers excellent examples. For counter-examples, refer to most technical journals and to standard documentation for the UNIX operating system.

What such examples and counter-examples show is that writing about difficult topics in simple language is an art. They also show that the long, convoluted sentence with polysyllabic or arcane words is verboten. (The previous sentence is a fairly good example of how *not* to write such prose.) Such language does not so much communicate as impress, and that only for only so long as we are willing to indulge its author and tolerate his or her indifference to our needs as readers. How indulgent do you feel while seated before a computer, experiencing a problem, and reading an incomprehensible sentence that supposedly holds the solution? The reaction of other readers, you can be fairly sure, would be similar.

3

Types of Users and the User-Documentation Match

Chapter 2 should have given you some insights into what goes on inside the typical documentation user. This knowledge can be very useful during documentation development. Unfortunately, to take the first step in this direction, we must deal with users a little more globally. We must, in a sense, simplify the way we think about them to get a handle on what type of documentation to develop. One way to do this is to think about users in terms of operator "stereotypes," i.e., classes of users. As everyone knows, stereotypes are bad.

"However," said the man...

Well, in their defense, the stereotypes discussed mark the limits on user populations and allow us to structure our thinking about not only them but every other type of user in between. By starting with stereotypes, we can get a handle on what type of documentation will be needed to support a program. We can fine-tune our definitions, as necessary. Given that we have defined users to this degree, we can decide, intelligently, exactly what type of documentation is needed. This process is sometimes referred to as making the "user-documentation match."

If you continue to wonder how the material in Chapter 2 fits into this process, it doesn't—at least not directly. However, knowing about such things as operator goals, short-term memory, and pattern recognition is very important when you sit down and start writing—as you will find out in later chapters, e.g., Chapters 7 through 11.

The first part of this chapter discusses types of users in terms of operator stereotypes and provides a simple scheme for classifying and thinking about the audience. The second part of the chapter tells how to make the user-documentation match.

Types of Users

One of the basic rules of writing is to know and target the audience (Figure 3.1). This rule certainly applies when creating user documentation and is important for several different reasons. First, the type of audience affects what type and amount of documentation are prepared. For example, unsophisticated users need a greater amount of tutorial and help information than experts; experts can often get by with reference information alone.

Second, the type of audience influences the depth of coverage—how much you must explain. Unsophisticated users who do not know how to insert a diskette need a lot more detailed explanation of procedures than UNIX operators.

Finally, the type of user may influence writing style. The inexperienced user is often insecure and in need of reassurance from documentation that speaks like a friendly, helpful teacher. The experienced user is less in need of reassurance, wants to get the facts, and may regard a "friendly" voice as condescending or stupid.

Thus, you must make certain assumptions about your audience before designing and writing documentation. Making these assumptions is

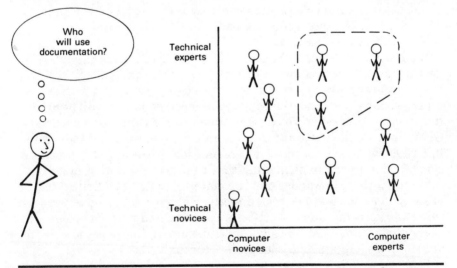

Figure 3.1   One of the first steps in developing documentation is to know and target the audience.

always dangerous but inescapable. One way to approach the problem is with operator stereotypes. Stereotypes are not real operators, but they mark the extremes of the operator population and are useful as starting points. They at least help you get an idea of what you are up against. Four stereotypes are presented here: computer professionals, professionals without computer experience, naive users, and skilled clerks (Figure 3.2).

The key dimensions of Figure 3.2 are *technical skill* and *computer skill*. By technical skill is meant background, education, and experience in the technical area of the software. This might be the programming language PASCAL, stock market analysis, record management, or any other topic software deals with. Technical skill does not necessarily relate to computers. For example, an accountant possesses a high degree of technical skill in accounting but might know nothing at all about computers.

By computer skill is meant experience with computers and application programs, particularly computers and applications similar to the one being documented. This does not necessarily relate to technical skill (unless the technical area is computers or programming). Thus, an experienced applications programmer would rate high in computer skill but low in technical skill with, for example, an accounting program. If the technical area is COBOL programming, the same programmer rates very high in technical skill, as he or she has been programming in COBOL since shortly after the discovery of fire.

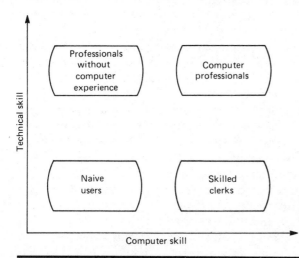

Figure 3.2 One way to categorize documentation users is in terms of their relative technical and computer skills. The four extremes are marked by the operator types shown in this graph. (*From Simpson*, Programming the IBM PC User Interface, *McGraw-Hill, New York, 1985.*)

Brief descriptions of the stereotypes follow. Bear in mind that operator stereotypes are oversimplifications and are mainly intended to help structure thought about the audience.

Computer Professionals

Computer professionals are programmers, systems analysts, and others who work daily with computers. They have done much programming, usually in many different languages. They have broader experience than any other group, and understand software and hardware concepts well. This group applies much of its previous experience when exposed to a new program.

Computer professionals lack patience. They want the essential information presented succinctly, accurately, and without trimmings. Thus, documentation written for computer professionals need not dwell on basics, but may be written at a fairly technical level. Good reference information is probably the single most important documentation needed by this group.

Professionals Without Computer Experience

Professionals without computer experience are nonprogrammer professionals, such as physicians, accountants, lawyers, and other professionals (including scientists and engineers) who do not have formal computer training. They are intelligent and well educated, and they know that a computer can help them do their job better. Typically, they do not have training in computer science, programming, or a scientific discipline. They may use their computer to keep patient records, manage a stock portfolio, calculate their taxes, or perform other analysis, planning, or management functions.

Unlike computer professionals, these users lack computer expertise; they do not have a particularly good understanding of what is happening inside of their computers. For that matter, they probably aren't particularly interested; they just want to get a job done. They also lack broad experience in using different types of programs.

Such users are not interested in knowing any more about the computer or program than necessary. It may be very difficult to get them to read documentation or follow written directions; often, they will attempt to forge ahead without it. Yet, this group needs and should use documentation far more than computer professionals, since they are less able to fill in gaps based on experience. One strategy for dealing with the needs of this group is to provide a range of overlapping (i.e., redundant) documentation. For example, divide the user's guide into sections that "spiral" upward in complexity as the reader progresses.

The first section might describe a range of features to get the reader started with simple text processing, and sections following might add more details to increase the user's ability to exercise program features. The key to this approach is to make the reader productive early by digesting a small amount of information. The alternative (and inappropriate) approach is to require the reader to digest a manual before being able to do anything useful.

Naive Users

Naive users know next to nothing about computers or about how computer programs are supposed to work. They seldom use programs. You should assume that their first exposure to a program is the one you are documenting. Naive users are children and adults who have little or no exposure to computers in their daily lives. When they sit down before a computer, it is usually to play a game or to use some simple home or entertainment program.

The most that you can assume about this audience is that they know how to turn their computers on and off (in some cases this may be stretching it). Moreover, it is extremely difficult to get naive users to read anything. Software for such users should be completely bullet-proofed and documented internally. External documentation should be kept as simple as possible. More to the point, the software should be simple enough so that it does not require much in the way of documentation—but this is a matter for software designers, not documenters.

Skilled Clerks

Skilled clerks are not programmers, but they use computers regularly and develop very strong user skills. Users falling into this class are word-processing operators, data-entry clerks, and others who use a program frequently enough to master it. These operators do not have a high degree of computer sophistication, but they do become highly skilled. They are like computer professionals in their interest in speed, since it is important in their daily work. Skilled clerks are expert operators but not programmers. In a sense, they are what naive users or professionals without computer experience can develop into after several years of experience.

Skilled clerks cannot afford to be careless or arbitrary about doing their jobs. Since they lack the sophistication of programmers, they need more documentation, and that documentation needs to be more complete. Like computer professionals, they need complete reference information, but like professionals without computer experience, they also need good introductory documentation such as user's guides.

Applying Operator Stereotypes to Documentation Design

Generalizations such as those just given about different user groups are helpful but must be applied with caution. You will never encounter a user with a label tattooed on his or her forehead and will seldom find it easy to categorize precisely the users for a program you are documenting. More often than not, you will discover that a program is being used by a range of users who do not fit into such handy categories. When the real world imposes itself so inconveniently, you must use your judgment and common sense to take the needs of all users into account.

Making the User-Documentation Match

There is no simple formula for matching documentation to users. What is needed is a straightforward procedure that takes into account certain properties of the application program, operating environment, and operators and provides as output a description of the types of documentation needed and the detailed properties of each. It would work like a sausage machine; you know, you put the offal, spices, and other ingredients in one end, turn a crank, and get the neatly packaged answers out the other end. Unfortunately, it's not that easy. However, we may apply certain more refined (and difficult) procedures in making the match, as described in the following sections.

Training Systems

Designing a documentation system is one aspect of designing a system. A system, you will recall from Chapter 1, consists of an interdependent set of components designed to achieve one or more objectives. One type of system of particular interest to documentation developers is the *training system*. A training system consists of all the elements needed to train a certain group of people to perform a task to a criterion level of performance. It consists of such elements as lists of training objectives, documentation, lesson plans, various instructional media, training exercises, and tests. Such materials have traditionally been developed by teachers or training developers, using idiosyncratic and somewhat unsystematic methods. Everyone who has been educated (presumably this includes everyone reading this book) knows that the effectiveness of education varies widely (and wildly) depending upon who designs and conducts instruction. It would seem that such variability is inherent in the nature of education for, despite the existence of graduate schools of education, no one has yet invented a magic sausage machine that works for training development.

Actually, that is not quite true. Several years ago the Department of Defense devised a training development approach called "Instructional

System Development" (ISD). ISD has since been adopted as the standard way of developing training courses throughout the U. S. armed forces. Reports from the training establishment suggest that the approach does work, but that it has drawbacks. ISD is complex and fills several volumes. It is also time-consuming and expensive to use. It is doubtful that it will soon be adopted outside the military. Moreover, some who have worked with it have reservations about its lock-step approach to training development and doubt that it is possible to systematize completely anything as complex as training development. That soldiers can march by the numbers does not mean that they will be able to develop effective training that way.

System Development Life Cycle

Of course, as documentation designers and developers, our interests extend beyond training. True, training is a part of what documentation is intended to support, but it has other functions as well, such as providing reference information for the experienced user. It is helpful, therefore, to look at how the systems approach is applied by human factors specialists during system development. This approach is admittedly an ideal and cannot always be applied in the real world, but it is a model to aim at.

Under ideal circumstances, when products are developed from scratch, the human factors practitioner likes to promote the use of the systems development cycle (Figure 3.3). This cycle begins with the designer specifying the *functions* to be performed by the system.

Next, the designer determines the most appropriate *allocation of functions* to the operator and equipment. Operators are assigned functions that complement the capabilities of humans, and the equipment is assigned functions that are least suited to the human operators. A good example of the former might be giving the human the functions involving inductive reasoning, and a good example of the latter might be giving the hardware or software the functions involving numeric computations.

The next phase of the product development cycle involves specifying the tasks to be performed by the people who operate the system. This is done by developing detailed lists of activities and representing them in flow diagrams and decision charts. Next, the *information requirements* associated with each task are specified. The purpose of this step is to determine what it is that the human will require in order to perform each task.

Developing user documentation is similar to the development of any other product intended for human users. Even though most documentation is developed only after the software has been written or is being tested, it is still appropriate to apply the basic concepts of the develop-

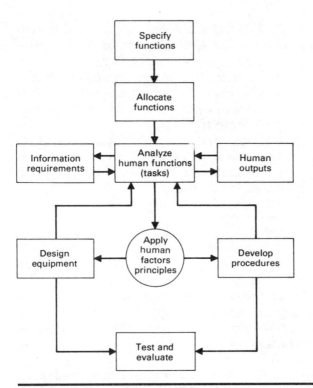

Figure 3.3 System developement life cycle.

ment cycle when developing documentation. Hence, the procedure described in the following incorporates these steps. This procedure takes into account the specific characteristics of the application, the characteristics of operators, and the probable operating environment, and allows us to home in systematically on the design of the documentation system.

The procedure is illustrated in Figure 3.4. Note that the procedure is meant to provide guidance in making design decisions and not intended to be followed rigidly or regarded as doctrine. This is a "top-down" approach to documentation design in the sense that it begins by examining the factors that govern what type of documentation is appropriate (types of users, scope of application, and operating environment) and then systematically proceeds to define the types of documentation and the detailed characteristics of each item (breadth and depth of coverage, organization, and format).

In what follows, each step of the procedure is described. To illustrate its application, assume that we are designing documentation systems for three different applications. The first is a computer game that will be used on a microcomputer such as the Apple II or Commodore 64. The second application is a database that will be used by individuals and operators of small businesses and will be implemented on a personal computer such as the IBM PC or Macintosh. The third is a version of the C programming language that will be used by programmers and computer science students on a VAX minicomputer that uses the UNIX operating system.

Step 1. Determine the Types of Users

Determine who will be using the application and documentation. Take all users into account, if you can. Attempt to classify the users systematically. If operator stereotypes fit, use them as a classification scheme. If stereotypes do not fit, devise a classification scheme that takes into account the key characteristics of operators, i.e., educational back-

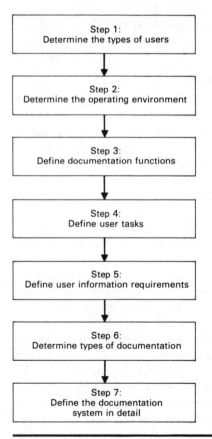

Figure 3.4 A procedure for making the user-documentation match based on the system development life cycle.

ground, intelligence, and experience with computers, application programs, and programming languages. Try to classify the users in terms of the properties shown in Figure 3.2: *technical skill* and *computer skill*. Determine the range of users in terms of these key properties; remember, it is seldom possible to classify all operators according to identical characteristics.

Most users of the game program will fit the stereotype of naive users.

In the database program, most operators will fit the stereotype of professionals without computer experience—individuals high in technical skill but low in computer skill. Some operators will simply do data entry and retrieval and will fit the skilled clerks stereotype.

The C programming language will be used by professional programmers and by students. The programmers will fit the computer professionals stereotype; the students may range from naive users to computer professionals.

It is common, as illustrated in the last two examples, for an application to have more than one type of user.

Step 2. Determine the Operating Environment

The operating environment is the setting in which the program is used as well as any characteristics of the program that may influence the manner of interaction between operator and program. The purpose of this step is to determine how the environment may affect the need for and utility of different types of documentation.

For the game program, the probable operating environment is a home where the operator will use the program alone or in the company of friends.

The probable operating environment of the database program is a small office, where it will be operated by a technical professional and data-entry operator.

The probable operating environment of the C language is a timesharing system, where the user will use either a terminal in a computer laboratory or an independent terminal connected to the computer with a line.

In the case of the game and database, program users lack direct access to people who can answer questions about the application (although the software manufacturer may provide a telephone hot line to answer questions). This implies that user documentation must be complete enough to support the user fully. In addition, each user of one of these programs is presumably an original purchaser and will have a complete set of documentation.

The timesharing environment of the C language implementation differs from that of the two microcomputer programs just described. First, it may offer the user recourse to technical and computer experts either face to face or via computer mail. Second, with this type of environment, it may not be necessary to provide all users with their own complete sets of documentation; certain documentation, such as reference manuals, can be shared. Third, the timesharing environment increases the cost-effectiveness of using within-program documentation.

Step 3. Define Documentation Functions

Documentation functions are the purposes for which the documentation will be used. The two major functional categories are training and reference. These functional categories may be subdivided further, if necessary, or new categories may be devised.

Most documentation systems include components designed to perform both of these functions, although the emphasis may vary considerably. The three hypothetical programs being used in our example should include documentation to perform both functions. It is clear, however, that the emphasis in each case will be on different functions: for the game program on training, for the database on both training and reference, and for the C language on reference.

Step 4. Define User Tasks

The tasks the documentation user must perform during program operation must be specified. The usual way of doing this is to analyze what the operator does while interacting with the program and compile a task list. Figure 3.5 shows a hypothetical list for the game program.

The task list consists of a set of task statements which are prepared in a standard format. Each task statement begins with an action verb. The subject of the activity is described in the second word in the task statement. The third part of the statement describes how the task is completed. The fourth part of the statement tells the purpose of the task.

By describing the tasks in this manner, the documentation developer will develop a very concrete understanding of what the user must do while using the program. The task lists can then be analyzed further (as follows) to define information requirements—which, in effect, amount to a specification for the information content of the actual documentation.

There are two benefits to developing task lists during the early part of documentation development. First, the lists define the content of the tasks; the task descriptions can later be used as the basis for procedural documentation. Second, the task lists can be used to define information requirements (see Step 5).

It is best to structure the tasks in the list chronologically, with those at the top of the list occurring earlier than those below. For example,

What its done? (action verb)	To what is it done? (object)	How is it done? (tools)	Why is it done? (effect or purpose)
Task 1. Select and "click".........	one of four direction symbols......	with cursor (and mouse)...........	to indicate desired direction of travel.
Task 2. Move or inspect............	individual objects visible on the screen	by entering text commands with the keyboard........	to acquire facts for continuing game
Task 3. Save	current game and status	using Save option on the menu (with mouse and curser)................	so that game can be continued later.

Figure 3.5 Hypothetical task list for game program.

early tasks concern gaining access to the system and getting started, and later tasks concern such matters as saving files and shutting down. The task statements should be quite detailed, if possible. For example, in describing the tasks for a spreadsheet program, the list would describe activities required to open a new file; provide labels for columns and rows; enter data in cells; define mathematical manipulations; modify labels, cell values, or mathematical operations; and generate output.

(Although it is desirable to perform task analysis before a system is developed, it can also be useful with existing systems. For example, Casey and Harris [1986] interviewed 30 users of a large computer-aided design system and identified over 300 tasks required to use the system effectively. By so doing, they discovered that most tasks were not adequately supported by existing documentation and that users were forced to acquire most skill on their own. As a result, they recommended the development of a concise pocket guide to ease the burden on users and on training personnel—who spent much of their time answering questions .)

Step 5. Define User Information Requirements

User information requirements are generated from the task lists. The information requirements define what the user must know to use the program effectively. These requirements may be viewed from two perspectives. The first of these is technical subject matter concepts. The second is computer concepts. (Incidentally, these are the dimensions, respectively, of the vertical and horizontal axes of Figure 3.2.) The purpose of this step is to determine how much knowledge (of both a technical subject-matter and computer-specific nature) the user must have to operate the application effectively. Documentation is then planned that will impart some or all of the necessary information to the user; what users may be expected to know already does not have to be documented, but the remainder must be covered.

In the game program, technical concepts encompass the history and rules of the game, the roles of players, and other information pertaining to the nature of the game, regardless of its particular computer implementation. Computer concepts are the computer-specific knowledge the user must possess to use the program. For the game, this includes such matters as how the game is loaded and executed from diskette, how its displays are interpreted, and how the user makes inputs with the keyboard or other input device.

For the database program, the technical concepts concern principles of record keeping, such as file content, organization, and indexing schemes. Computer concepts concern matters such as configuring the program to the particular computer; loading and executing the program; and data input, display interpretation, and subprogram selection.

For the programming language, the technical and computer concepts have considerable overlap, although there are distinctions. The technical concepts concern such matters as the difference between an operating system and programming language; the properties of the C programming language; and the functions of text editor, compiler, libraries, and other components of the program development environment. Computer concepts in this case concern the specific nature of the UNIX C implementation being documented, e.g., how the text editor works, how the compiler is evoked, and differences between the version of C being documented and standard C.

Readers who have done formal training development will recognize that this step is analogous to determining the skill and knowledge requirements of a job. In this case, the "job" is to use the program effectively, and the skill and knowledge requirements are defined in a very broad fashion.

Figure 3.6 shows one possible format for developing a list of information requirements related to the performance of a single task. This particular example relates to the operation of a computer system used to obtain and process data during oil field operations.

Step 6. Determine Types of Documentation

There are some rules of thumb for matching documentation to users based on user stereotypes. The first of these is that each type of user

Function to be completed	Operator information requirements	Operator outputs
23. Assignment of names to data columns	1. Input channel numbers 2. Vehicle numbers 3. Vehicle numbers for each input channel (format cable assignment printout so that operator can use it to name the data columns).	1. Type vehicle numbers into cells. Toggle across cells with Tab key.

Figure 3.6 A possible format for developing a list of information requirements related to the performance of a single task.

needs complete documentation of everything in the program that might concern him or her. This does not mean that all types of documentation (user's guide, reference manual, help screens, guided tours, etc.) must be prepared for every program; it does mean that appropriate documentation must be prepared for each type of user of a program. Since many programs will have more than one type of user, different—and usually overlapping—documentation may be prepared for different user groups (this is the case for the database program described later in this section).

The documentation needs of different user groups differ somewhat. Naive users need complete coverage of everything, since it cannot be assumed that they know about computers, other application programs, or the technical subject area of the program. Conflicting with this guideline is the reality that most naive users will be disinclined to refer to or use documentation. Thus, the program must be designed to minimize the need for documentation, and the documentation must be designed to cover everything that is necessary. (A tough combination but not impossible. Refer, for example, to Macintosh applications such as *MacWrite* and *MacPaint* and their documentation.)

Professionals without computer experience usually know about the technical subject area (e.g., accounting principles, computer programming), and so its coverage in their documentation can be kept brief; however, in other areas they usually require the same breadth and depth of coverage as naive users.

Computer professionals usually need the least "hand-holding" type of documentation, but need complete reference information.

Skilled clerks are more difficult, for in some ways they are like naive users and in other ways like computer professionals; i.e., they have limited computer expertise, but a high degree of expertise in what they do. To prepare documentation for this group, you must have a clear understanding of what tasks they perform and how frequently. The main rule for skilled clerks is to provide them with solid reference information in both full and quick-reference forms; quick-reference information—cards, guides, job performance aids—is especially important.

Given that we have these guidelines, we may apply them within the context of the information requirements defined in the previous step. In a sense, these requirements are the shopping list of what might be covered in documentation. What actually is covered is governed primarily by the type of user.

Using these guidelines, let us decide what documentation to provide for the three applications being used as examples. Start with the game. Because most users will be of the naive type, documentation must be kept to a minimum. It would be desirable for all documentation to be internal because many of its naive users will not read written documentation anyway. Because the program will be operated by an individual without ready access to help from more experienced users, it is important for it to be as "turnkey" as possible; i.e., it should be designed to minimize the need for documentation. Thus, documentation must cover all essentials for configuring and operating the program successfully. Fortunately, because the scope of the program is fairly narrow, complex documentation is unnecessary.

Let us go through the list of documentation possibilities and consider what we might provide for this program. The possibilities mentioned in Chapter 1 are the user's guide, which commonly contains background, procedural, and reference information, and which may contain a tutorial; reference information in the form of the reference manual, reference guide, quick reference card, and the job performance aid; the help screen, which contains a single screen of reference or procedural information; help menus, which are organized sets of help screens; and guided tours, which present an animated demonstration of program features.

For the game, we decide to prepare a short user's guide and a help screen. The guide will provide information on setting up the program and a description of the game and its rules. Within the program, one or two help screens will be provided to remind the user of the rules and how to play. The game is simple, and reference information, help menus, and a guided tour are unnecessary. Because of the audience, the documentation provided must be kept simple and short. At the same time, because the user will be unable to go elsewhere for additional information, documentation must be clearly written and answer all of the questions that the user might ask. (For a more complex game we might do things differently. For example, if it is a battle simulation with complex rules, it might be necessary to add reference information concerning types of characters and their properties, scenarios illustrating the game in action, and perhaps a tutorial or guided tour.)

For the database, we decide to prepare a user's guide, reference manual, reference guide, and a set of help menus (Figure 3.7). The guide will provide information on setting up the program, background information on databases, theory of operations of the program, a tutorial, descriptions of procedures, and some basic reference information. The guide must be written to satisfy the needs of both its audiences: professionals without computer experience and data-entry operators. Both may be regarded as computer-naive, but the first audience will take technical responsibility for program setup, operation, and management; and the second audience will be primarily concerned with efficient, accurate data entry. Thus, the first audience will be concerned with the entire user's guide, and the second primarily with its tutorial and procedures. The database has its own programming language, which requires considerable reference information. The user's guide will contain some of the reference information in the form of examples and descriptions of key words and commands, but most reference information will be put in a separate manual which will be aimed primarily at sophisticated users. Key information from the manual will also be condensed into a quick reference guide which can be used at the computer. The help menus will be aimed mainly at data-entry clerks and will

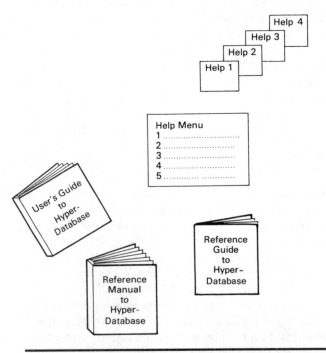

Figure 3.7 Documentation for a database program: a user's guide, reference manual, reference guide, and set of help menus.

provide procedural information (alternatively, a set of job performance aids might be used).

For the C language, we decide to develop a detailed reference manual and a set of help menus. A user's guide is unnecessary because the language will use the standardized UNIX operating environment and C language, both of which are documented elsewhere. Professional programmers and students may refer to these documents if needed. However, our version of both UNIX and C have extensions and special features that need to be documented fully in a reference manual. Fairly extensive help menus will provide reference information concerning both UNIX and C. These are required because it is impractical to provide all users with complete reference manuals at their terminals. The help menus will be designed to answer common questions that might arise; for more detailed information, the user must leave the terminal and review a complete reference manual that is stored in some central location.

Step 7. Define the Documentation System in Detail

Once you have scoped the types of documentation needed, you must define each documentation item in detail. To accomplish this, several additional questions must be asked.

First, you must determine the breadth of coverage of each documentation item. What topics should be covered? You can make this determination by examining the task lists and information requirements.

Second, you must determine the depth of coverage of each item. Given a topic, what can be assumed about the reader's existing knowledge and how much is it necessary to explain? Clearly, the answer to this question may vary from item to item and topic to topic within an item, depending upon the audience and the extent of coverage elsewhere.

Related issues that should be considered at this point are the tone and writing style. Both of these are subjective factors but very real to the reader. The tone may, for example, be that of a helpful friend, a gentle but exact teacher, or a no-nonsense drill sergeant. Style is reflected in the chosen lexicon and its use in prose. For example, in presenting information to naive users, the choice may be to use a strictly nontechnical vocabulary (or explain each technical term used in passing) and short, simple sentences. Alternatively, in writing for a sophisticated audience, the choice may be to use technical terms without definition and to structure sentences more elaborately.

Third, how should each item of documentation be organized? This can be done in several ways and varies with the type of documentation being developed. For example, a user's guide is often organized into sections devoted to the major issues the user must understand, e.g., system configuration, principles of operation, program organization, tutorial, procedures for each major program function, reference information, and index. Reference manuals are usually organized by program functions, alphabetically by command, or in other ways that permit quick access to information. Quick-reference information is usually organized similarly. An individual job performance aid is usually designed to support performance of a single task, and a set of these aids to cover a range of key tasks. Help screens are usually organized like quick-reference information or job performance aids. A set of help menus usually works like the table of contents of a book and leads to a larger body of information elsewhere which may reflect various data locations, such as portions of a user's guide.

Fourth, you must determine the format of the documentation you provide. This requires decisions concerning such factors as document size, construction (e.g., bound or looseleaf), type styles, type and amount of graphics used, and indexing.

The key questions have been identified but not discussed in depth; Chapters 7 and 8 will address these questions more fully.

Chapter 4

The Documentation Development Process

This chapter discusses the documentation development process, a systematic way to plan, develop, evaluate, and maintain a documentation system. The chapter deals with documentation development mainly from the management perspective. It is aimed at project managers, editors, and others concerned with seeing that good documentation products are developed on time and within budget.

The key to fulfilling management's responsibilties is having the right people to do the job; thus, the chapter begins by discussing the documentation development team. Sections following sketch the key steps in documentation development. The methods and procedures offered in this chapter are meant to be suggestive rather than prescriptive and are intended mainly to raise your consciousness about some important issues to address. Feel free to modify what is suggested to suit your project's unique requirements and your working environment. Weigh these issues carefully; all of them are important and should be of concern.

The first section of the chapter discusses the functions of the documentation development team. The second section presents three hypothetical case studies showing how these functions might be assigned to actual people in three quite different organizations. The third section describes a step-by-step documentation development procedure. The final section discusses documentation updating.

The Documentation Development Team

The documentation development team is the group responsible for performing a documentation development project. In large firms, this team may consist of several people who have job titles and are expected to do certain specific types of jobs (Figure 4.1). In small firms the "team," so called, may consist of a single person who tries, more or less, to do it all.

In many firms, job titles do not mean very much. For example, a program manager may at various times act as a manager, system designer, technical liaison to other working groups, and so forth. Likewise for individuals with other titles. To avoid the ambiguity inherent in these titles, the following discussion focuses on job functions, i.e., sets of duties that are assigned to people. It is not necessary (or likely) that each function be assigned to a separate person, but it is necessary that the function be assigned to and performed by somebody. These team functions are illustrated in Figure 4.2 and discussed briefly in the following sections.

Team Management

The team management function is to carry out the traditional management activities for the documentation team. These responsibilities include planning and assigning tasks, organizing and supervising team members, coordinating activities within the group, and controlling work, i.e., eliminating bottlenecks and ensuring a smooth work flow.

In simple terms, team management works with the team to define the job, then sees that the job gets done efficiently and on time. The "job"

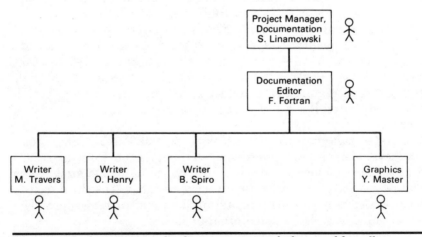

Figure 4.1   The documentation development team may be large and formally organized, as shown here, or quite small, with one person doing everything.

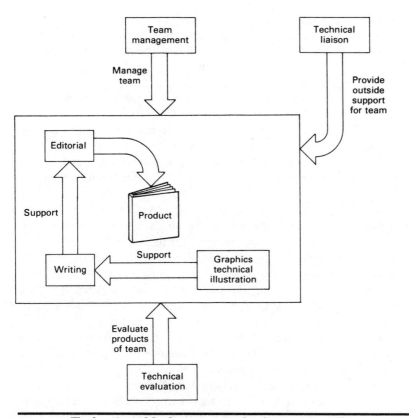

Figure 4.2   The functions of the documentation development team. These functions may be assigned in many different ways, but all must be performed if documentation is to be effective.

goes well beyond the production of end products, such as user's manuals. It also includes conducting the analyses required to define the documentation system (see Chapter 3), and laboratory or field evaluation of end products (see the following and Chapter 12). Management also ensures that the team has access to the tools it needs to do the job (see Chapters 5 and 6).

Technical Liaison

One of the realities of the documentation team is that it performs a support activity in an organization, the primary activity of which is software creation. The team needs the help of software creators—system designers and programmers—to produce its end products. Technical liaison provides a smooth and effective working relationship between software creators and documenters. The person performing technical liaison may belong to either group but will be more effective if he or she is a designer or programmer; in that case, he or she will be able to answer many technical questions directly and will also have more influence among designers and programmers.

The person performing technical liaison has two key responsibilities on the documentation project: (1) providing technical support to the documentation team and (2) ensuring technical accuracy.

He or she gives *technical support* to the documentation team by seeing that it is provided with operating versions of the program being documented, whatever documentation has already been prepared by its designers and programmers, and by making qualified members of the programming staff readily available to the documentation team.

Clearly, the documentation team cannot do its job in a vacuum, and so it needs to be able readily to tap into the technical knowledge base that exists within the design and programming staff. By "readily" is meant that the programming staff understands that a certain amount of its time will be required and is willing to provide the time on reasonable notice. Without belaboring the point, it is worth noting that this understanding and willingness to help are not usually available without strong support on the part of technical management. Anecdotes suggest that the documentation departments of many firms inhabit a world regarded as second class by their technical counterparts and have difficulty getting the technical support they need to do their job. (You know this is a problem in your organization when writers and editors complain about the difficulty of obtaining the answers to technical questions from designers or programmers unwilling to spend any time with them. There are other obvious signs of this problem as well, and if they are allowed to persist, it makes the job of the documenters difficult and reduces the effectiveness of the end products. Too often, when a writer cannot obtain an answer from someone who knows, he or she will ignore the issue or gloss over it when writing the documentation.)

He or she ensures *technical accuracy* by reviewing or having qualified members of the programming staff review work in progress; i.e., drafts of documentation under development. This is best done on a formal basis, but may be done informally if designers/programmers and documenters have good working relationships and the former do not feel that supporting the effort is an intrusion on their time. The design and programming staff should be informed by memo or in a meeting that certain of its members will be expected to support the documentation effort, to devote a specified amount of time to it, and that reports (e.g., annotated drafts, rewrites of some material, etc.) are to be generated. Formalizing the working relationship will smooth work flow and reduce the potential for organizational conflicts.

As the foregoing illustrates, technical liaison has both technical and managerial concerns. On the technical side is ensuring that documenters get the answers they need in order to write and continue their efforts. On the managerial side is ensuring that programmers and documenters have a clear understanding of their working relationship and that both work together in harmony.

Editorial

The editorial function is to ensure the editorial quality of end products. This function is active continuously before, during, and after documentation development. Editorial contributes to consistency and quality before development by creating and maintaining documentation standards—a set of rules and examples that writers can follow in creating new documentation (see Chapter 5). Editorial contributes during development by reviewing work in progress and giving guidance to writers. Editorial contributes after development by acting as the final filter for drafts and refining them to ensure completeness, accuracy, continuity, and conformity with documentation standards.

Writing

Writers are the principal laborers on a documentation project. In addition to their obvious task of writing, they perform several related tasks: They review technical documentation, become experts on the software they are documenting, work with designers and programmers to obtain answers to technical questions, and support the design team in creating internal documentation. They are also the logical group—along with editorial—to perform the analyses required for documentation system definition (see Chapter 3).

Graphics and Technical Illustration

Virtually all user documentation can benefit from suitable artwork: graphics and technical illustrations. Creating this material is the function of the graphics designer and technical illustrator.

Knowing how to use art effectively to support the text or to make a point on its own requires some sophistication (see Chapter 9). Preliminary design of art is usually done by writers and editors, but creating the final, finished product may require the help of a professional. However, the need for professional artists and illustrators might be in decline today because of the widespread availability of inexpensive and powerful graphics tools on microcomputer (e.g., Apple Computer's *MacPaint* and *MacDraw* applications; see Chapter 6).

Technical Evaluation

The editorial function ensures the editorial quality of end products.

However, documentation must also be evaluated from a technical perspective to ensure that users are able to understand it and use it effectively on the job.

The scope of technical evaluation will vary depending upon the type of documentation, its intended audience, and several other factors. Formal, hands-on testing of the documentation with representatives of its audience is not only desirable—it is important. Conducting a proper technical evaluation requires some sophistication in research methods, selection of subjects, protocol development, data collection, and data analysis. In some cases, the skills of an experimental psychologist may be called for.

In practice, technical evaluations are probably one of the weakest areas for most documentation development teams and deserve greater attention than usually given. Technical evaluation is discussed in detail in Chapter 12.

Assigning Documentation Functions Within Organizations

Let us consider how the functions just described might be assigned to actual people in three hypothetical organizations: Mom & Pop's Microworks, SmallCo Software, and MidCo Miniware. These case studies will be used to show how the functions might be assigned to actual employees.

Case Study 1: Mom & Pop's Microworks

Mom & Pop's is a two-person company that creates and markets a small number of specialized educational programs out of a converted garage. It is typical of small firms with small staffs. This staff performs all product creation, development, marketing, management, support, and customer service functions, and its organization is loose in the extreme (Figure 4.3).

Mom, a former schoolteacher, writes the programs, and Pop, a former engineer, answers the telephone and handles orders. Mom's programs are technically sound but Pop spends half of his time on the telephone answering questions from confused schoolteachers who don't understand the photocopied set of "User's Notes" that goes with each program to explain how it works. Moreover, a potential distributor has told Mom that he will not carry her software until it is packaged more professionally and provided with adequate documentation.

Mom and Pop decide that Pop will write the documentation since Mom is busy writing software, Pop is a better writer, and Pop, moreover, is well aware of the types of problems users are having. Mom will

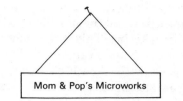

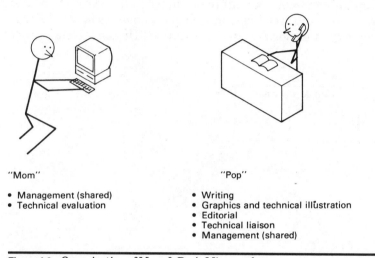

"Mom"

- Management (shared)
- Technical evaluation

"Pop"

- Writing
- Graphics and technical illustration
- Editorial
- Technical liaison
- Management (shared)

Figure 4.3   Organization of Mom & Pop's Microworks, a
two-person software company with loose organization.

answer Pop's technical questions and review what he writes, thereby
performing both the technical liaison and editorial functions. Mom and
Pop together will define end products, set schedules, and monitor
progress, thereby sharing the management function. Pop will write and
do graphics (using a Macintosh and laser printer). The technical evaluation function cannot be performed in house, so Mom makes contact
with a local elementary school. She works an agreement with the principal whereby she will provide free software and documentation in
return for observing software being used in class, having teachers
complete a usability questionnaire, and conducting interviews with
teachers to identify weaknesses in the documentation.

Case Study 2: SmallCo Software

SmallCo Software is a seven-person software firm that creates and
markets specialized program development utilities for software devel-

opers. The staff includes three programmers, a secretary, an accountant, a person who handles hot-line calls, and the president, who is also the system designer and who does marketing. This staff is more specialized than Mom & Pop's but still fairly loosely organized (Figure 4.4).

The reference manual that goes with SmallCo's main product, *Astound!*, was written by a programmer in his spare time based on his rather cryptic personal notes, and even the most ardent admirers of the program have complained about its incompleteness, obscurity, and lack of illustrations.

The president sees the need to rewrite the manual. Three options are available: assign a member of staff to do the job, hire someone, or use a consultant. The staff is too busy, the job is too small to justify hiring, and so the president decides to use a consultant. He conducts a search

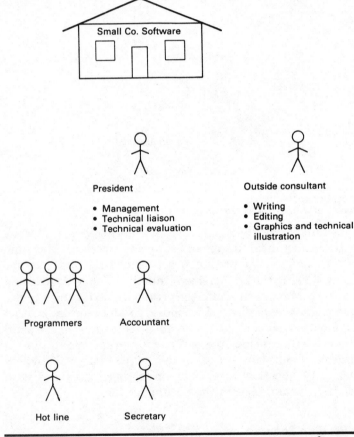

Figure 4.4 Organization of SmallCo Software, a seven-person software company using an outside consultant to perform documentation development.

of qualified consultants and eventually finds one with several years of experience and good references who enthusiastically praise her work. She fulfills the functions of writing and editing and, through a subcontractor, handles graphics. The president handles management, liaison, and evaluation. When drafts of documentation are completed, the president arranges to have them tried out by some programmers who are unfamiliar with the program. He collects their comments, relays them to the consultant, and she revises the documentation accordingly.

Case Study 3: MidCo Miniware

MidCo Miniware is a 70-person software firm that creates and markets a broad range of application programs for office-based micro- and minicomputers. Its programs include a word processor, database, spreadsheet, a network, and several support programs. All of these programs are designed for end users. MidCo's staff is organized along traditional lines, with separate departments for management and administration, marketing, programming, and support (Figure 4.5). The marketing department includes an editor, two writers, and an artist, and handles program documentation for MidCo's products. MidCo is fairly typical of

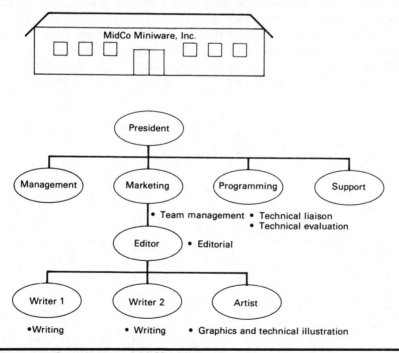

Figure 4.5 Organization of MidCo Miniware, a 70-person software company with formal staff organization.

medium- to large-sized companies with structured organizations and a high degree of specialization in the staff.

Within this organization, there are well-established procedures for creating user documentation. Each time a new product is being created, the department heads meet and develop a product-development plan that includes a user documentation component. This component provides for continuous involvement by the documentation team as the product is developed. Team members attend product briefings, are given access to the design and programming staff, and are provided with product descriptions, design documentation, and preliminary versions of the program as it evolves.

Development team functions in MidCo are clearly defined. Technical liaison is handled by the programming department head; team management by the marketing director; and editorial, writing, and graphics by members of the marketing department. Technical evaluation is a formal part of the product development plan and is handled by the programming department.

The Documentation Development Process

The document development process is a systematic way to plan, develop, and evaluate a documentation system (Figure 4.6). Much of this process has already been discussed in this book. Making the documentation-user match (see Chapter 3) is part of it. Development processes are also implicit in the hypothetical case studies of Mom & Pop's Microworks, SmallCo Software, and MidCo Miniware. Of these case studies, the most

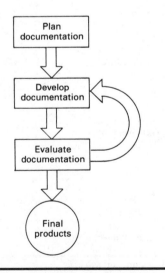

Figure 4.6 The documentation development process (general).

complete process discussed is that of MidCo Miniware, but MidCo is a fairly structured, medium-sized company, and the same process could not be fully adopted in smaller or less-structured companies.

Truth is, despite the authoritative title that heads this section, there is no such thing as a single documentation development process. Anyone who claims otherwise is naive, has myopia, or belongs to a large bureaucracy that requires its members to swear allegiance to rule and procedure. However, there are certain tasks that should always occur during documentation development, regardless of where it happens. This section focuses on these tasks. It does not matter whether you work in a company like Mom & Pop's, SmallCo, or MidCo, or for the Martian Defense Ministry, for that matter—you still need to perform certain tasks. These tasks are illustrated in Figure 4.7 and discussed in the following sections.

Step 1. Form the Documentation Development Team

Documentation is developed by people, so the first and most obvious step is to decide who will do the job (Figure 4.8). As development proceeds, some people may leave the team and others join it, but the team must exist in some form before starting anything.

The skill and manning requirements of the team cannot be fully defined until the types of documentation required are established by completing step 2 (make the user-documentation match, which follows). However, it is necessary at the start of the project to know who will perform the step 2 analyses. Thus, at the outset, team members should be assigned to perform the functions of technical liaison, project management, editorial, and writing. Assignments for the functions of graphics and technical illustration and technical evaluation can wait until the completion of step 2.

Step 2. Make the User-Documentation Match

The user-documentation match, discussed in Chapter 3, consists of steps for defining the types of documentation to develop based on the types of users, the operating environment, user tasks, and information requirements (Figure 4.9). The procedures for making the match are incorporated herewith (as a sort of subroutine; refer to Chapter 3 for detailed information).

The product of this step is a definition of the types of documentation needed and a fairly detailed definition of each, i.e., breadth and depth of coverage, organization, and format. Once the match has been made, the scope of the documentation development project will be apparent.

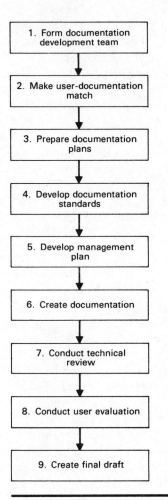

Figure 4.7 Steps in the documentation development process.

The documentation team assignments can then be modified accordingly. For example, if the match indicates that extensive internal documentation (e.g., help menus) will be required, then someone with expertise in that area can be added to the team.

Step 3. Prepare Documentation Plans

Documentation plans define the scope and content of each documentation item (Figure 4.10). They are developed based on the analyses conducted during step 2. A separate plan is prepared for each item. Each plan includes a content outline and guidance concerning the intended

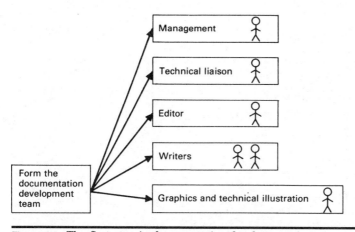

Figure 4.8 The first step in documentation development is to form the documentation development team—assign team responsibilities to individuals.

audience, depth and breadth of coverage of each topic, use of graphics, and source materials (if any) on which the item is to be based. In addition, where several items of related documentation are being developed (e.g., reference manual, guide, and quick reference card), the extent of overlap should be indicated to prevent duplication of effort.

Each plan will eventually be provided to a writer and used as the basis for preparing a particular item of documentation. This goal should be kept in mind as the plans are developed; they must be sufficiently detailed to provide the guidance needed to produce the intended products.

Developing these plans is a management/editorial function and, in principle, they should be developed by the project manager or editor. In practice, it is usually more efficient for the project manager and editor to sketch the plans, and to have writers develop detailed plans. Plans developed this way can then be reviewed and revised, as necessary, before developing actual documentation.

How detailed should the plans be? This depends mainly on the development environment. In a highly interactive environment (such as Mom & Pop's), a broad outline may suffice. In a more structured environment—particularly one in which the project is large and many people will be involved—it is essential for plans to be very detailed.

Step 4. Develop Documentation Standards

Documentation standards are a set of rules and examples that writers can follow in creating new documentation. Developing these standards is an editorial responsibility. Writers follow these standards in prepar-

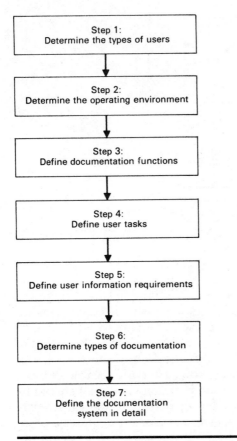

Figure 4.9 Procedure for making the user-documentation match.

ing their documentation. The standards ensure consistency in what is developed and reduce the amount of editing and rewriting later. The standards include rules, examples, and where available, other documents which may be used as models.

The standards cover such matters as page formats (e.g., page numbering, headings, average line length, lines per page), writing style (e.g., average sentence length, tone, voice, vocabulary guidance), and graphics (e.g., type, use of callouts).

Step 5. Develop Management Plan

The management plan defines the "what," "who," "when," and "how" of the documentation project (the "where" is usually self-evident). Developing this plan is a management responsibility, but the planner will need inputs from editors and technical liaison as well.

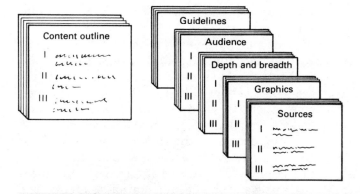

Figure 4.10 Documentation plans define the scope and content of each documentation item. They include a content outline and guidance concerning the intended audience, depth and breadth of coverage, use of graphics, and source materials.

The plan will include some type of time-line chart (such as a PERT or Gantt chart) and a written component that incorporates the documentation plans developed during step 4. The plan specifies what documentation items will be produced, who is responsible for each item, when the item is due, and the how of production. The what and who parts are straightforward. The when and how require a little elaboration.

First, when: Documentation is usually developed in sections or parts, and each part is developed in stages. The following is a possible progression:

- Create first draft—writer
- Create rough graphics—writer
- Editorial review—editor
- Create working draft—writer and editor
- Create working graphics—artist
- Technical review—technical liaison
- Revise working draft—writer and editor
- Conduct user evaluation—technical liaison
- Create final draft—writer and editor

A given project may include more or fewer steps, depending upon its specific requirements. Note that editorial and technical reviews and the user evaluation may require recycling to earlier stages, and that the progression will not always run smoothly; some slack must be built into the schedule to allow for delays.

Second, how: The how of documentation development concerns both the mechanics of production and any support or materials that the writer needs to produce the particular item. The mechanics are fairly straightforward; e.g., the writer is to produce text files and paper copy using *WordStar* or some other standard word-processing program. Support and materials may be problematical, i.e., the writer may need the technical support of a programmer or the availability of a working prototype of the program. Where these dependencies exist, they should be defined explicitly in the plan. This makes it easier for technical management to assess the needs of the documentation team and the impact of delays on the documentation project. A PERT chart makes such dependencies obvious and is a good management tool. (Chapter 5 discusses managment tools such as PERT and Gantt charts in detail.)

Once the management plan has been developed, it is reviewed within management, editorial, technical liaison, and other levels, and then revised and finalized. How this review process occurs is very much a function of the particular organization and its operating style. However, the current wisdom of modern, enlightened managers is that a management plan works best when it reflects inputs from personnel at all levels affected by the plan.

Once a satisfactory management plan has been developed, it is disseminated and implemented. Schedules are posted, personnel are given formal assignments, and work begins. As things move along, progress will be recorded, and management will periodically revise the plan, disseminate changes to the staff, and so forth.

Step 6. Create Documentation

The sequence previously outlined shows that documentation items are developed not in a single step, but in several steps involving initial creation, editorial and technical review, evaluation, revision, and so forth. The final products may involve several iterations before they are ready to be shown to the world. However, we may, for purposes of this discussion, simplify things slightly and treat creation as if it were a unitary activity.

Initial creation of documentation involves the first few steps outlined previously:

- Create first draft—writer
- Create rough graphics—writer
- Editorial review—editor
- Create working draft—writer and editor

- Create working graphics—artist

Although the initial product may reflect inputs received from designers and programmers, it is primarily a first attempt by writers, artist, and editor to produce a documentation item. Inevitably, there will be gaps to fill and errors to correct later. A few comments on the last point. Writers and editors should always attempt to produce the most technically accurate and complete documentation possible. Labeling an early effort a "draft" does not absolve its author of the usual journalistic responsiblity. More to the point, it is likely to place a greater burden on technical reviewers, strain the relationship between editorial and technical staffs, and make things more difficult for everyone.

Step 7. Conduct Technical Review

The objective of the technical review is to identify and correct technical errors and omissions in the preliminary documentation. The review is arranged by technical liaison and may be conducted by the individual performing that function or by members of the design and programming staff. Technical reviewers read and annotate the documentation provided and may, in some cases, provide inserts or rewrites of certain material.

Reviewer comments are eventually passed back to writers and editors so that corrections can be made. Following revision, a working draft of the documentation item is produced. As noted earlier, more than one review cycle (or iteration) may be necessary before an acceptable working draft is produced.

Step 8. Conduct User Evaluation

When an acceptable working draft of the documentation item has been produced, it should be subjected to a formal user evaluation. This evaluation can take a variety of forms, depending upon the scope and nature of the documentation (Figure 4.11). (User evaluations are discussed in detail in Chapter 12.)

```
• direct methods
   • Interviews
   • Subject logs
   • Questionnaires
   • Rating scales
Direct methods
   • Observations
   • Written tests
   • Performance tests
```

Figure 4.11   Some of the possible ways of collecting data during a formal user evaluation of documentation.

For simple programs with uncomplicated documentation, a field trial of the documentation may be adequate. This involves recruiting a sample of representatives of the user population, providing them with program and documentation, observing their attempts to use the system, making notes, and interviewing users afterwards.

For more complex programs or programs with more extensive documentation, it may be necessary to conduct small-scale experiments in which users are required to perform certain critical tasks and data are collected and subjected to formal statistical analyses. Although this type of evaluation is quite unusual in practice, it is becoming increasingly common and is advisable for programs that will be widely used or for which error consequences are serious. (Take note if your documentation deals with software for running nuclear power plants, navigation systems, fire control systems, or financial databases.)

Step 9. Create Final Draft

Following the user evaluation, the final draft of each documentation item is prepared. As in editorial and technical reviews, more than one iteration may be required before it is possible to create the final draft. If users have serious difficulties with documentation during the user evaluation (step 8), then it may be necessary to repeat part or all of the evaluation with successive documentation revisions. The "final" draft, as such, is one that users can use effectively.

Documentation Updating

Written documentation should be updated just as software (and internal documentation) is updated. Most updating of documentation should occur when updates to software are made available. All too often, the user is supplied with an updated version of a program and not an updated version of the supporting documentation.

It is unacceptable to the user to receive an update in the form of a printed list of modifications. What are required are new or replacement pages or new documentation. In other words, make it possible for the user to get rid of the outdated information and replace it with current information. Update lists are frequently sent along with an update disk and are supposed to be inserted in the front section of a manual. Presumably, the user is to read the update list—which may go on for 20 pages— and remember all the changes it contains. Then he or she refers to the manual, as usual, keeping in mind that certain parts of it no longer apply.

One of the advantages of providing documentation in ring binders is that the user can remove or replace pages. Binders also make it relatively easy for the developer to change the documentation. The replacement pages should be accompanied by a set of instructions telling how to incorporate the new or replacement pages into the document. A summary of the new or revised features of the program should also be provided. The design and architecture of documentation are discussed in detail in Chapters 7 and 8.

5

Management Tools for Documentation Development

This chapter presents an overview of several different management tools which may be used to support a documentation development project. The chapter is divided into two sections. The first discusses manual tools, and the second computer-based tools. Manual tools discussed are Gantt and PERT charts, checklists, and documentation standards. Computer-based tools discussed are planning and management programs, spreadsheets, outline processors, database programs, and project-specific dedicated programs. While this chapter does not attempt to describe all of the computer-based tools available, it does discuss a representative sample of programs for the IBM PC and compatibles and for the Macintosh computer.

Manual Tools

Manual tools discussed in this section are Gantt and PERT charts, checklists, and documentation standards.

Gantt and PERT Charts

Both Gantt and PERT charts are widely used in industry for managing projects. The Gantt chart (Figure 5.1) is the simpler and older of the two. It was invented around the turn of the century by Henry Gantt. The PERT (Program Evaluation and Review Technique) chart (Figure 5.2) was devised in the late 1950s to handle the complex planning and control requirements of the Polaris missle program. These charts differ

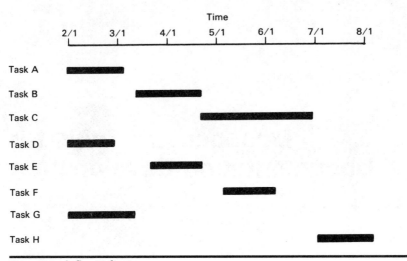

Figure 5.1 A Gantt chart.

in construction, but both can be very useful to project managers.

Gantt Chart.   The Gantt chart (Figure 5.1) lists tasks down the left edge and time across the top. Tasks are represented as horizontal bars in the rows. The task start date is at the left edge of the bar, completion date at the right edge of the bar, and everything in between represents performance time.

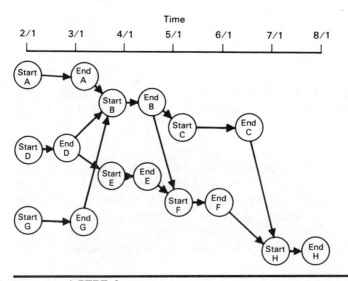

Figure 5.2 A PERT chart.

Gantt charts were originally devised for scheduling production operations in which the tasks were fairly predictable and independent. As each task has its own, separate row, chart format does not readily lend itself to showing interrelationships among tasks. For example, there is no standard way of using the chart to show that task 1 must be completed before task 2, that tasks 5 and 6 must be completed before 7, and so forth. This limitation may or may not be a problem, depending upon the particular project. Clearly, it is not a problem if all of the tasks are independent. However, as dependencies increase, the chart becomes increasingly limited as a management tool.

The importance of dependencies to effective project management increases with uncertainties in individual tasks. For example, if you are managing a documentation project in which several people are working on different documents, each having separate dependencies on the availability of technical support and an evolving piece of software, then a breakdown at any point may have a ripple effect throughout the entire project. In this case, the dependencies are critical. On the other hand, if you are managing a small-scale project with a few people, the dependencies are probably not as critical.

Gantt charts often include "milestones"—key dates by which certain project goals are to be accomplished. For example, a Gantt chart for a documentation project will usually include a prominently marked symbol for the completion of the program user's guide, reference manual, or other main deliverable. Figure 5.3 shows a Gantt chart for a documentation development project following the process described in Chapter 4.

Though the Gantt chart is mainly thought of as a management tool, it is also very useful in communicating project goals and progress to the documentation team. It is simple enough to be transparent on the surface. Hence, it is common practice to develop one of these charts and to post it prominently so that team members can see how work is progressing. PERT charts can also be used for this purpose, but they are more complex and not as easy to interpret. Thus, even if the project is managed primarily with a PERT chart, it is a good idea to develop a Gantt chart for communication.

PERT Chart. The PERT chart (Figure 5.2) resembles and is in fact a network. Nodes (usually drawn as circles) represent events, and links (actually vectors, since they have arrowheads and are directed) represent activities. Events are specific, measurable occurrences and can be tied to dates. Examples of events are the start or end of a task, the point at which a support service (such as technical review) is required, and the completion of a deliverable item. Task process is what goes on between one or more events.

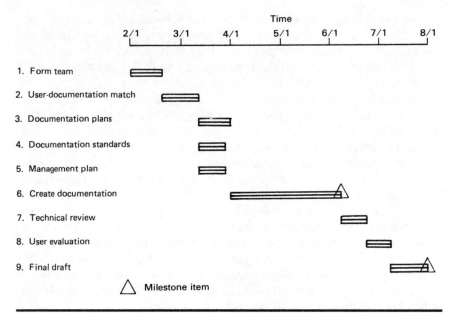

Figure 5.3 A Gantt chart for a hypothetical documentation development project (compare with Figure 5.5).

The PERT chart lends itself well to projects in which there is a high degree of interdependence among tasks. An event which has several other events dependent downstream can be linked to the others with arrows. Interdependencies become very obvious when charted. Moreover, as an analytical technique, PERT charting can be very useful in identifying critical events, i.e., those events which have broad downstream impact. A Gantt chart for the same project simply lacks the information necessary for identifying these interdependencies; the manager must derive and remember it mentally.

PERT charts often contain patterns. A series of dependent events (like dominos) takes the form of a string of pearls (Figure 5.4a). A single event prerequisite to two or more downstream events looks like a crossroad (Figure 5.4b). Multiple events prerequisite to a single event are like merging lanes of traffic (Figure 5.4c). Events often proceed in parallel, and the total network can begin to resemble a road map of physical geography. The road-map metaphor is not farfetched, for just as traffic tends to become bottlenecked at crossroads, so does the progress of work tend to be tied critically to nodes shared among several tasks. Once a PERT chart has been created, it is fairly easy to identify these critical points in a development project.

As with Gantt charts, the utility of PERT charts depends upon the particular development project. The PERT chart becomes increasingly

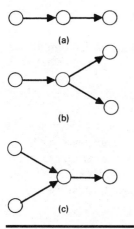

Figure 5.4 Common PERT chart patterns: (*a*) series, (*b*) burst, and (*c*) merge.

important and useful as project complexity increases—unlike the Gantt chart. Complex projects need PERT charts. Gantt charts, when used as communication tools and to chart the flow of different tasks, remain useful even when PERT charts are used. Figure 5.5 shows a PERT chart

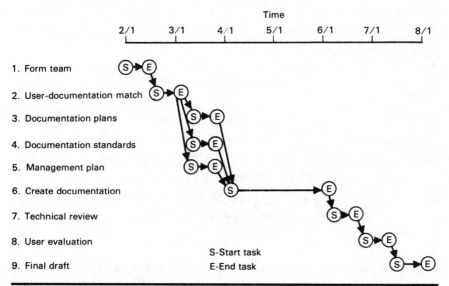

Figure 5.5 PERT chart for a hypothetical documentation project (compare with Figure 5.3).

for a documentation development project following the process described in Chapter 4.

PERT charts can be used to determine critical paths, calculate elapsed times, assign probabilities to events, and to perform several other analytical functions not touched on here. For more information on their use, consult a good management text, such as Maynard's *Industrial Engineering Handbook*.

The preparation of Gantt and PERT charts has traditionally been a somewhat tedious exercise involving paper, pencil, and drawing tools (or sticky or magnetic tiles on large boards). Chart preparation has been much simplified in recent years by the appearance of software packages that automate the process. Planning and management software is discussed in the next section.

Checklists

Organized people, it is often said, tend to be list-makers. They make lists to keep from overlooking the many things they need to do during the day, week, or month. A list reminds them to do certain things and, once a thing is done, it is checked off. As long as it remains on the list, unchecked, it is a prod. Having the item on the list is no guarantee that it will get done, but not having it there increases the chance it won't.

Checklists can be very useful on a documentation development project because many details must be attended to. They are also a way of communicating to the development team what is to be done on project tasks.

Management checklists.   Project managers will find checklists useful for such activities as the following:

- Coordination of support for development tasks (e.g., making phone calls)

- Completion of events (e.g., ensuring that the first draft of the user's guide is done on June 5, as scheduled)

- Content of documentation items (e.g., that the reference manual contains the type of material specified in its outline)

- Production event scheduling (i.e., ensuring that draft materials are edited and proofed, artwork is prepared, index is completed, copy is sent to printer, etc.)

Developer checklists.   Writers and others creating documentation will find it useful to prepare checklists which define the components of each task assignment (the same as the manager's content checklist) and any related events (such as contacting a subject matter expert). Such checklists are somewhat redundant with other materials used during a development project. A document content outline, for example, tells what a document must contain, and the team member responsible for that document (or part of that document) can refer to it to determine what to cover. Likewise, if a PERT chart is used on the project, it tells much of what must be done. (A Gantt chart is not as informative.) However, the checklist will contain some things that outlines and PERT charts do not, such as defining how the developer is to coordinate work with others. The relationships among these three tools are illustrated in Figure 5.6.

There are no simple rules for deciding what checklists to use—or if any should be used at all, for that matter. This tool, like others available to a project manager, becomes increasingly important as the project grows in size. The more things there are to do and the more people to coordinate, the more important checklists become to ensure that everything is done, as planned, and on schedule.

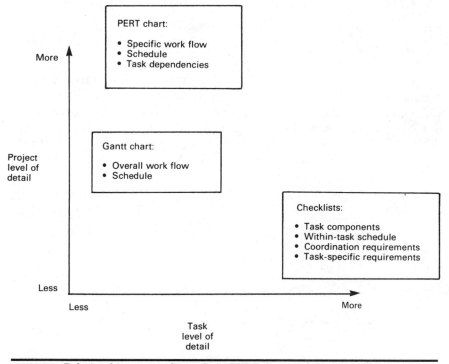

Figure 5.6 Relationships among Gantt chart, PERT chart, and checklists: Gantt and PERT charts provide different levels of detail concerning the overall project, with PERT being most informative. Checklists provide the most specific information about individual tasks, but little information about the overall project.

Documentation Standards

Documentation standards are a set of rules and examples that writers can follow in creating new documentation. They do not define the content of the document, but do define how it will look, be written, and work. The creators of documentation use these standards in preparing their documentation. The standards ensure consistency in what is developed and provide explicit or implicit guidance concerning how the item of documentation is to be designed, formatted, and written. While there are no "standard" standards, as such, one may think of these standards as consisting of three separate components: (1)general reference materials, (2)project-specific guidelines and rules, and (3)models (Figure 5.7).

General reference materials.   General reference materials include such materials as the following:

- Dictionary
- Thesaurus
- English language usage reference materials
- Computer terms and usage reference materials

The first two items on the list are obvious requirements for every documentation developer's individual bookshelf.

English language usage reference materials include such documents as the *Associated Press Style Manual*, Strunk and White's *The Elements of Style*, or technical writing books containing the conventions that will be followed in preparing documentation. The particular selection depends upon the project.

Computer terms and usage reference materials include such docu-

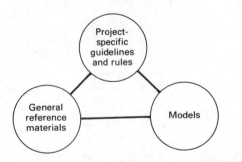

Figure 5.7 Components of documentation standards.

ments as dictionaries of computer terminology, documents defining the standards for a particular language (e.g., Kernighan & Ritchie's *The C Programming Language*), and other documents that will be followed in determining the appropriate terms and usage of a particular programming language or operating system. Again, the selection of documents depends upon the project.

All materials in this category are selected rather than developed from scratch. Their purpose is twofold: (1) to provide the team with answers to questions concerning terminology and usage and (2) to ensure that documentation is developed with due recognition to industrywide standards. It does not make much sense to define terms anew in your documentation or to develop new ways of expressing the syntax of a particular command or command statement. Doing such is not only unprofessional but will increase the difficulty of using the document. Hence, appropriate general reference materials should be made available to and used by documentation developers.

Project-specific guidelines and rules. In addition to general reference materials, certain project-specific guidelines and rules must be developed for the project as a whole and for each individual item of documentation. The content of these guidelines and rules will vary with the project but, overall, they address the issues discussed in Chapter 7 (Documentation Design) and Chapter 8 (Documentation Architecture). Moreover, before these standards can be developed in their entirety, the content, organization, and depth and breadth of coverage of the document must be defined and the physical structure and format of the final product(s) must be decided upon. The guidelines and rules concern some or all of the following issues:

- Document modularity
- Structure of introductions, tutorials, and reference sections
- Use of advance organizers
- Use of concrete examples
- Use of tropes
- Quick-reference considerations
  - Table of contents
  - Indexing
  - Heading numbering scheme (if used)
- Graphics conventions
  - Types of graphics used
  - Callouts

- Location (e.g., margin or embedded)
- Frequency of use
- Structural conventions
  - Titles, headings, subheadings
  - Pagination
  - Use of running headers and footers
  - Justification (left or full)
  - Type font and size
  - Use of typographic cuing (e.g., boldface, underlining)
  - Margin, header, and footer size
- Instructional style
- Language human factors rules
  - Active versus passive voice
  - Average sentence length
  - Use of compound sentences
  - Positive versus negative constructions
- Rules for use of acronyms and abbreviations
- Glossary of project-specific terms and phrases

Most of the items listed are discussed in Chapters 7 and 8 and may form the basis for your documentation standards. While it will take a considerable effort to develop the guidelines and rules for your project, doing so will ensure greater consistency in the final products and considerably reduce the editorial changes required. In short, this effort is well spent and will result in more cost-effective documentation development.

Models.　A model is an existing item of documentation similar in form and content to one being developed. If such models exist, they can be of great help to the developer since they show, in concrete form, what is expected in terms of a new document. Rules and guidelines tell how things should be, but models show. They are very powerful tools indeed.

Chapter 10 of this book describes several items of user documentation which may be used as models. The items were selected from a fairly large set (approximately 100 programs). While these are certainly not suitable universally, they are good models. The documentation manager and developer should always be on the lookout for models that might be used in house.

Computer-Based Tools

Several different desktop computer programs are available to support project managers. These fall into four categories: planning and management programs, spreadsheets, outline processors, and databases. In addition, if resources are available, it may be possible to create a dedicated (i.e., project-specific) program. Planning and management programs are used to develop Gantt or PERT charts and various management-related reports. Spreadsheets are used primarily for financial planning, but many can also be used to create charts. Outline processors are used to organize ideas. Databases are used to store and access data. Dedicated programs are developed in-house to serve the specific requirements of a project.

This chapter focuses on desktop applications for the IBM PC (and compatibles) and the Macintosh. Similar programs are available on larger computers, although they are much more expensive. The discussion is meant to illustrate the types of capabilities available, not to recommend any particular item of software. The fact that a product is mentioned is not an endorsement of it; it simply means that the product falls into the category being discussed and is a good example of the particular type of software.

Planning and Management Programs

There are several project planning and management programs on the market. The majority of these are available for the IBM PC, although there are also a few for the Macintosh. Most cost less than $500. Some of the programs can generate only Gantt charts, but the more sophisticated ones can generate PERT charts and several different types of management reports. The programs normally define a project in terms of the relationships among tasks, available resources, and time. Each project may be broken down into tasks, and each task requires certain resources. Given the resources, the program can calculate the time required to complete a task. Moreover, if the program is able to handle dependencies among tasks, critical paths can be determined. While such programs cannot do the actual planning, they simplify the process somewhat and greatly reduce the work required to change the plan. (And, as every manager knows, Murphy's law of management requires that every plan always changes.)

The way planning programs typically work is shown in Figure 5.8.

The first step in using such a program is to list the tasks and resources required by the project. Resources may be people, teams, equipment, or other entities used in performing the work. If costs are to be computed, cost information is also entered. A start or end date is specified; planning may be forward (from start date) or backward (from end date). These entries, obviously, cannot be made by the program, and still represent considerable work for the planner. However, the program will

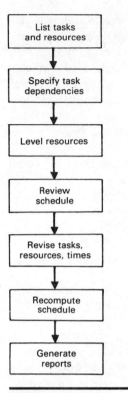

Figure 5.8 Typical sequence of steps in using a planning program.

use these data to calculate dependent dates and workloads and save the user that work. The entries are usually made with a Gantt chart-like input screen.

Next, task dependencies are specified. This is done by indicating which tasks must be performed before others can be started.

The program then does "resource leveling," i.e., determines how much time each task will take based on the available resources. At that point, it provides output in the form requested by the user.

The user reviews the schedule provided by the program, makes the necessary revisions to tasks, resources, or time, and has the program recompute the schedule. This revision-recomputation process is continued until a satisfactory schedule is obtained.

Reports are then generated for managing the project. The types of reports available depend upon the particular program. Usually, the program generates a Gantt chart (see Figure 5.8). It may also be able to generate a PERT chart (Figure 5.9) and various task-specific reports which may be used to manage individual tasks, determine resource allocation and usage, compute costs, or compare actual versus planned performance. Figures 5.10*a*, *b*, *c*, and *d* show a sampling of the reports available with *Timeline* (Breakthrough Software).

The available project managers vary considerably in capabilities. The less sophisticated ones are useful only for managing small, simple projects. Usually, they are unable to generate PERT charts, are more limited in the number of tasks and resources they can handle, may not provide cost information, and generate fewer reports. The more sophisticated ones have greater capabilities. Among these programs are *Harvard Total Project Manager* (Software Publishing Corp.), *Timeline*, *Project Manager Workbench* (Applied Business Technology Corp.), and *PMS-II* (North American MICA, Inc.) for the IBM PC; and *Micro Planner Plus* (Micro Planning Software, Ltd.) for the Macintosh. For a good comparative review of IBM PC software, see the February 11, 1986 issue of *PC Magazine*. *PC Magazine* gave good reviews to all of the project managers it checked, but rated *Timeline* high for its capabilities and reasonable price ($495). *Microsoft Project* (Version 1.02) was the least expensive program reviewed ($250), of more limited capabilities, but adequate for simpler projects. *Micro Planner* is one of the more powerful management programs available on the Macintosh but, according to

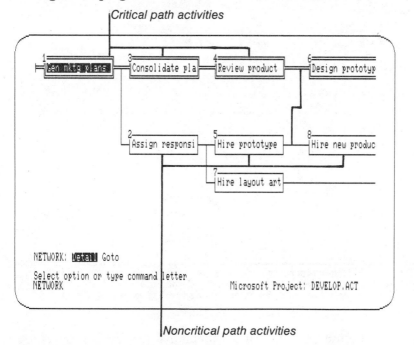

Figure 5.9 PERT chart generated by a planning program. (*From* Microsoft, [user's guide], *Microsoft Corporation, 1985.*)

Task Detail Report

```
Schedule Name:   Preliminary Design of Product A
Project Manager: B. Humphrey
As of date:      8-May-85 10:00am      Schedule File: DK:MANRPTS

Client Contact is B. Lauren (415-555-3829)

PROJECT START

          ASAP        In Future    MileStone

          1

                      Start            End
                      -----------      -----------
          Date:       8-May-85 10:00am 8-May-85 10:00am

          CRITICAL (no slack)

          Tasks which come before:    Tasks which come after:
          --------------------------  --------------------------
                                      :Client Meeting (1)

:Client Meeting (1)

          ASAP        In Future    1 day

          1

                      Start            End
                      -----------      -----------
          Date:       8-May-85 10:00am 9-May-85 10:00am

          CRITICAL (no slack)

          Resource:                   How much:    Cost:
          --------------------------  ----------   ----------
          Cathy Nash (Coordinator)          1.00      240.00
          Joe Burkhart (Analyst)            1.00      320.00
          Sharon Sullivan (Writer)          1.00      280.00
          James Thomas (Editor)             1.00      109.09
          Rental of Meeting Room at Hotel   1.00      600.00
          Miscellaneous Fixed Costs       100.00      100.00
              Total Cost ...............................  1,649.09

          Tasks which come before:    Tasks which come after:
          --------------------------  --------------------------
          PROJECT START               :Research


Time Line Task Detail Report                              Page 1
```

(a)

Figure 5.10 A selection of reports generated by the *Timeline* planning program: (*a*) Task Detail, (*b*) Resource Table, (*c*) Cost Report by Resource, and (*d*) Actual Versus Planned. (*From Timeline Manual, Breakthrough Software Corporation, 1985.*)

InfoWorld (November 11, 1985) it is difficult to learn and use, especially for the occasional user. One of the simplest Macintosh planners is *MacProject*, a program adequate for small-scale projects.

Resource Table Report

```
Schedule Name:   Preliminary Design of Product A
Project Manager: B. Humphrey
As of date:      7-May-85  5:20pm        Schedule File: DK:MAN20

Client Contact is B. Lauren (415-555-3892)

Resource                                         Maximum            Cost
or Cost    Full Name                     Type    Available  Compute Rate    Per       Accrue
---------- ----------------------------- -------- --------- -------- ------- --------  --------
Assemblers Assemblers - Pool of 5        Resource    5.00  Variable 12.00   1 Hour    Prorate
CN         Cathy Nash (Coordinator)      Resource    1.00  Variable 45.00   1 Hour    Prorate
HP         Harry Pierce (Illustrator)    Resource    1.00  Variable 32.00   1 Hour    Prorate
JB         Joe Burkhart (Analyst)        Resource    1.00  Variable 4200.00 1 Month   Prorate
JT         James Thomas (Editor)         Resource    1.00  Variable 2250.00 1 Month   Prorate
Machinist  Machinists - Pool of 4        Resource    4.00  Variable 37.50   1 Hour    Prorate
Misc Cost  Miscellaneous Fixed Costs     Cost              Fixed                       At Start
Paper      80 lb. bond (per ream)        Cost              Unit     4.25              At Start
RH         Randy Hughes (Writer)         Resource    1.00  Variable 18.00   1 Hour    Prorate
Room Rent  Rental of Mtg Room at Hotel   Cost              Variable 65.00   1 Hour    At End


Time Line   Resource Table   Page number 1 of 1
```

(b)

Figure 5.10 *(Continued)*

The programs mentioned above should give you a sense of what is available in the marketplace. Since products change and new products are introduced, you would be well advised, if interested in purchasing one, to examine more current reviews than those cited and to check out the programs personally. If you plan to manage a complex project, you

Cost Report by Resource

```
Schedule Name:   Preliminary Design of Product A
Project Manager: B. Humphrey
As of date:      7-May-85  5:20pm        Schedule File: DK:MAN20

Client Contact is B. Lauren (415-555-3892)


Resource        Rate    Per          Amount
----------  ----------  ----------  --------------
CN            30.000    1 Hours       1,680.00
JB            40.000    1 Hours       2,880.00
JT         2,400.000    1 Months        327.27
Misc Cost                               100.00
Room Rent     75.000    1 Hours         600.00
SS            35.000    1 Hours         280.00
==========                          ================
TOTAL                                 5,867.27


Time Line   Cost Report by Resource   Page number 1 of 1
```

(c)

Figure 5.10 *(Continued)*

Actual Versus Planned

```
Schedule Name:   Preliminary Design of Product A
Project Manager: B. Humphrey
As of date:      8-May-85 10:06am        Schedule File: Dk:MANRPTS

Client Contact is B. Lauren (415-555-3829)

Compared against plan, DK:MANRPTS.Te0, of 8-May-85 6:35am .


-------------------------------------------------------------------------------
Took longer than planned:
-----------------------------Planned------------Actual-------------------------

:Research               4 days          5 days


-------------------------------------------------------------------------------
Took less time than planned:
-----------------------------Planned------------Actual-------------------------

:Design (s)             2 weeks         8 days


-------------------------------------------------------------------------------
Milestones that started later than planned:
-----------------------------Planned------------Actual-------------------------

PROJECT START           8-May-85  9:00am   8-May-85 11:00am


-------------------------------------------------------------------------------
Other tasks that started later than planned:
-----------------------------Planned------------Actual-------------------------

:Client Meeting (1)     8-May-85  9:00am   8-May-85 11:00am
:Research               9-May-85  9:00am   9-May-85 11:00am
:Define All Items      15-May-85  9:00am  16-May-85 11:00am
:Design (s)            15-May-85  9:00am  16-May-85 11:00am


-------------------------------------------------------------------------------
Milestones that started earlier than planned:
-----------------------------Planned------------Actual-------------------------

APPROVALS (1)           3-Jun-85  9:00am  31-May-85 11:00am


-------------------------------------------------------------------------------
Other tasks that started earlier than planned:
-----------------------------Planned------------Actual-------------------------

:Do Long Lead Items    24-May-85  9:00am  23-May-85 11:00am
:Design Review         30-May-85  9:00am  29-May-85 11:00am


Time Line Actual-vs.-Planned Report                               Page 1
```

(d)

Figure 5.10 (*Continued*)

need a capable program. If not, you are better off with one of the simpler ones.

Spreadsheets

The original spreadsheet program was *VisiCalc*. Many people today regard it as the reason for the success of the personal computer, particularly the Apple II. Since its appearance in the late 1970s, the spreadsheet has undergone a number of refinements, but its basic structure and utility remain unchanged.

A spreadsheet, as the name suggests, consists of a matrix of cells (Figure 5.11). The cells may contain characters (such as column headings), numbers (e.g., the price of a commodity), or formulas. The formulas may perform various operations on cell contents, define a cell in relation to other cells (e.g., the value in the cell is defined as the sum of the contents of several other cells), or perform other operations.

The user may manipulate one or more items in the spreadsheet and determine the effect elsewhere. This makes it fairly easy to ask "what-if" questions and obtain quick answers—without having to go through tedious recalculations by hand.

The most widespread use of spreadsheets is in financial planning and management. A program such as this has obvious utility to the real estate investor who wants to know what the return on investment will be five years down the road and who must take into account at the outset such factors as initial investment, interest rate, projected rise in the cost of utilities and maintenance, and a host of other factors. Likewise, a spreadsheet is valuable to the project manager who needs to know how

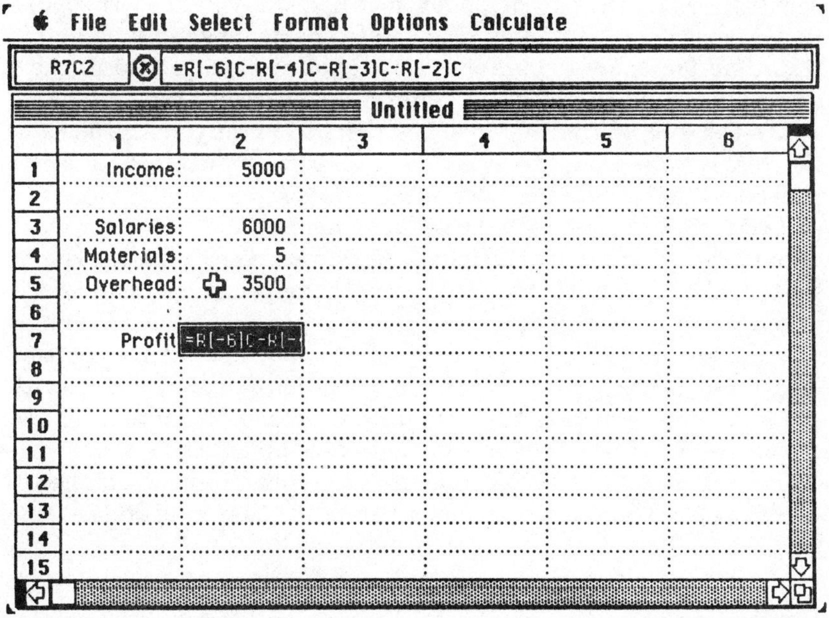

Figure 5.11 A screen from the Macintosh version of *Microsoft Multiplan*. A formula is being entered. (*From Simpson*, Programming the Macintosh User Interface, *McGraw-Hill, New York, 1985.*)

a delay in one aspect of a project will affect the bottom line (some project management software does this automatically). Financial concerns such as this matter to any manager responsible for budgets (and what manager isn't?).

If you are concerned with budgets and have not used a spreadsheet, then you can probably benefit by learning more about them and trying one out. These programs are very popular and much has been written about them, including several good how-to books. Today most managers are familiar with at least one of these programs, and using them is part of the job.

Simple spreadsheets still exist. *Microsoft Multiplan* is a good example. The capabilities of many of these programs are being expanded. For example, *Microsoft Excel* also incorporates a built-in database and graphics capabilities. So-called "integrated" applications such as *1-2-3* (Lotus Development Corp.) and *Framework II* (Ashton-Tate) include a word processor and database in addition to the spreadsheet. While an integrated application makes it simpler to transport data among the three applications, usually the capabilities of any single subapplication (e.g., the word processor) are more limited than those of a stand-alone program.

In addition to their use for financial management, spreadsheets can be used to create charts. Most were not designed for this, and they are not the best tool for the purpose, but they will do the job. The less sophisticated spreadsheets can be used to create charts by simply using the cells as areas for text or lines. For example, you can create a Gantt chart this way by entering dates in the cells on the top row of the sheet, task names in the cells on the left edge, and then fill in the cells to the right of the tasks with lines corresponding to performance times. Some spreadsheets will create the horizontal bars for you.

A PERT chart can be created in similar manner, but the connecting links must later be drawn in by hand. One advantage of creating charts this way is that it is fairly easy to modify them; you simply call up the spreadsheet, move things around, shift the scale, add or delete things, and you have a new chart. You don't have to pencil in changes or send the chart back to the art department for a revision. Creating charts with spreadsheet programs is not universally recommended. Planning and management programs (previously mentioned) are much better for this since they do more than produce a chart. Graphics tools (see Chapter 6) make drawing easier. But spreadsheets will, as they say, do the job.

Outline Processors

Outline processors are programs designed to facilitate the creation, editing, and organization of outlines. They are useful both as management tools and as production tools. Though they are sometimes called "idea processors"—particularly in advertisements—the more humble name has stuck. Their design makes them easier to use than word processing programs for the types of operations common during early planning and outlining, i.e., entering short blocks of text, moving the blocks around, organizing them in different ways, changing dependencies and subordination, sorting them, and so on.

The programs are useful for a number of different purposes. Obviously, they can come in handy during documentation outlining. Start with document divisions or chapter titles. Enter the subtopics in a particular chapter. Then "hide" the subtopics temporarily to work on the next division. Continue in this manner until the preliminary outline has been created. Along the way or afterward, "unhide" the lower levels of the outline, review them, reorganize, and so forth. What makes this particularly easy is that the program provides built-in tools to show subordination (by indentation), to perform moves, to hide and unhide various levels, to sort, and to perform other manipulations.

An outline processor can also be useful for creating a table of contents, an index, or a glossary—particularly the latter two.

Outline processors come in various forms—as dedicated programs, as utilities within other programs, as desk accessories—and are available for virtually all desktop computers. One of the earliest of the lot, a dedicated program and a long-time best-seller, is *Think-Tank* (Living Videotext); the manufacturer has since come forth with *Ready!*

Framework (Ashton-Tate) incorporates an outline processor into an integrated program. *Freestyle* (Select Information Systems), *Fact Cruncher* (Infostructures), and *MaxThink* (MaxThink, Inc.) are extensions of the basic outlining concept with additional features. *MaxThink* is primarily an outliner, *Freestyle* is a word processor with strong outlining capabilities, and *Fact Cruncher* combines the features of an outliner with a database. Each of these programs, though different, incorporates outlining features. In addition, there are many other such programs on the market.

If you are unfamiliar with outline processors, it would probably pay to investigate further. They are useful not only to managers, but also to those developing documentation. Hence, you should have one available for the documentation development team to use. For most purposes, one of the simpler ones will do nicely.

Database Programs

Database programs are used to store, organize, modify, and selectively retrieve data. The data may be any information of importance to the user: a list of names, personnel records, titles of books and articles, pages of text. Some database programs can store very long documents or even pictures.

Considerable work is involved in creating a database: The content must be entered by typing it in or by transferring it from another database, it must be kept updated, and a computer is required to retrieve the data. Manual filing systems can be used for the same purpose, although a database may be more efficient if many people make use of it. In addition, some ready-made databases can be accessed on disk or via modem. The utility of these varies with the particular project.

Figure 5.12 shows the structure of a hypothetical database. A database consists of one or more files. Files are usually organized into records, which are collections of related data elements (such as names, telephone numbers, addresses, etc.). Records are defined in terms of fields; each field consists of a single data element. An index is a key used to access file records. For example, an alphabetic index is commonly used to access a file, the records of which contain names.

A database program is flexible in terms of what it contains and how its contents are organized; these factors are under the user's control. For example, by adapting program features, the user may use the same program to track a parts inventory, maintain personnel records, or manage a library.

The simpler databases are computerized filing systems. Examples of such programs are *PFS: File* (PFS Corp.) and *Microsoft File*. Data are entered, indexed, and retrieved using the index.

Often, however, the user cannot devise an indexing system that will meet all possible future data-access requirements. When this is the case, it may be desirable to use a relational database, i.e., a program that permits data to be accessed via the normal index route or via relationships among its data fields. For example, one might use such a program to search a personnel file to identify all professional employees who have worked for a firm for 2 to 4 years. The search requirement implies a relationship: employee type (i.e., professional) and length of employment (2–4 years). A relationship such as this is specified on the spot, during the search. Tomorrow the interest may shift to another

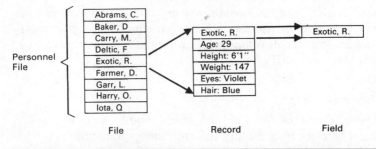

Figure 5.12 Structure of hypothetical database. The database consists of separate files. Each file consists of records, and each record consists of related data elements called "fields."

relationship, e.g., production-line employees earning less than $8 per hour. It is common to specify the relationship using logical operators (AND, OR, NOT) and relational operators (less than, more than, equal to, etc.).

There are many different database programs, and they vary greatly in complexity, power, and ease of use. To be useful, the program must give the user flexibility, but this flexibility tends to make the program complex and difficult to use. The program must be customizable; it must be possible for the user to specify features built into conventional programs. For example, the user must be able to define the content of the database, design record formats for data input and display, and specify field type and content. A relational database must permit the user to define the desired search relation—and this may pose serious problems to program users unfamiliar with logical and relational operators. For simple record-keeping tasks, a filing system—even a manual one— is often preferable.

Again, the utility of a database program (or an integrated application) depends upon the particular documentation development project and what type of information needs to be tracked. On small-scale projects, its utility is doubtful; on larger ones, it may be quite valuable. (Manual record-keeping systems, though they date to antiquity, still have much going for them. Not the least of their virtues are that they require little training to use, don't require computers, and cannot be destroyed by power failures.)

Project-Specific Dedicated Programs

A dedicated program is one designed expressly to perform a specific type of task. Planning and management programs, spreadsheets, outline processors, and databases do not fall into this category because they are general-purpose programs that must be tailored by the user to fit task requirements. Such programs may be quite good and may, in many cases, fulfill all the necessary requirements. On the other hand, sometimes they do not quite fit or are too much work to customize to the specific job. When this is the case, a dedicated program may be the answer.

You may, for example, need to generate certain types of plans or reports that cannot be created easily with one of the general-purpose programs. In this case, it may be cost-effective to develop an in-house program expressly for the intended purpose. Developing custom software can be expensive, and the practicality of doing so depends mainly on the relative cost of performing the task by traditional methods versus using a new, dedicated program, with the cost of software development amortized over the expected life of the dedicated program.

6

Production Tools for Documentation Development

This chapter provides an overview of several different desktop computer-based production tools which may be used to support a documentation project. The chapter is divided into four sections. The first section discusses hardware and software considerations relating to these tools. The second section discusses writing tools: word-processing programs, spelling checkers, and on-line thesauruses. The third section discusses drawing tools: drawing programs and image banks. The final section discusses desktop publishing.

While this chapter does not attempt to describe all of the computer-based production tools available, it does discuss a representative sample of programs for the IBM PC (and compatibles) and for the Macintosh computer.

Hardware and Software Considerations

This book focuses on software for the IBM PC (and compatibles) and for the Macintosh computer. Both machines have become "standards" in a way—widely used in business, industry, science, and elsewhere

Interestingly, they are seldom used by the same people. For some reason, a person usually embraces one or the other, seldom both. Among some people, the Macintosh is regarded as a machine for the computer novice, and the IBM PC one for sophisticated users. The reason probably is the Macintosh's graphics-oriented user interface—icons, menus, mouse—but may also have something to do with the machine's California origins in a company once run by very young, non-IBM types.

People who truly understand both machines see things differently. The Macintosh is a superb machine for graphics-oriented applications, better by far than the IBM PC. On the other hand, with text-oriented applications, it's quite a different story. Not only are there relatively few word-processing programs for the Macintosh, but many of those available have limited power. Thus, one way of comparing the machines more meaningfully is to think of one as a graphics machine and the other as a text machine.

While not everyone is crazy about the Macintosh user interface, something very similar has been made available on the IBM PC. The GEM (Graphics Environment Manager) operating system can be used on IBM PCs to achieve much the same icon, menu, and mouse environment as on the Macintosh. A small number of GEM-based, Macintosh-like programs are beginning to appear for the IBM PC. Likewise, a set of related Microsoft products (*Windows*, *Write*, and *Paint*) offer Macintosh-like features on IBM PCs and compatibles. The opposite is not occurring, at least not yet. For example, no one has yet written a powerful, keyboard-based word-processing program for the Macintosh.

Hardware differences also have some important implications. The IBM PC with high-resolution monochrome display offers probably the best all-around text display of *any* desktop computer, but is incapable of doing graphics. The characters appear fully-formed on the screen and can be tolerated throughout a full working day without danger of eyestrain. The IBM display monitor is of reasonable size (12-inch diagonal) for extended work. One serious drawback of the monochrome monitor is that it is available only with green phosphor, which rather demands that it be used in subdued light. The ideal high-resolution monitor for working in an office would present black characters on a white background (like the Macintosh); these can be used in normal lighting without eye adaptation problems.

The IBM PC with a graphics card and color monitor is capable of graphics and color. Unfortunately, this combination results in much poorer legibility than the high-resolution monochrome display—not recomended for use over an extended period of time. The IBM PC, PC XT, and PC AT keyboards—particularly those used on the later machines—are excellent, although some of the keys on the original machine were small and poorly located (e.g., the Return key); most of the problems have been corrected with the AT. It is full-sized, has an excellent feel, has function keys, and has several special-purpose keys—including cursor keys arranged in a sensible fashion.

The Macintosh, in some respects, scores more poorly in the hardware department than the IBM PC. On the positive side, it's a very compact machine, with a sharp, high-resolution, black-on-white display and a keyboard with good feel. Use of the mouse-controlled cursor is intuitive and fast. There is also little to remember in the way of keyboard commands and the like. On the negative side, the display of pre-Macintosh II versions is too small (9 inches) and the keyboard is nonadjustable and lacks many of the keys it needs to be useful to skilled keyboardists. The Macintosh II, with its larger monitor and improved keyboard, overcomes these shortcomings.

In case you think the authors are biased on the IBM PC versus Macintosh question, you're absolutely wrong. We must be even-handed. One of the authors uses an IBM PC almost exclusively and the other a Macintosh. Part of this book was composed on one type of computer, and the rest on the other type. We've also had to face the incompatibility problem. (Ultimately, we piped everything over to the Macintosh, mainly to simplify editing and reproduction.)

Is one machine better than the other?

Yes. For serious, prolonged work with text-only applications, the IBM PC is much better. For graphics-based applications or for applications mixing text and graphics (e.g., desktop publishing), the Macintosh is better. These are opinions, obviously, and many readers will disagree, but this is how we see it. Since each machine has its particular strengths, it probably makes more sense to think of the two as complementary rather than competing alternatives. A documentation development team should have access to both.

Does this rule out the use of minicomputer- or mainframe-based applications for documentation development? Certainly not, if the applications are available or reasonably priced, relatively easy to learn and use, and offer special features not found on desktop computers. Otherwise, it probably makes more sense to use desktop computers for documentation development. Our best guess is that desktop applications are more suitable for most such projects. The cost, ease of learning and use, and capabilities of desktop applications give them the edge over minicomputer- or mainframe-based applications.

Writing Tools

This section discusses word processors, spelling checkers, and on-line thesauruses. The most powerful writing tools are available for IBM PCs and compatibles, so this section tends to emphasize IBM PC–based software. Some Macintosh software is also covered.

Word-Processing Programs

Document developers need a word-processing program, obviously. Which one should be used? There are three basic considerations: (1) compatibility, (2) capability, and (3) usability (Figure 6.1).

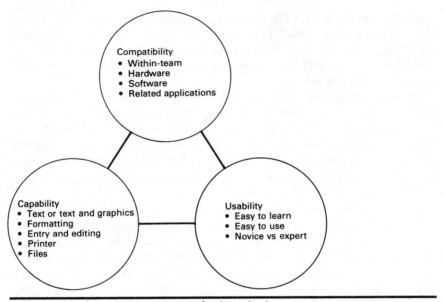

Figure 6.1 Word-processing program selection criteria.

Compatibility.   The output produced by the program must be compatible both within the team and with whatever hardware and software are being used. Within-team compatibility is maintained by using the same word-processing program. Authors working on different parts of the same document should be able to transfer files back and forth. Editors should be able to edit a writer's draft on their systems.

To some extent, incompatibility problems can be overcome by converting files to a standard format (usually ASCII) and transferring them from one machine to another by wire or modem. In order to do this, the word-processing programs must have a way of producing files in common formats. Having this capability does not justify letting every writer and editor use the word-processing program of choice. It is much more efficient to use the same program.

In some cases, a degree of incompatibility is inevitable. For example, if the documentation development team employs separate graphics and word-processing systems (e.g., Macintosh and IBM PC), then complications arise in transferring files. Hence, in selecting software it is essential to consider the compatibility factor.

Capability.   The word-processing program must be capable of performing the task required. Usually, it makes little sense to demand that the program do more than required, since this has additional implications in terms of usability. Powerful programs are usually more difficult to learn and use than simple programs.

What capabilities are essential? This depends very much on the types of documentation being developed. If the word processor must be able to handle both text and graphics, then hardware as well as software choices must be made. Word-processing programs for the IBM PC and compatibles are mainly restricted to text alone (Microsoft *Windows*, *Write*, and *Paint* are exceptions, as are some GEM-based applications). The logical choice is one of the Macintosh word-processing programs (e.g., *MacWrite* or *Microsoft Word*). Alternatively, if text and graphics will be handled separately, the options are more open.

Given that one does not have the requirement just stated, exactly what other capabilities are needed? Every user of a word processor can compose a list (presumably on the favorite word processor), and so no list is complete. One of the key requirements is usability (see next section). Given this, the other main areas of concern are text formatting, entry and editing, file handling, printer support, and the availability of special features (Dickinson, 1986). In each of these areas, several dozen specific features could be listed. However, let us focus on a few of the key ones.

For text formatting, the program should handle text justification and variable margins, page lengths, and spacing; permit and display needed character formats (plain, underline, boldface); permit tabbing; allow running headers and footers; and readily permit text format to be varied within the document, preferably with style sheets. The program should be able to reformat a document quickly.

For text entry and editing, the program should readily permit text to be entered and edited (delete, insert, move, copy, save to disk) by character, word, sentence, paragraph, and block. It should be possible to move the cursor freely around the screen—by character, word, line, and to top and bottom of screen and document. Cursor movements should reflect cursor key actions exactly, e.g., the "up" arrow moves the cursor directly up. It should have a fast find, search, and replace utility.

For printer support, the program should be able to drive the types of printers used and in the formats required, e.g., 12-pitch proportional spacing.

For file handling, the program should be capable of handling documents of the size required, permit file merging, and be able to save part of the working file, as well as read and create ASCII files.

Special features might include a spelling checker, dictionary, thesaurus, the use of keyboard macros, footnoting, automatic file saving, or on-screen mathematical calculations.

While many word processors offer an enormous number of features, sheer power is not an appropriate index of how good the word processor is. There is no point in having more than is needed. What is important is to have what is needed. Moreover, given that you find a program with the perfect combination of features, the selection problem does not end there. The program must be usable—in the fullest sense of the word.

Usability.   The word "usability" is used here to mean ease of learning and use for the full user audience. Usability is reflected in a number of attributes: speed, internal consistency, demand on user memory, the number of keystrokes required to accomplish an operation, error protection, the "intuitiveness" of the program, and so forth.

A usable program is easy to learn and easy to use. However, usability is not the same for all users. Experienced, full-time word-processor operators will find more sophisticated programs (e.g., *WordPerfect*) preferable to the simpler ones (e.g., *MacWrite*). For the novice or occasional user, preferences are usually the reverse. In short, what is usable depends upon the user.

For most documentation development, the users will fall between these extremes—neither highly sophisticated nor novice users. Hence, the logical choice of a word processor for them is a program somewhere in the middle range of complexity. Arguments can be made, of course, in favor of the simplest or most powerful programs. If a documentation team is formed of people with limited prior word-processing experience, it may pay to use one of the simpler programs, especially if it has the capabilities needed. Alternatively, if the team consists of highly skilled users of word processors, then a more sophisticated program may make sense.

Reviewing the reviews.   Word-processing programs are widely used and one of the most reviewed of software species. Moreover, it doesn't matter which program you personally prefer, you will be able to find reviews favoring or condemning it. Software reviewing is a cottage industry, commonly done by individuals with little perspective of the entire field. Hence, all reviews are suspect. At this writing, there are approximately 100 word-processing programs for the IBM PC and a handful for the Macintosh. In addition to dedicated word-processing programs, there are several integrated applications for these computers which offer word-processing capabilities. If we discount the integrated applications and focus on the dedictated programs, we still face considerable difficulty in making a choice.

One of the most wide-ranging reviews of IBM PC software was conducted by *Software Digest* in its January 1986 issue. The magazine reviewed 25 different dedicated word processors based on several criteria, including ease of learning, ease of use, error handling, overall performance, and versatility. One of the products of this monumental effort was a power versus ease-of-use chart (Figure 6.2). As the figure shows, power and ease of use are at odds. As power increases, ease of use decreases, and vice versa. The perfect word processor would be marked by a box at the upper right corner of the chart—a region conspicuously blank. However, some programs did much better than others in terms of power, usability, or the combination of both they offer.

Software Digest rated nine programs at the top of the list in its overall evaluation. The highest possible score was nine points. The programs and their numeric ratings are shown in Table 6.1

Interestingly, except for *PFS:Write* and *WordPerfect*, these nine programs are not among the most well-known or best sellers. Missing from the list are several much more popular programs, including *Word-Star*, *Microsoft Word*, and *MultiMate Advantage*. You figure it out. The message seems to be that popularity does not readily translate to capability, usability, or the other attributes of a good program. Note that the authors of this book are reporting data, not making recommendations.

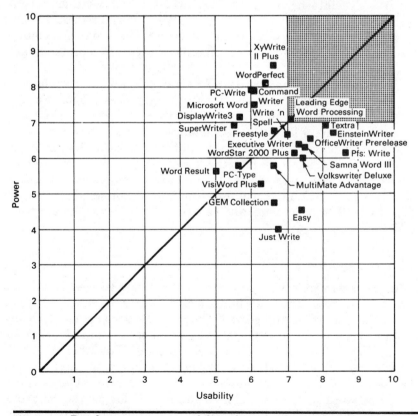

Figure 6.2 Rated power versus usability chart for 25 word-processing programs. (*From* Software Digest Ratings Newsletter, *Software Digest, January 1986.*)

TABLE 6.1.   Top-Rated Word-
Processing Programs for the IBM PC

Rating	Program name
7.8	PFS: Write
7.8	EinsteinWriter
7.6	Textra
7.4	XyWrite II Plus
7.2	OfficeWriter (prerelease)
7.1	Executive Writer
7.1	Leading Edge Word Processing
7.0	WordPerfect
7.0	Samna Word III

SOURCE: *Software Digest*, January 1986.

The review just discussed covered only 25 programs and evaluated them based on its criteria. You must make the decision based on your own.

For the Macintosh, there are two widely used word-processing programs: *MacWrite* and *Microsoft Word*. *Word* has more features and is more powerful. Among other things, it permits the user to open multiple documents in separate windows, has more keyboard commands, and offers greater flexibility.

However, at this writing there is no Macintosh word processor for text processing in the same league as the best word processors for the IBM PC. (The IBM and Macintosh versions of *Microsoft Word* are entirely different programs, with little resemblance to one another but name.) When it comes to handling mixed text and graphics, the story is different. Here, the Macintosh has the clear advantage over an IBM PC–based word processor. All of the available Macintosh word processors have strong graphics capabilities and, for example, allow the use of pictures within documents and several different type fonts, styles, and sizes.

Spelling Checkers

Spelling checkers are utility programs that compare the words in a text file with those in the checker's built-in dictionary and identify those in the text file that are unrecognized. The program does not so much say that a word is misspelled as that it is ignorant of the word. Some of the unrecognized words will, of course, be misspelled, but others will not. However, in responding to the spelling checker's alert, the user must in each case tell it what to do: ignore the word, add it to the dictionary, change the word in the text, etc. Of course, the longer the checker's dictionary, the less likely it is to ring false alarms, i.e., alert the user to correctly spelled words that are unrecognized. In the early days of spelling checkers, the vocabularies consisted of tens of thousands of words. Today, many of the dictionaries are many times that size.

The use of spelling checkers with technical prose is problematical. First, user documentation contains many words not in the everyday vocabulary. The more technical the prose, the more this is true. Writing a reference document for a computer language, for example, will produce spelling-checker alerts on almost every word in the language.

Second, the people who write user documentation are usually skilled word-processor operators who presumably know how to spell already. Using a checker takes time. If most of this time is spent adding words to the dictionary or telling the checker to ignore unrecognized words, little is gained and much time is wasted. Alternatively, if someone who is a poor speller uses a spelling checker in the mistaken belief that it will help them improve the spelling in their document, they will gain less than they think. Ultimately, the user must decide whether each word producing an alert is misspelled or not; if the person deciding cannot spell, correct decisions are unlikely.

People who are good spellers sometimes use spelling checkers to look for typographical errors. This is a sound strategy. However, it may take more time than reading carefully through the document. And considering that, during the course of development, a document will usually be reviewed by several people, most of the spelling errors should eventually be caught.

Whether or not a spelling checker can be useful depends partly upon the foregoing considerations, but also upon the particular speller itself. For the speller to be of potential utility to a documentation project, it must meet at least three requirements: (1) use a large dictionary, (2) permit the dictionary to be updated, and (3) be fast. A large dictionary is one containing at least 100,000 words.

Updating of the dictionary should be possible in at least two ways. First, it should be possible to add words to the dictionary as the document is being checked by giving an "add" command. Second, it should be possible for the checker to add words to the dictionary that are provided to it in the form of a text file provided by the user.

How fast the checker works can be assessed in a number of ways. The first of these is how long it takes to check a document. Computers with large, random-access memory have the edge in this department because they can pull the dictionary into memory and access it instantly. If the computer has a small memory, then it must read the disk more frequently to look up words. Speed is also governed by the efficiency of its code. Finally, speed can be assessed from the user's viewpoint.

From the user's viewpoint, the most efficient way for spelling to be checked is to turn on the checker and come back later when the checker is finished to review an alphabetized list of words the checker has flagged as possibly misspelled. The user then goes through the list, word by word, and decides what to do, dispatching the correct words, adding new words, making the necessary corrections, and so forth.

There are at least two alternative ways for a checker to work. The first is for it to check spelling as words are typed in, sort of looking over the shoulder of the writer and alerting the user each time it finds something potentially wrong. This is not an efficient way to use a checker: Beside the obvious problems caused by slowing down production, the user may begin to resent the program. Forcing someone to use this type of checker is like having Big Brother present. The second alternative, and probably the most common, is for the checker to go through the document from beginning to end, generating alerts as it goes, and requiring the user to respond to each alert in turn. The problem here is that the checker requires the user to be in attendance while it works, rather than letting the user deal with alerts after all checking has been done.

We examined a handful of spelling checkers while writing this book and cannot offer recommendations regarding any specific products. Of those examined, *MacLightning* (Target Software) for the Macintosh had sufficient speed, dictionary size, and convenience to be of practical utility. *Spellswell* (Greene, Johnson, Inc.) is also an adequate checker for the Macintosh. A good checker for IBM PCs is *Webster's New World Spelling Checker* (Simon & Schuster). However, many of the spelling checkers examined are limited in speed or dictionary size, or are simply difficult to use.

There are many excellent spelling checkers available, so readers should not regard our judgments as definitive. Moreover, checkers will undoubtedly improve as the computers they reside in improve. (Too bad the same cannot be said about the spelling abilities of their users; the decline of literacy and all.) Eventually, when desktop computers become fast enough and have enough memory, someone will write one of these programs with every word in *Webster's* (how about the *Oxford English Dictionary*?), and then we can expect to find them truly useful. For the moment, however, our enthusiasm for them is very restrained.

On-Line Thesauruses

An on-line thesaurus is a computerized synonym finder. The utility of these on a documentation development project is even more problematical than that of spelling checkers. You look for synonyms to find the uncommon word or to find an alternative way of saying things. These are both stylistic concerns and have little to do with word meaning. In fact, language human factors (see Chapter 8) discourage the use of synonyms for the sake of internal consistency in a document.

Nonetheless, there are valid reasons for using a thesaurus. One of these is to find the right word when you know the one you're thinking of does not have exactly the meaning you intend. At that point, you can go to your bookshelf and take down the thesaurus. Alternatively, you can use a computer-based thesaurus, if you have one. If you look for synonyms frequently, you might save some time with a computer-based thesaurus.

We reviewed two computer-based thesauruses for the IBM PC: *Webster's New World On-Line Thesaurus* (Simon & Schuster) and *Word Finder* (Writing Consultants). *Webster's* contains 90,000 synonyms for 9000 key words. *Word Finder* contains 100,000 synonyms for an unspecified number of key words. (For comparison purposes, *The New Roget's Thesaurus in Dictionary Form* (Third Edition) contains about twice this number of key words.) Both of the programs can be used in lookup form, like hardcover thesauruses. In addition, they make it fairly easy to replace a word with its synonym.

Is such a program necessary during documentation development? Probably not, especially if it means disk swapping or reducing your word-processing capabilities to employ it. It makes a lot more sense to keep a hardcover thesaurus—along with a dictionary—close by your computer. Alternatively, it might come in handy during the writing of nontechnical prose, such as marketing copy, articles directed at a general audience, novels, and so forth.

Drawing Tools

This section discusses drawing programs and image banks. The most powerful and easiest-to-use drawing tools are available for the Macintosh, so this section tends to emphasize Macintosh-based software. Some IBM PC software is also covered.

Drawing Programs

This subsection discusses several different drawing programs. Each subsection focuses on a particular program to use as an example. However, these examples are meant to represent a class of programs; other programs with similar capabilities are available. The first subsection ("Sketchers") focuses on *MacPaint* (Apple Computer, Inc.). The second subsection ("Charters") focuses on *Microsoft Chart*. The third section ("Drafters") focuses on *MacDraft* (Innovative Data Design, Inc.).

Sketchers. The "sketcher" label is not meant to imply that such programs are toys; all of them are very powerful. They permit the user to create free-form drawings using various tools, to access common geometric figures and straight lines, to fill areas with patterns, and to manipulate the resulting drawing in various ways. *MacPaint* is an excellent example of the class. This program is very easy to use and has been much copied. Drawing is done exclusively with the mouse, but text can be inserted with the keyboard.

The *MacPaint* drawing screen is shown in Figure 6.3. The "palette" on the left edge contains 20 icons, the lower left corner a series of lines, and the bottom edge 38 boxes with patterns. The 20 icons are used to perform several different classes of functions. The lasso, dotted box, and hand are used for figure movement (Figures 6.4a and b); the dotted box alone, to select a portion of the screen for a graphics operation; the capital A, to activate the keyboard for text entry; the bucket, to fill an area (Figure 6.5); the spray can, paintbrush, and pencil, to draw (Figure 6.6); the line, to draw a straight line between two points; the eraser, to erase; the boxes, ellipses, and so on, to draw the specified figure (Figure 6.7).

The main graphics functions, specified by the icons on the left edge of the screen, are constrained by the selected line widths and patterns on the lower edge of the screen and may be further constrained with the "Goodies" menu. The patterns are generated by drawing instruments and used for fill; they govern the format of the dots laid down on the screen. The Goodies menu enables the user to, among other things, lay down an invisible grid to aid in making the drawing symmetrical, edit

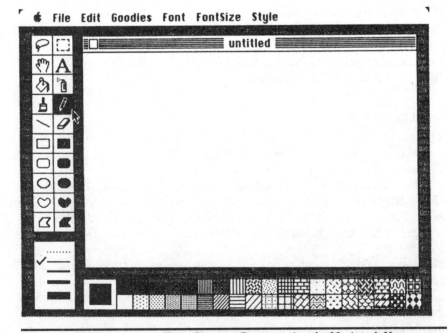

Figure 6.3 *MacPaint* screen. (*From Simpson*, Programming the Macintosh User Interface, *McGraw-Hill, New York, 1986*.)

Figure 6.4 *MacPaint* figure movement operations with (a) lasso and (b) hand. (*Palm trees from DaVinci Landscapes series, Hayden Publishing Company, 1984.*) (*From Simpson, Programming the Macintosh User Interface, McGraw-Hill, New York, 1986.*)

the pattern at the pixel level (Figure 6.8), change brush shape, and create mirror images while drawing. The Edit menu has special options to enable the outlined part of the drawing to be inverted, filled, flipped sideways, or rotated (Figures 6.9a and b). The features of *MacPaint* have since been extended in the applications *FullPaint* (Silicon Beach Software) and *SuperPaint* (Ann Arbor Softworks).

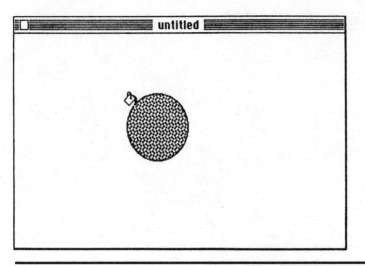

Figure 6.5 Use of paint bucket to fill an area. (*From Simpson,*
Programming the Macintosh User Interface, *McGraw-Hill, New
York, 1986.*)

Windows Paint (Microsoft) for the IBM PC offers features similar to
MacPaint on the IBM PC computer. The *Windows* operating environment—in contrast to that of the usual MS-DOS–based program—is
similar to that of the Macintosh, with *Windows*, pull-down menus, use
of the mouse, and so on.

Figure 6.6 Rank amateur's attempt to illustrate drawing with
spray can (upper), paintbrush (middle), and pencil (lower). *(From
Simpson*, Programming the Macintosh User Interface, *McGraw-
Hill, New York, 1986.)*

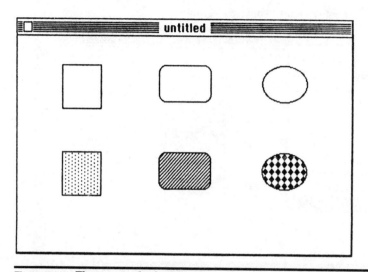

Figure 6.7 Three standard *MacPaint* figures—rectangle, rounded rectangle, ellipse—in open and filled forms. (*From Simpson*, Programming the Macintosh User Interface, *McGraw-Hill, New York, 1986.*)

Prodesign II (American Small Business Computers) offers somewhat-more sophisticated drawing capabilities for the IBM PC but in the MS-DOS operating environment. The program permits the use of a mouse

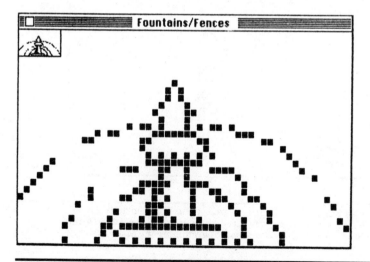

Figure 6.8 FatBits expansion of top of fountain shown in Figure 6.9. (*Fountain from* DaVinci Landscapes *series, Hayden Publishing Company, 1984.*) (*From Simpson*, Programming the Macintosh User Interface, *McGraw-Hill, New York, 1986.*)

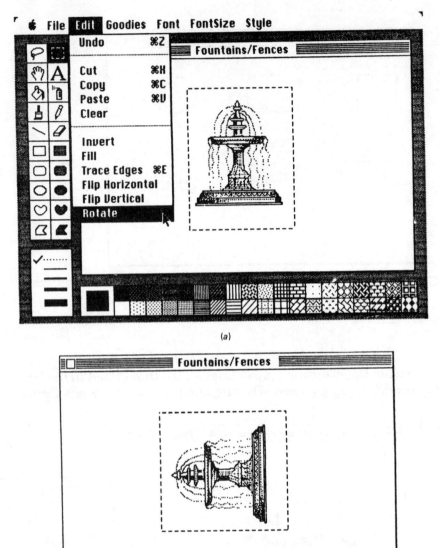

Figure 6.9 *MacPaint* Edit menu with (*a*) selection of Rotate option and (*b*) results of rotation on figure. (*Fountain from* DaVinci Landscapes *series, Hayden Publishing Company, 1984.*) (*From Simpson,* Programming the Macintosh User Interface, *McGraw-Hill, New York, 1986.*)

or graphics tablet for input but relies heavily on keyboard commands; it is modeled after minicomputer-based CAD (Computer-Aided Design) systems. *Sound Presentations* (Communication Dynamics), another MS-DOS–based program, offers similar capabilities. Both programs can be used to produce professional-quality output, in color, and on dot matrix printers or plotters. A sampling of output from *Sound Presentations* is shown in Figures 6.10*a* and *b*. Black-and-white reproduction hardly does these figures justice; both were produced by a plotter in color.

Charters. Charters are used to draw charts, graphs, plots, and other graphic representations of data. They are available in stand-alone form or as separate applications within some programs (e.g., *Microsoft Excel*). They simplify considerably the process of translating numeric data into graphic form to draw such figures as pie charts, bar and column charts, scatter plots, area charts, and to plot data. Such data representations can also be created with a sketching program such as *MacPaint*, but doing so requires much more work and results in less accurate figures. A charting program, if properly designed, converts the raw numeric data into graphic form directly, automatically performing such operations as scaling, point positioning, and formatting. *Microsoft Chart* for the Macintosh is a good example of the genre.

With *Chart*, data coordinates are initially entered into a data-input table (Figure 6.11). Pull-down menu options may be used to format the resulting data in various ways, add legends, and provide other pertinent data on the chart. Chart type is specified by selecting an option from the Gallery menu (Figure 6.12). This figure shows that the Line... option has been activated, displaying the available line-chart display options to be displayed in a separate window. One of these is selected and the data are displayed in this format (Figure 6.13*a*). Figures 6-13*b, c, d, e,* and *f* show various other representations of the same data set.

Drafters. Drafting programs are specialized drawing programs for creating large-scaled drawings. They usually provide grids to enable drawings to be sized precisely, and drawing and editing tools to enable the construction of accurate line drawings. *MacPaint*, though it offers a grid and some such tools, is limited to small drawings and is not really equipped for this purpose. Alternatively, it provides a greater variety of drawing tools (e.g., paintbrush, spray can, pencil) for creating more varied drawings. If the intent is to create large, accurate, scaled drawings, a drafting program is more suitable. *MacDraft* (Innovative Data Designs, Inc.) for the Macintosh is one such program.

The working environment of *MacDraft* (Figure 6.14) is similar to that of *MacPaint* (see Figure 6.3). Various drawing tools are located along the left side of the screen and the headings of pull-down menus are along the top. A significant difference is the availability in *MacDraft* of horizontal and vertical scroll bars, enabling the screen window to be moved readily around the document. Another significant difference is the dotted grid lines on the screen. Grid lines provide a visual reference for

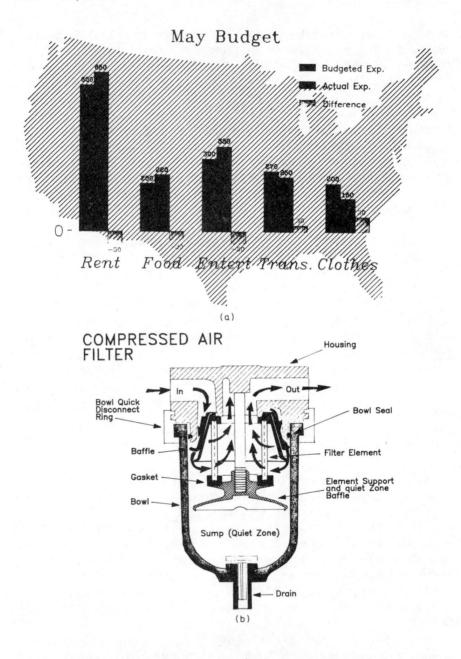

Figure 6.10 Sample graphics from *Sound Presentations* program, both produced with a plotter: (*a*) budget and (*b*) cross section of filter. The originals were in color. (*Communication Dynamics, Inc.*)

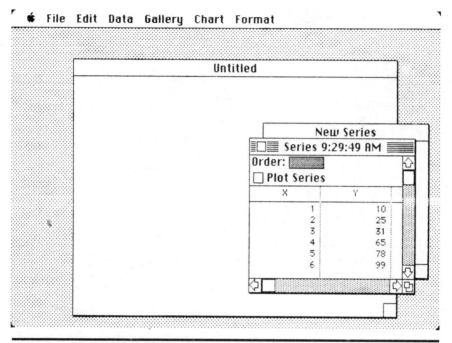

Figure 6.11 *Microsoft Chart* data-input table.

accurate placement of lines and objects on the screen; moreover, the program restricts drawing to comply with grid lines.

MacDraft, among other things, permits more refined scaling, rotation, and zooming of drawings than *MacPaint*. These features are particularly important in constructing accurate drawings.

Figures 6.15*a*, *b*, *c*, *d*, and *e* show a sequence of drawing and editing operations used with *MacDraft* in the course of creating an organization chart.

MacDraw (Apple Computer, Inc.) offers features similar to *MacDraft* and, based on our experience, is more trouble-free. The IBM PC–based programs discussed under the "Sketchers" heading can also be used for drafting purposes (see Figure 6.10*a* and *b*).

Image Banks

Image banks are sets of graphic images or fonts which may be incorporated into drawings using an application such as *MacPaint*. The images are available for a variety of subjects, varying from the whimsical to the highly serious. The images offer a level of detail or sophistication requiring considerable time or talent to create. Hence, if appropriate images can be found, they may save the documentation developer considerable time.

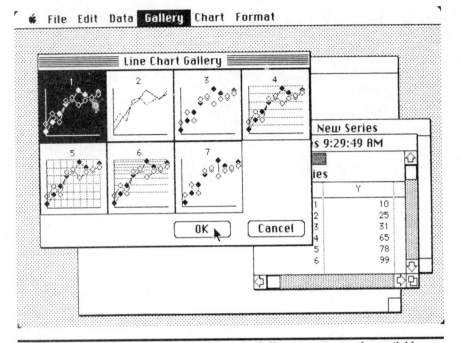

Figure 6.12 Selecting a chart-type option from the Gallery menu causes the available display formats to be displayed in a separate window. In this case, the Line chart option has been selected, and the first of seven available display formats has been chosen. The resulting chart is shown in Figure 6.13*a*.

The most complete set of images currently available is the *DaVinci* series, published by Hayden software. These deal mainly with interior design, landscapes, and representations of building exteriors. The *DaVinci* series also offers a set of graphic fonts which may be use to generate images via the Macintosh keyboard.

ClickArt (T/Maker Graphics) offers a series of graphics images for use in publications and elsewhere. Images of a wide variety of animate and inanimate objects are available.

Image banks are available in greatest quantity and variety for use with the Macintosh. Many of the packages appear to be aimed at destkop publishers. Some of the packages may also be useful in the development of computer user documentation.

Desktop Publishing

Desktop publishing is a computer-based system for composing and producing documents consisting of mixed text and graphics. The systems are relatively inexpensive compared to traditional typesetting, manual

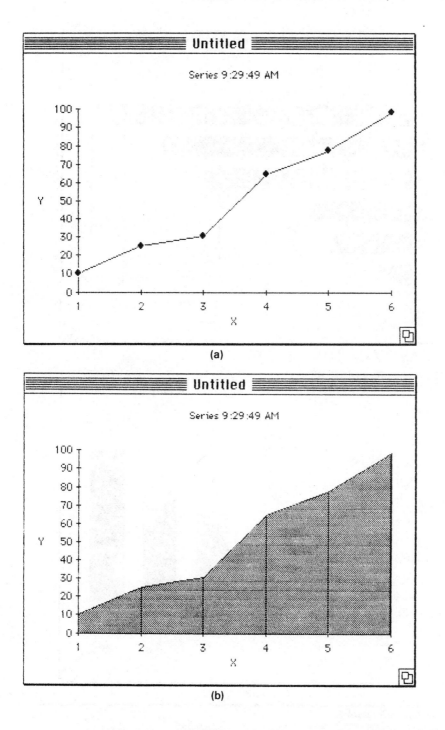

Figure 6.13 Several *Microsoft Chart* displays of the same data set: (*a*) line, (*b*) area, (*c*) bar, (*d*) column, (*e*) pie, and (*f*) scatter plot on log-log coordinates.

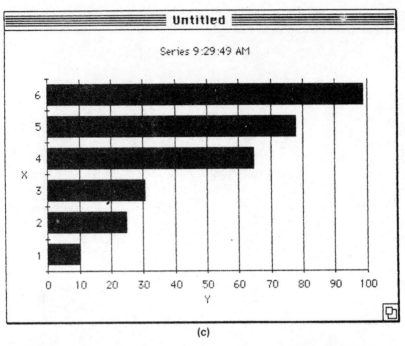

(c)

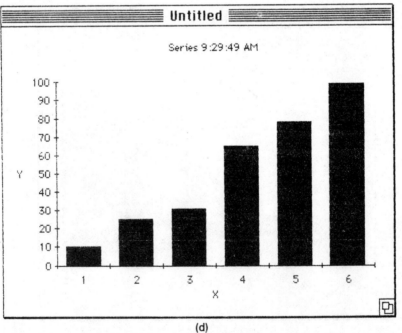

(d)

Figure 6.13   (*Continued*)

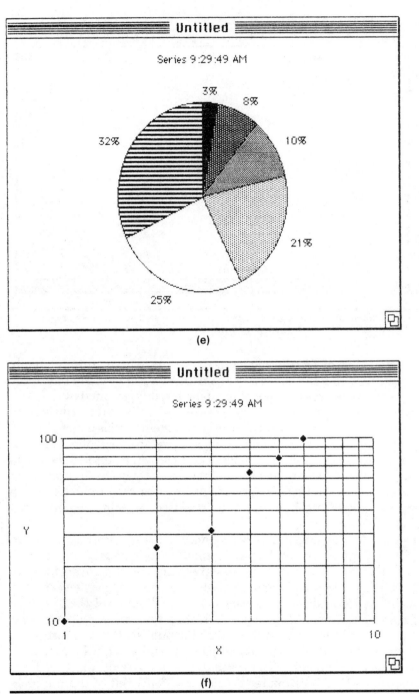

(e)

(f)

Figure 6.13 *(Continued)*

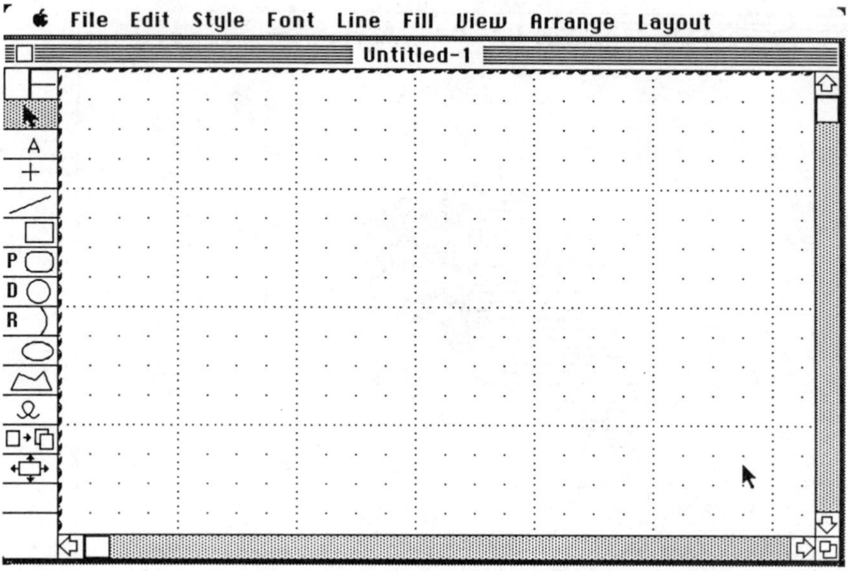

Figure 6.14 *MacDraft* drawing environment: Drawing tools and functions are on the left, pull-down menus on the top, and the drawing grid in the center.

composition, and offset printing methods, and have been growing rapidly in popularity duing the last few years. Although it is doubtful that these systems will take over the publishing industry, it is certain that they will have a significant impact, particularly on organizations that produce documents in small volume. As software user documentation is often produced in limited quantity, desktop publishing systems should dominate this as well as many other publishing fields. Their use can result in substantial savings in dollar costs, time, and equipment, as compared to traditional publishing methods. Moreover, publishing can be done in house, which offers that unique combination of both increased flexibility *and* increased control.

Over 2.5 trillion pages of technical documentation were produced in the United States in 1984 (Davis, 1986). The majority of this was produced—often in limited volume—by firms and the government to support products and equipment. These corporate and government publishers produced far more pages of printed material than book or magazine publishers. Desktop publishing systems may very well change radically the way such material is published in the future.

The advantage of desktop publishing may not lie so much in the ability to support initial publication as in the ability to revise existing documents. Davis (1986) estimates that about 55 percent of the life-cycle costs of documentation are associated with document creation, 10 percent with initial publication, and 35 percent with system management and support. A significant part of this support involves documentation updating.

When integrated into a total documentation production system including compatible word processors and graphics packages, the desktop publishing system forms the final link, giving documentation developers control of the entire documentation creation and publication process. Xyvision, a software manufacturer, estimates that users of such integrated production systems can anticipate cost savings of 30 to 50 percent over traditional production methods (Davis, 1986). The ultimate savings are a function of many factors, including the costs of equipment, software, and converting over to the new system; production volume; and the number and type of documentation revisions anticipated.

Desktop Publishing System Components

A desktop publishing system consists of four major components (Figure 6.16). First, there is a moderately powerful desktop computer having random-access memory of one megabyte or greater. The computer includes a video display, keyboard, and one or more graphics input devices (e.g., mouse, graphics tablet, light pen, digitizer).

Second, the system uses a device for permanent storage of large amounts of data. Most systems operate best with a hard disk, but many can be used with dual floppy disk drives, given adequate random-access memory. Desktop publishing systems are notorious for using up large amounts of both random-access memory and disk space; hence, adequate amounts of both are required if they are to be used with documents more than a few pages long.

Third, the system includes one or more output devices. An impact dot matrix printer may be used, but the output device of choice is a laser printer. The image resolution of a laser printer is about 300 dots per inch, in contrast with 80 dots per inch for a good-quality impact dot matrix printer (Figure 6.17). The resolution of a phototypesetting machine is about 1000 to 2000 dots per inch. Current laser technology does not provide the same quality as typesetting, but its resolution is adequate for many printing jobs, particularly for small- to medium-sized printing jobs. Laser printers contain xerographic scanning and toner deposition devices and operate much like a photocopying machine. Output is produced by selectively applying toner to paper at the pixel level, thus producing any desired combination of text and graphics. Unlike copying machines, they can be interfaced with and controlled by a computer.

Fourth, the system uses software, i.e., a desktop publishing program. Many such programs exist, and they represent a wide range in terms of price, capabilites, and ease of use. It is prudent to select a program capable of handling large, complex documents. Most user documenta-

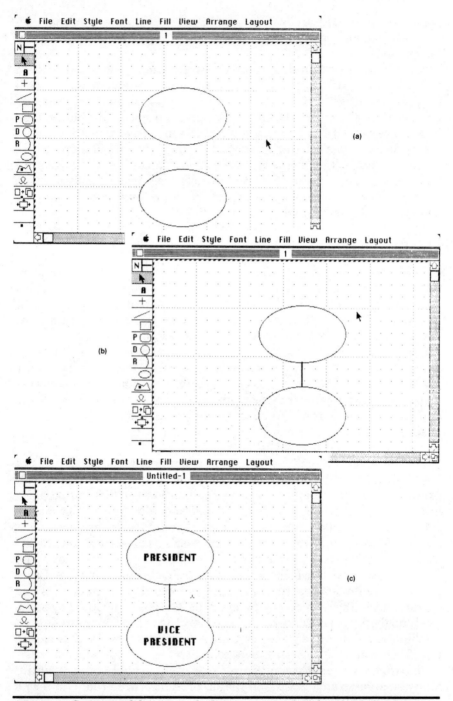

Figure 6.15 Sequence of drawing and editing operations used with *MacDraft* in creating an organization chart: (*a*) drawing an oval, (*b*) connecting the ovals with lines, (*c*) adding text, (*d*) scrolling the chart, (*e*) viewing the chart as a whole, (*f*) automatic chart reformatting.

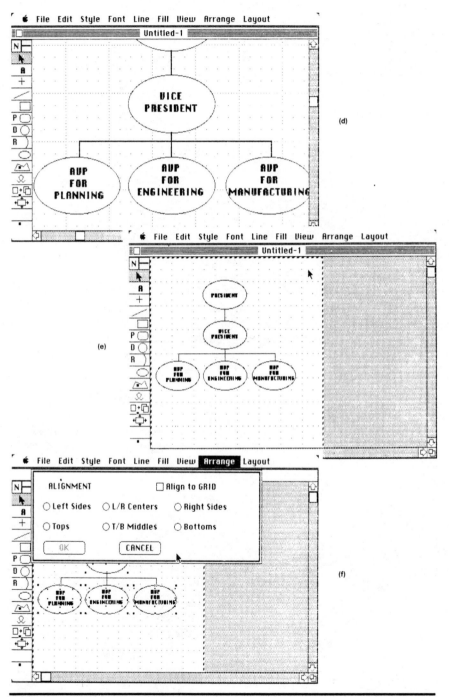

Figure 6.15 (*Continued*)

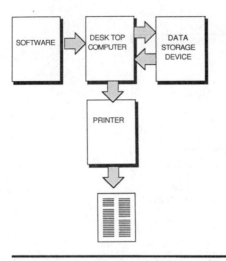

Figure 6.16 Components of desktop publishing system.

tion is lengthy, requires mixed text and graphics, and must be periodically updated. Many of the available programs are intended for developing brief newsletters and flyers, and will not adequately meet the needs of someone developing, say, a user's manual. The initial investment in a more sophisticated package will be more than offset later by savings in personnel and production time.

Functions of Desktop Publishing Systems

Desktop publishing systems enable one individual to perform the functions of three: illustrator, paste-up artist, and typesetter (Biedny & Berman, 1986). The actual user of the system may be an author, editor, or artist.

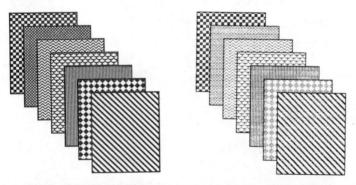

Figure 6.17 Comparative outputs of laser and impact dot matrix printers.

The illustration function may be performed with graphics application packages such as described earlier in this chapter. Though these may be used separately from the desktop publishing program, they are an important component of the desktop publishing process and one of the reasons it is feasible.

The paste-up function is performed with the desktop publishing program, which permits the user to move and position headlines, blocks of text, and figures and tables to compose pages.

The typesetting function is performed with the same program, which permits screen images of composed pages to be transferred electronically to paper.

Integrating these three functions reduces the likelihood of communication breakdown along the way. At the same time, it presents certain pitfalls, for not everyone is skilled in the three areas of illustration, paste-up, and typesetting. If the person using the desktop publishing program is deficient in one or more areas, it will show in the resulting document. Each of the three areas requires skill, knowledge, and the application of certain rules to produce a professional-quality end result. A graphics program does not make anyone an illustrator, though it may help; many people are incapable of developing professional-quality graphics with these programs. The same sort of thing is true of the paste-up and typesetting functions.

The evidence of misuse is before us in the ill-conceived products of newsletter publishers who get carried away with their desktop publishing systems: documents with poor page composition, inadequate graphics, too many different type fonts and styles, too many drop shadows, and too much or too little of whatever else makes for a usable and attractive document.

Desktop publishing systems are powerful tools, but the user must still acquire the skills and apply the professional standards of the illustrator, paste-up artist, and typesetter. One approach is to assign the desktop publishing system to a person already possessing skills in one or more of the traditional areas. For example, have an illustrator or paste-up artist use the system as a tool. Have writers and editors prepare text with a compatible word-processing program and drafts of art by hand or with a computer-based graphics application. The assigned user of the desktop publishing system then creates the final illustrations and composes the document from the text files and illustrations. This approach also permits one "document integrator" to support many different writers.

Desktop Publishing Technology

This subsection examines the hardware and software aspects of desktop publishing technology.

Hardware. Though many factors have contributed to the growth of desktop publishing, one of the most important is the laser printer. As this book is written, these machines—typified by the Apple Laserwriter and Hewlett-Packard laser printer—are rapidly growing in popularity, increasing in power, and dropping in price. Impact dot matrix print quality is usually equal to or slightly better than the computer video image, but laser printer output is superior. In addition to the improved quality of filled and shaded areas, the superiority of the laser printer can be seen in diagonal lines, where "stair-stepping" is less evident. Some printers—both laser and impact dot matrix—can perform "pixelation," i.e., smooth rough edges during printing (Wesley, 1986). Apparent print quality can be improved by photographic size reduction. However, care must be taken not to reduce legibility in the bargain (see Chapter 8).

Currently, the clear leader in low-cost desktop publishing is Apple Computer, with the Macintosh computer and Apple Laserwriter printer. IBM–PC-based systems exist and are undergoing rapid development, but are playing "catch-up" to the Macintosh computer's lead. Bobker (1986) contends that the Macintosh is the "best buy" in a desktop publishing system costing less than $15,000 (a price sure to drop) and having adequate hardware (computer, hard disk, laser printer) and software support. (As one of the major cost items is the laser printer, a developer can reduce costs considerably by using an impact dot matrix printer during development and having the final laser-print copy made by a photocopy or print shop.)

Scull (1986) contends that there is a tremendous difference in "elegance and functionality" between Macintosh and MS-DOS machines that is widely recognized and readily apparent to the user. Although a number of Macintosh lookalike programs have been developed for MS-DOS machines, they have not yet reached the level of functionality of Macintosh desktop publishing programs. The graphics-oriented Macintosh is particularly well suited to page design and layout.

One serious limitation of the Macintosh—and of MS-DOS systems as well—is limited random-access memory and permanent storage capacity. Ideally, it should be possible to contain an entire document—or, at a minimum, each section or chapter—on a single diskette, and to access any page of the document without disk swapping. At least 1 megabyte of random-access memory and a hard disk are recommended.

Software. There are three basic types of desktop publishing programs (Lu, 1986): (1) mark-up languages, (2) graphics-based without pictures, and (3) graphics-based with pictures. Mark-up languages, like command languages, require the user to design pages with command words and statements. The commands are difficult to learn and use, and the fidelity of the video display in representing the final product is limited. Graphics-based programs without pictures permit the user to display, move, and format text, but not to display or manipulate graphics. Graphics-based programs with pictures permit full manipulation and display of both text and graphics and offer the greatest degree of visual fidelity to the final product; this is the predominant form of desktop publishing program for the Macintosh and the one on which our discussion will focus.

The most distinctive feature of this type of program is its visual fidelity, which is true to the maxim "What you see is what you get." Moreover, the Macintosh-style user interface permits page composition and manipulation in ways analogous to the traditional ways with manual methods. The user points at objects with a mouse pointer, "drags" them to different locations, "cuts" and "pastes" parts of the document, and performs other operations in an intuitive and natural way.

What follows are brief descriptions of three currently popular desktop publishing programs for the Macintosh: *MacPublisher* (Letraset USA), *ReadySetGo* (Manhattan Graphics), and *PageMaker* (Aldus). Note that desktop publishing software is rapidly evolving and that these are simply being used to illustrate the discussion. By the time you read these words, these programs may have changed and other programs will certainly be available. However, these three models are useful for comparing and contrasting approaches to desktop publishing.

Of the three programs, the original version of *MacPublisher* provides the least visual fidelity. The user works with a split screen containing source material on one side and page layout on the other. The program is limited to documents of 32 pages or less. Longer documents require multiple files. The program organizes a document like a newsletter—as an issue consisting of articles. The user cannot change fonts, column width, or style within an article. Headlines must therefore be a separate "article" if they are to be of larger size than text.

The original version of *ReadySetGo* is inexpensive, has good visual fidelity, and is ideal for short documents. It uses a precise measurement system, allows tab settings within text blocks, and displays all results to the user (Figure 6.18). Drawbacks are limited document size, limited display size (approximately one-half of a page), and an awkward method of scrolling. It is best suited for flyers and short newsletters, and is not a good choice for a large document, such as a computer user's guide. A more recent version (version 3.0) is more highly regarded and contains many advanced features.

PageMaker is available for both the Macintosh and IBM PC. The original Macintosh version provides excellent visual fidelity but, according to Meilach (1986), with the IBM PC version "what you see is more or less what you get." Text and graphic files from other sources (e.g., word processor, graphics program) can be cut and pasted onto pages, or the text and graphic capabilities within *PageMaker* can be used to

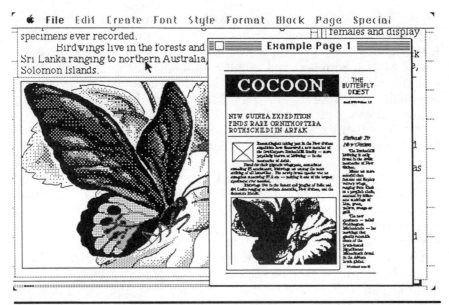

Figure 6.18 A sample screen from Manhattan Graphics' *ReadySetGo* desktop publishing program.

create pages. Like many other such programs, document size is limited. As with the other programs, enhancements are provided with new releases.

In a comparison of early versions of these programs, *PageMaker* was found to be quickest for both page layout and printing time (Goodman, 1985) (Table 6.2). None of the programs provided either kerning (see Chapter 8) or automatic hyphenation, though many useful features have been recently added.

A description of desktop publishing would not be complete without a few words about *Post Script* (Adobe Systems). *Post Script* is a publishing language built into the Apple Laserwriter and many other laser printers (except Hewlett-Packard, Corona, and Canon printers) that "allows the printer to have complete control over every dot on the piece of paper that is going to be printed" (Onosko, 1986). The program creates type fonts, styles, points, lines, and mathematically derived curves. *Post Script* can be used directly or accessed by desktop publishing programs to overcome some of the limitations.

TABLE 6.2. Comparative Printing Times (minutes) for Three Macintosh-Based Desktop Publishing Programs

Program	Layout time	Printing time	Total time
PageMaker	2:31	3:05	5:36
MacPublisher	8:17	4:48	13:05
ReadySetGo	16:33	5:44	22:17

Source: Goodman (1985).

Most existing publishing programs permit the user to print in a variety of page sizes, such as 8 1/2 by 11 inches, 11 by 17 inches (tabloid style), and European page sizes A4 and B5. However, the Apple Laserwriter is limited to 11- by 14-inch pages. To overcome this limitation (without manual cutting and pasting), some users are turning to other *Post Script* machines for final output. One of these is the Linotronic 100-300 series from Allied Linotype, a *Post Script* machine that will print large pages but which costs considerably more than a laser printer. Onosko (1986) believes that *Post Script* is rapidly becoming the industry standard.

Desktop Publishing System Recommendations

This section offers recommendations for the selection of hardware and software to use in a desktop publishing system.

The system should permit full-page display and simple scrolling. The original Macintosh suffers from an undersized video display. The Macintosh II, however, provides a 12-inch monochrome or 13-inch RGB color monitor, a much superior choice for a desktop publishing package. In any event, the publishing program should not require the user to scroll in order to view a single page. Many Macintosh programs provide full-page viewing in reduced form—but are difficult or impossible to read. Until this limitation is overcome, the Macintosh is less than ideal for desktop publishing.

The video display should accurately portray the printed page and it should be possible to manipulate text and graphics on the page in "intuitive" and "natural" ways. These criteria argue for a Macintosh-like user interface as opposed to a typed-in, command-based system. As a rule, requiring the user to recall commands or perform mental manipulations to figure out what the final printed page will look like will increase task difficulty and errors. Command-based systems may be faster and more powerful than those with a Macintosh-like interface, but take longer to master, are more difficult to use, and are less desirable for most desktop publishing applications. Alternatively, if the system will be operated by a full-time, dedicated operator, this criterion may be relaxed in favor of the increased speed and power potentially available with a command-based system.

A "wish list" of features and capabilities for a desktop publishing system would include speed, large document size, powerful word-processing and graphics capabilities, compatability with other word-processing and graphics applications, variable type fonts and styles, the ability to integrate text and graphics, page measurement and placement features, automatic left and right justification, kerning, automatic layout templates, and free-form heading and graphics arrangement.

How long a document should the system be able to handle? Clearly, for user documentation projects, one able to handle fewer than a dozen pages is inadequate. Alternatively, documents longer than about 50 pages are not usually necessary, given the divisions common in user documentation. Moreover, documents longer than this become difficult to manage. For most applications, a desktop publishing system should be capable of handling about 40 to 50 pages at a time.

The system should be able to import text and graphics from other applications: word-processing programs, graphics applications, outline processors, and other programs used during documentation development. Although desktop publishing programs can usually generate both text and graphics, they offer less flexibility than separate applications. Importing such files is seldom a problem with the Macintosh because most of its word-processing and graphics applications can transfer files back and forth. It is simpler to create and edit text or graphics with these applications than with a publishing program, the features of which are more limited. Hence, the publishing program should be used as the final step in the documentation development process—to integrate text and graphics and to compose pages.

Documentation Design

This chapter presents the basic principles of documentation design. These principles come mainly from human factors design methodology and design guidelines. They apply in the design of any written documentation. Topics covered in this chapter include information design principles, organizing and structuring information, routing, establishing context, instructional styles, use of concrete examples, tropes, and writing and editorial obligations. Though many of the examples in this chapter focus on the user's manual, keep in mind that the principles apply equally to the design of other forms of documentation, e.g., tutorials, reference guides, job performance aids, help screens, and so on.

Information Design Principles

Howard (1981) argues that information—e.g., user's manuals—should be designed according to three basic principles: (1) content, (2) organization, and (3) format. The *content* principle concerns the breadth and depth of coverage. Content is best represented as a topic diagram—an outline drawn in the form of a flowchart . A topic diagram gives a "top-down" view of the content of a document, with breadth shown by the horizontal dimension and depth by the vertical. The greater the number of topics, the greater the breadth. The greater the level of detail in a topic, the greater the depth.

The obvious advantage of developing a topic diagram is that it provides a clear picture of the breadth and depth of coverage. A more subtle but perhaps more fundamental effect is that it imposes systematic, hierarchical organization on the information content. If the material is disorganized—for example, if a series of related topics are treated in a disconnected way—the topic diagram will show it very clearly.

The *organization* principle concerns user orientation while using the document. The user should be able to tell where he or she is at any point in the document as well as have a good concept of where he or she is headed. The flow from one topic to the next should be logical and should follow the flow of the task or the subject of discussion. To satisfy these requirements, the developer must define document structure before creating content.

The *format* principle concerns the manner of information presentation—in simple terms, how words and pictures will be used to present information content. At the outset, before writing begins, the information designer must make decisions on such issues as page layout, the use of graphics, fonts, document structure, indexing, tabs, and so forth. The best place to define such matters is in documentation standards (see Chapter 4).

Organizing and Structuring the Information

Key factors during documentation development are organization and structure (Figure 7.1). Organization refers to the process of grouping or arranging parts to form a whole. Structure refers to the arrangement of parts or elements and, in particular, the physical characteristics of the document.

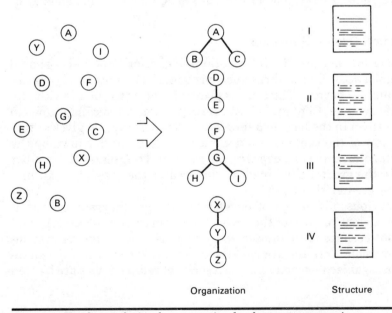

Organization   Structure

Figure 7.1 Key factors during documentation development are organization and structure.

The overall content of a document should be determined based upon the requirements of the user and the stated objectives of the document. For example, decisions on such matters as developing separate reference and tutorial manuals or combining them in the same document, creating quick reference guides, and providing help menus should be based on an analysis of user tasks (see Chapter 4). Appropriate documents and documentation mix vary based on the type of users, operating environment, type of application, and other factors, as described in Chapter 3.

Breadth and Depth of Coverage

Breadth and depth of coverage should be determined based on user information requirements (see Chapter 4). Breadth of coverage must be sufficient to satisfy the information requirements, as well as any prerequisite skills and knowledge that the particular audience may lack. Depth of coverage is determined similarly.

Unfortunately, there are no simple rules of thumb for determining depth and breadth for all documents. Given the information requirements, the documentation designer must consider the characteristics of the probable user and the operating environment, make decisions, and then develop the documentation.

However, the process should *not* end there. Somewhere along the line the documentation should be tested with actual users (see Chapters 4 and 12) to assess how well it works. Shortcomings in documentation will be reflected in poor operator performance. That is the signal to take a second (or third or fourth) look at the previous breadth and depth decisions and to revise documentation accordingly.

Planning and Outlining

Documents should be planned carefully before being developed. A written outline and a topic diagram are both very useful planning tools. As with many other aspects of the document, the key to both is clear definition of user information requirements.

The main purpose of outlining is to ensure that all required topics are addressed by the document in appropriate depth and in a logical and orderly manner. Careful planning can prevent many of the defects of documentation—if the effort is expended to do the job properly.

Outline preparation can be facilitated by using some of the management tools described in Chapter 5. For example, outlines can be constructed and revised very readily using outline-processor software. Topic diagrams can be generated using project planning tools. These tools are not necessary but can be helpful. You can develop a written outline with a word-processing program or even with pencil and paper, if you're so inclined. Likewise for the topic diagram.

An outline is a working tool and will require revision during documentation development. But, as the man said, "The plan may not be perfect, but it's a plan and we can change it if we need to—it's better than no plan."

Case in Point: Organizing and Structuring a User's Guide

To illustrate the organizing and structuring process more concretely, let us take a specific case: developing a user's manual for an application program used on a desktop computer. In this case, it is often possible to provide all relevant material within a single set of covers, e.g., tutorial, program description, reference information. What should this manual contain, and how should it be organized? Houghton-Alico (1985) contends that a user's manual should contain about 16 parts (Figure 7.2). In addition to material dealing directly with the program and its use, the document must contain disclaimers, copyright notices, and other nontechnical information. A narrative overview of the program and supporting diagrams of the program should be provided. Many manuals contain information on how to use the manual. Manuals for nonexpert users usually include a tutorial. The organization of the remaining elements varies. Some manuals contain a single chapter of procedural and reference information; others contain many sections, each dedicated to a major system feature, e.g., characteristics of the user interface, types of output, problem solving, and so on.

In an earlier book, one of the present authors described the content of an "idealized" user's guide, which was divided into three parts: (1) introduction, (2) tutorial, and (3) reference material (Simpson, 1985) (Figure 7.3). Among the recommendations are to provide introductory

```
1  Preface, disclaimer, copyright, etc.
2  System overview
3  System process diagram
4  Introductory note on how to use the manual
5  Tutorial (step by step)
6  The computer interface
7  List of sequential entry procedures by function
8  List of update procedures
9  List of output procedures
10 Sample output
11 List of error messages
12 List of commands
13 List of communications protocols
14 Data dictionary
15 Glossary
16 Index
```

Figure 7.2 Houghton-Alico (1985) recommends that user's manuals be organized according to the 16-part scheme shown here.

```
1 Introduction
  • Objectives of guide
  • Guide organization
  • How to use guide
  • Definitions of terms
  • Equipment requirements
  • Program overview
2 Tutorial
  • Divide into modules
  • Exercises for major features of program
  • Each module takes one hour or less
3 Reference information
  • Divided into appendices
  • Appendix for each type of information
```

Figure 7.3   Simpson (1985) recommends that user's manuals be organized into three main parts, as shown here.

material giving the objectives of the guide, describing its organization, giving instructions for use, defining terms, specifying equipment requirements, and providing a program overview. The tutorial is divided into sections corresponding to modules, with each section consisting of a block that can be completed in about one hour, and providing the user with step-by-step instructions for using different features of the program. The final section of the guide contains reference information and related appendixes for each major class of reference information.

Although the two authors just cited conceptualize a user's manual somewhat differently, their suggested content and organization are practically identical. Nonetheless, such manuals can be designed in many other equally valid ways. There are no standards or rules of thumb for documentation content and organization. This is probably just as well, for, as previously stated, these matters should be decided based on the users, the program, the operating environment, and other factors—not on the basis of some preordained plan.

The Importance of Modularity

An important aspect of organization is modularity; this is implicit in the recommendations of the two authors just cited. Modularity, in this context, means dividing the document into separate, stand-alone sections that allow the user to select and use those sections fitting his or her particular interests and needs (Figure 7.4).

All too often, documents are developed for a particular class of user: the novice or, more commonly, the expert. A novice-oriented document exasperates the experienced user seeking concise answers to questions. Tutorials, though they may support the needs of novices nicely, are

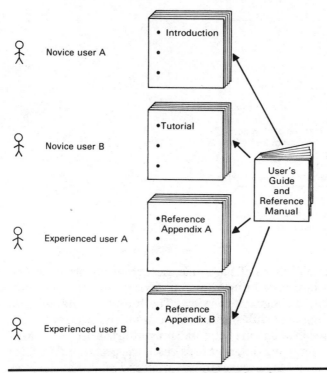

Figure 7.4 The document should be modularized so that the user can select the sections fitting his or her particular interests and needs.

anathema to experts. Indexes for tutorial-based documents are often inadequate for the expert; a topic listed in the index may be followed by a long list of page numbers, showing where information on the desired topic may be found, requiring the user to read through them all to find what is needed. Modularizing the information can reduce such problems.

The negative side effects of integrating tutorial and reference information can be reduced somewhat by page formatting; e.g., by highlighting key points with graphic techniques such as boxes, a two-column format with the points listed in the left margin, colored type, or other imaginative techniques to make certain portions of the text stand out (Simpson, 1985). However, it is desirable to provide these two functions—tutorial and reference—in separate modules.

Organizing Around the Task

It is best to organize user documentation around the task; the flow of the document should parallel the flow of the tasks that the user must perform. (This does not apply to reference information defining the words in a computer language but does apply to the use of those words to form commands and perform higher-level procedures.) The basis for such organization is the task analysis (see Chapter 4), which provides a list of operator tasks and suggests how these tasks may be organized. The task data can be translated into a scheme of document organization.

To illustrate, Figure 7.5 is the flowchart of the tasks performed during the setup and operation of an oil field management computer. Each time the system is used, the operator must perform the preparation procedures in the list. The appropriate documentation organization is obvious; it must follow the natural order of the task.

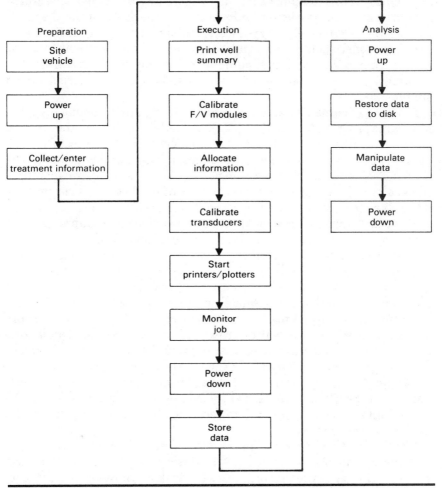

Figure 7.5 A flowchart of tasks performed during the setup and operation of an oil field management computer.

Even when the task sequence is unpredictable, it is desirable to organize material around logical task sequences. For example, the user of a computer-aided design system might use a modeling program in an enormous variety of ways. Still, user interactions with the computer can usually be broken down into functional sequences. The user starts with a blank screen and must initiate the program. Next, the user might (a) review an existing design, (b) modify a design, or (c) create a new design. After performing any one or a combination of these subtasks, the user must shut the system down.

Although the precise sequence of interactions cannot be predicted, the phases of operation can be specified and the material can be organized accordingly. For example, users who will create a drawing from scratch should be able to find relevant information in the early part of the reference section. Conversely, users interested in reviewing or modifying an existing model should find what they seek in later sections. Just as information on saving files should follow information on creating files, information on other advanced features should follow information on simple features.

Devising documentation for another drawing environment—Apple's MacPaint program for the Macintosh computer—offers another case in point. This free-form drawing program permits the user to create, modify, and delete graphic features in an infinite number of ways. The drawing screen consists of a screen with a palette (a set of drawing functions) along the left edge, a series of lines at the lower-left corner, and 38 boxes containing patterns at the bottom. How can one explain the use of these drawing features when the task sequence is so unpredictable?

One of the ways is by examining the available functions, devising logical groupings, and basing organization on those groupings. In this particular case, the 20 icons in the palette along the left edge can be grouped functionally: the lasso, dotted box, and hand are used for figure movement; the dotted box to select a portion of the screen for a graphics operation; the capital A to enter text; the bucket to fill an area; the spray can, paintbrush, and pencil to draw; the line to draw a straight line between two points; the eraser to erase; and the boxes, ellipses, and so on, to draw the specified figure. Likewise, the lines at lower left are used to change line width, and the 38 boxes at the bottom of the screen are used to set the fill pattern. Hence, by looking a little more deeply at the individual functions, an organizing scheme can be devised to use as the basis for the document.

Ideally, the flow of topics from one to the next should be natural and relatively transparent to the user. Basing the topics on the task supports this since the text organizes the task for the user. Alternatively, a document that does not follow task-based organization requires the user to create his or her own organization. Recall from Chapter 2 that one aspect of human learning is that users form mental models of the external world. You facilitate the formation of accurate models by making them explicit. One way to do this is to organize text logically. Two consequences follow from doing otherwise: you make more work for the user, and the user forms less accurate models.

Routing

Routing refers to the practice of directing the reader to a different section of a document to obtain information necessary for the task at hand, i.e., the text equivalent of a computer subroutine.

Human "Stack Overflow"

One of the authors had a recent bad experience with routing. His daughter's ancient Volkswagen experienced an electrical failure that he diagnosed as the result of a bad generator. Being handy with old BMWs, the author reasoned he could fix the problem. He bought a generator and a repair manual. Chapter 5 of the manual describes generator replacement. The second step of the procedure is to remove the fan shroud; the procedure for this is given in another chapter. Routed to that chapter, the author discovered the deck lid had to be removed before the fan shroud, a procedure given in yet another chapter. Having gotten this far, the author could not remember where he had started, but discovered he had to remove the carburetor, a procedure given in still another chapter. At that point the author reached the human equivalent of stack overflow, roused his son, and induced him to do the rest of the dirty work.

Routing is time-consuming and irritating to anyone who uses documentation. If you do it, you run the risk of losing the reader. Although some routing is necessary to avoid major redundancies in text, doing too much can be a serious inconvenience to the user. If the required explanation is not excessive, it is preferable to repeat it rather than to route the reader elsewhere.

How to Reduce the Need for Routing

One of the best ways to reduce the need for routing is to base document organization on user task sequences, as discussed. If sections of the document follow the natural sequence of user tasks, there will be less need to route the reader elsewhere.

Another way to reduce routing is the use of foldout pages (Figure 7.6) (Mosier, 1984). Foldouts can, for example, be contained in an appendix and referenced in the text. When the user needs to see two sources of information or perhaps the text in the original section of the document and an illustration, the illustration can be contained on a foldout.

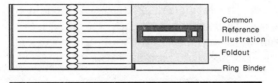

Figure 7.6   Foldouts can be used to reduce the need for routing within a document.

Foldouts can also be good for explaining the functions of other matters that may require explanation at several different points in the text, such as a keyboard rundown. Basically, any figure, checklist, table, or other descriptive element that might be referenced in several scattered locations should be considered as a good candidate for the foldout treatment.

Establishing Context

Research into language comprehension indicates that context plays an important part in understanding. To give a practical example: Saying "I will kill you" to your opposite in a tennis match has quite a different meaning than saying the same words to someone on the exercise field of a state penitentiary. In simple terms, the meaning of a statement is governed not just by the words themselves, but also the context in which they are uttered. This, incidentally, is one of the key differences between interpersonal dialogs and dialogs carried on with computers. Computers are very literal-minded and have little appreciation of context; for them, words have consistent meanings (different operating modes may change the effect of a command, but commands always mean the same thing to a computer).

Context in Interpersonal Dialog

Humans are highly sensitive to context. In interpersonal dialog, the context is defined by the physical and verbal environment and the social and psychological world in which the language user operates (Ochs, 1981). The physical environment is the setting in which communication takes place, be it the tennis court, a page in a manual, or a screen within a computer program. The verbal environment is where in the sequence of communication a particular communicative act occurs. The social and psychological world govern the accepted meanings and interpretations of language.

To illustrate how verbal environment works: Different meanings will be ascribed to the "I will kill you" threat if you precede it by saying either "I mean this" or "This is a joke." Of course, for context to govern meaning, the reader or listener must know (a) the current context and (b) what that context means. Hence, one of the requirements of developing user documentation is to provide this information.

You can define the current context in a number of different ways: by using headings with obvious meanings (e.g., "Introduction," "How to Open a File," etc.), by defining it in text, and by using flowcharts or other graphic representations to show where the user "is" within the document (like a subway map). What the context means will, in some cases, be obvious but in others may need an explanation. For example, if the heading for a section defines a specific task ("How to Open a File"), then it may be obvious. In many other cases—perhaps in most—the meaning of the context must be stated. This is done by putting the material being presented into perspective. The way to do this is to tell the reader how the present subject relates to what came earlier and what comes next. How, for example, does opening a file relate to the higher-level task being performed? When is it done and for what reason?

Creative and Inferential Interpretation

What does the heading just given mean? It is composed of two somewhat abstract adjectives, a conjunction, and an abstract noun. You probably have some notion of its meaning, and so does every other reader, but since the words of which it is composed are nonconcrete, you can't have a very specific sense of its meaning. Whatever meaning you have attached to it is due to your powers of creative and inferential interpretation. You cannot know precisely what the heading means because it has not yet been explained. Yet, you can *create* and *infer* a meaning.

Problems are not limited to abstract language alone. They also occur because readers come to a written page with different assumptions and expectancies. A study by Smith (1981) illustrates this point very nicely and somewhat humorously. Smith showed three groups of subjects (engineers, housewives, Human Factors Society members) a picture of a refrigerator, the door of which was hinged on the right side, and asked them whether the door was "left-opening" or "right-opening." The results are shown in Table 7.1. The engineers and housewives tended to call the refrigerator "right-opening," presumably because its hinges are on the right. The human factors specialists, more than the other two

TABLE 7.1. **Responses of Three Groups to the Question "Is this a left-opening door or a right-opening door?"**

	Engineers	Housewives	Human Factors Society Members
"Left"	36%	41%	56%
"Right"	64%	59%	44%

Source: Smith (1981).

groups, tended to call the refrigerator "left-opening," presumably because its handle is on the left and it is opened from left to right. Differences among groups were not statistically significant because a small sample size was used, but the results illustrate that people do not always see things the same way. Where such confusions may result, the only reasonable course is to define and, if possible, illustrate potentially ambiguous terms.

One of the ideas implicit in context is that language is not a fixed thing that always means the same thing. Mathematics does have fixed meanings—which is one of the reasons it is used when communication must be precise and explicit. But normal human language is otherwise. For vague terms such as "creative" or "inferential" to be interpreted in common ways, you must define them. In fact, this requirement extends to more concrete words as well. The bottom line is that if you do not say what you mean, precisely, your reader will create or infer a meaning of his or her own.

Headings and Titles

A key contextual cue is the selection and placement of titles and headings. Titles and headings should be explicit and used liberally. This helps the user stay oriented during reading and provides locational cues for browsers who are leafing through a document in search of a specific subject. It also gives the reader a little "breathing room" between sections. It is undesirable to present long blocks of text under a single broad heading; it is much better to break up the text into smaller blocks, based on the ideas being presented. Titles and headings are also important as advance organizers, as described in the next section.

Advance Organizers

An advance organizer (AO) is information presented prior to a task in which the reader will be required to gather and organize information. The AO provides a structural framework presumed to help the reader perform this task effectively. AOs can take many different forms. The table of contents of this book is an AO for the book as a whole. The introduction to this and other chapters in this book tells in summary form what topics will be covered and is an AO for this chapter. A map is an AO for a trip. A diagram such as shown in Figure 7.7 is an AO for the structure of a program. And a syntax diagram such as shown in Figure 7.8 is an AO for a discussion of command syntax.

There are no prescribed rules for designing an AO. The only specific requirement is that the AO be given *before* the material containing the information content; for example, a summary at the end of a chapter is not regarded as an AO (Wickens, 1984). Posttext summaries certainly do not have a negative effect on comprehension, but the evidence shows that they do not improve comprehension.

In verbal communication, the posttext (i.e., after the talk) summary may be of value. Spoken words place greater stress on human short-term memory than do written words, which can be reviewed at will. The Army sergeant's prescription for an effective lecture—"Tell them what you're going to tell them, tell them, tell them what you told them"—still makes sense. However, in written communication, the emphasis should be on the first two steps, not on the last.

Do AOs work? Sometimes yes, sometimes no. Research concerning AOs has largely focused on their utility as learning aids. This research has yielded mixed results and led to doubts that AOs work. In the most recent complete review of the literature on the subject, Mayer (1979*a*, 1979*b*) concluded that they work but under particular conditions. The conditions are that the AOs are used with material that is unfamiliar, technical, or otherwise difficult for readers to relate to their existing knowledge base. They are of little help if the reader is already knowledgeable in a particular domain. For example, if readers are command language experts, you would expect to gain little by using AOs to support text concerning command syntax; if readers are command language novices, you would expect a gain. As documentation users often vary in terms of knowledge and experience, the best practice is to use AOs.

Some of the common forms of AOs are described in the following three sections.

Descriptive titles and headings. Research has shown that descriptive titles have a positive impact on reading comprehension. For example, Dooling and Lachman (1971) examined reading comprehension for passages with and without prior presentation of a title defining the passage's theme and found that the title significantly aided comprehension for information relevant to the title.

Introductory summaries. Introductions which summarize what is to follow are quite useful AOs for most readers. The summary should describe the route to be taken and the landmarks along the way, i.e., the topics to be covered. That is, it tells how what follows is organized and what it contains. It may also specify relationships among the material to follow; where there are many such relationships, a diagram may be more effective than words alone to tell the story (see next section).

The introductory summary provides the user with a framework to support learning from the material to follow. Each major section should be preceded by either an outline or a narrative description of the section's content. In some cases, a diagram may be helpful.

INTRODUCTION

Q&A has five major modules: **Your intelligent assistant**, **Write**, **File**, **Report**, and **Utilities**. Figure I-1 shows the Q&A Main Menu where you select which part of the program to work with.

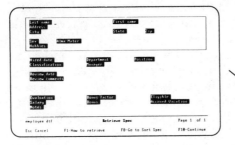

FILE: Design and build databases; then retrieve and sort information to your specifications

REPORT: Arrange and print columnar reports based on information from your database

WRITE: Prepare, store, retrieve and print word processing documents, including mail merge documents

Figure 7.7 A "map" showing the five main modules of Symantec's *Q&A* integrated application. A diagram such as this serves as an advance organizer to the structure of the program. (*From* Q&A Instruction Manual, *Symantec Corporation, 1985.*)

Q&A's MAIN MODULES I-3

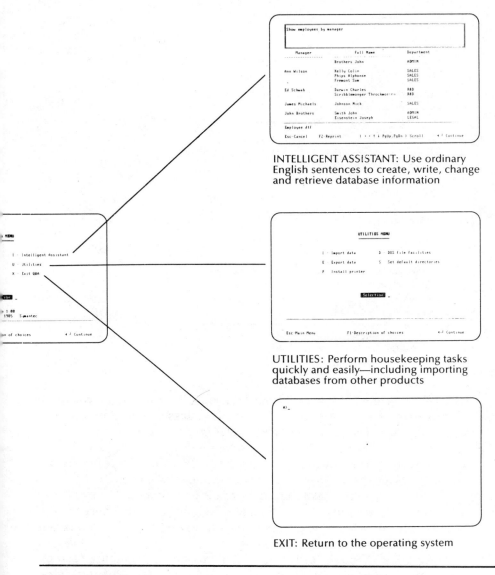

INTELLIGENT ASSISTANT: Use ordinary English sentences to create, write, change and retrieve database information

UTILITIES: Perform housekeeping tasks quickly and easily—including importing databases from other products

EXIT: Return to the operating system

Figure 7.7 (*Continued*)

Format Notation

We will use the following notation to indicate how the DOS commands should be formatted:

- You must enter any words shown in capital letters. These words are called *keywords*. You can enter keywords in any combination of uppercase and lowercase letters. DOS automatically converts keywords to uppercase.

- You must supply any items shown in lowercase *italic* letters. For example, you should enter the name of *your* file when *filename* is shown in the format.

- Items in square brackets ([ ]) are optional. If you want to include optional information, you do not need to type the brackets, only the information inside the brackets.

- Items separated by a bar (|) mean that you can enter one of the separated items. For example:

  ON | OFF

  Means you can enter ON *or* OFF, but not both.

- An ellipsis (. . .) indicates that you can repeat an item as many times as you want.

- You must include all punctuation (except square brackets and vertical bars) such as commas, equal signs, question marks, colons, slashes, or backslashes where shown.

Figure 7.8 An advance organizer for a discussion of command syntax. (*From* Disk Operating System Quick Reference Card, *IBM Corporation, 1983.*)

Descriptive pictures. Bransford and Johnson (1972) have demonstrated that pictures or text presented prior to a text passage increase comprehension of the passage. Unlike text, a picture can present an entire set of concepts and their relationships in a wholistic fashion (see the discussion of pattern recognition in Chapter 2). Hence, a diagram is very powerful for presenting complex, interrelated concepts.

In certain cases the need for a diagram is self-evident. Consider, for example, the criticality of having a wiring diagram when performing electrical troubleshooting. In many cases the need for a diagram is not as obvious, but its benefits still exist.

Flowcharts—though falling into disfavor among computer scientists—are still quite useful for presenting concepts and their relationships and can be very helpful AOs. Figure 7.9 is a flowchart

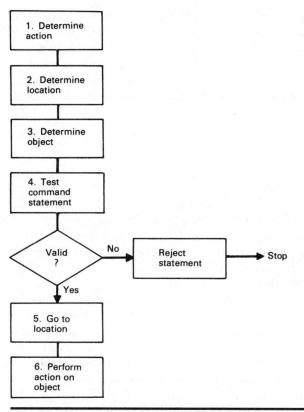

Figure 7.9 Use of a flowchart to present a simplified picture of how a computer unpacks a typed-in
command.

designed for computer novices to illustrate the sequence of actions occurring within a computer as a command is unpacked by a hypothetical
command interpreter. Although this sequence is not technically accurate
or complete, it does provide a framework for understanding how a
computer digests a command and can be useful to the learner.

Many other types of AOs can be envisioned and created, so do not feel
bound by those described. Use them, if possible. In creating your own,
keep in mind the ground rules: (1) they come before, not after; and (2)
they are effective when the material is unfamiliar, technical, or otherwise outside the readers' knowledge base.

Instructional Styles

An instructional style is a particular manner of presenting information.
Different styles are variously suited to different types of users, informa-

tion content, and types of programs. Houghton-Alico (1985) describes four common styles: (1) "cookbook," (2) screen-based, (3) playscript, and (4) foundation. These styles and their variants have evolved not so much from educational research as from practice. However, they are worth examining as schemes for presenting information. A document does not have to be of one type entirely; its various parts can employ different styles, as necessary, as well as other styles.

Cookbook

Cookbook-style manuals are used mainly to present information for highly structured tasks that follow a prescribed sequence. They are largely tutorial in nature and cover such tasks as data entry, editing, and output generation. The information is presented as a sequence of numbered steps, with each step beginning with an action verb. Graphics showing the computer screen in realistic form are used liberally to support the discussion and show the effects of user actions.

The cookbook style can also be represented graphically, and if alternate steps are possible based on particular conditions, it is probably advisable to support the presentation with a flowchart. The explicit, step-by-step orientation of a cookbook-style presentation is much more effective than embedding the steps in an extended paragraph that forces the reader to extract them. Despite its somewhat pejorative label, the cookbook style is the logical candidate for presenting procedures in computer documentation; this is the style used in job performance aids and that should be used in most other procedural descriptions.

Screen-Based

Screen-based instruction is similar to cookbook but is used in more restricted situations—for example, when the user is being shown how to enter data from a written form. Input procedures are described with short, numbered steps, with each number corresponding to a data-entry field on an illustration of the computer screen.

Playscript

Playscript style is usually used in situations with many alternatives that cannot be easily specified using a simple sequence of steps or a flowchart. A matrix is used specifying desired end results, conditions, and appropriate actions. The user refers to the matrix to determine what actions to take to accomplish the particular objective. Figure 7.10 shows a simple type of playscript used in the Apple Macintosh Plus manual (Apple Computer, 1986). Conditions are listed down the left side and actions across the top. The results

	Drag document	Drag folder	Drag application	Drag disk
To folder on same disk	Moves it there	Moves it there	Moves it there	
To folder on different disk	Copies it there	Copies it and its contents there	Copies it there	
To a different disk	Copies it there	Copies it and its contents there	Copies it there	Copies it there, replacing any existing contents
To a hard disk	Copies it there	Copies it and its contents there	Copies it there	Copies it there, adding to any existing contents
To trash	Discards it	Discards it and its contents	Discards it	Ejects the disk and, if it's not the current startup disk, removes its icon from the desktop

Figure 7.10   A sample page of a playscript presentation. (*From* Macintosh Plus [user's guide], *Apple Computer, Inc., 1986.*)

of each action under different conditions are shown in the cell at the intersection of the row and column for a particular condition and action.

Foundation

Foundation style is used when procedures are too complex or variable to be described in simple sequences of steps. Documents using this style do the following:

1. Explain what users can do with the system

2. Describe program outputs and other products

3. Describe the available tools and procedures for use

4. Present examples of different types of uses of the program

5. Contain reference data

Most manuals for flexible, interactive programs, such as word processing and drawing, are well suited to foundation style. For example, with a two-dimensional drawing program such as *MacPaint*, the drawing tools can be used in many different ways, and no single procedure can be prescribed for all possible situations. Hence, documentation must deal with procedures at a functional level. As noted in the earlier discussion of *MacPaint*, the various drawing tools perform classes of functions that can be described in documentation separately.

Use of Concrete Examples

Many users initially attempt to use programs without first referring to documentation. If they do refer to it, often they look for an example representing a situation similar to one they face and attempt to apply the example. Thus, examples are extremely important to the user. The more specific and concrete, the better.

Since the operating environment of a computer user involves one or more computer displays, examples usually benefit from a graphic representation. It is difficult to provide too many examples or too much graphics in user documentation. Naturally, graphics cannot replace good text, nor should they be considered a substitute. The two must go together, with the graphic supporting the point made in the text or adding an additional dimension.

Tropes

Tropes are figures of speech that liken one object to another. Among them are simile, metaphor, and analogy. These are quite important to creative writers. Aristotle, among others, regarded a writer's ability to use metaphor as the single most important measure of artistry. Writers of computer documentation do not usually regard themselves as artists, nor do most writers of technical prose for that matter. (Some critics may think otherwise; for example, some of T. E. Lawrence's technical prose has been reprinted for critical perusal based on its literary merits.) Nor, probably, should they. Artistry in expression has little place in technical writing. One of the objectives of the artist is to suggest meanings beyond those presented literally. The technical writer works to reduce ambiguity to the maximum degree possible—and this is an uphill battle, as noted earlier in this chapter.

Given the foregoing, what place can tropes possibly have in user documentation? Actually, they can be quite useful, but not when used for artistic effect and not when used carelessly. To use them properly, we must view them in a "nonartistic" sense. Moreover, we must think of them as modes of expression that extend beyond figures of speech—to think of them in pictorial terms, for example. Many researchers have begun to explore how people use tropes to support learning. They can be useful learning tools because they allow a person to apply their existing knowledge to a new situation. For example, when you tell someone that the control structure of a computer program is like a network of roads and that you make turns by selecting menu options, the person can refer to his or her knowledge of road maps and make several additional inferences about program control networks without being told about them specifically (Figure 7.11).

Figure 7.11 Use of a metaphor allows the learner to apply existing knowledge to a new domain.

As previously mentioned, tropes, though they come in different forms, liken one object (object A) to another (object B). The attentive reader then applies knowledge of B in understanding object A. To use the trope to support learning, object B must meet certain requirements. Since all objects are in fact different, there will be ways in which A and B differ. Hence, the trope is inexact. Carroll and Thomas (1982) suggest that certain guidelines be followed in using metaphors for instruction. The metaphor needs to be transparent, natural, and map properly to the domain. *Transparent* means that the metaphor is both familiar and obvious. *Natural* means that it applies readily to the referent. *Mapping properly to the domain* means that the overlap between the metaphor and the referent is sufficient to support instruction but not such as to cause the reader to draw inappropriate conclusions. Though these recommendations are given with reference to the metaphor, they can be extended to other types of tropes, such as the simile and analogy. All of them must be used carefully, however.

Like practical examples, tropes can support instruction and can often be very powerful in cutting through complex concepts. The obvious example, of course, is the Apple Macintosh computer, the operating system of which is in fact a metaphoric representation of a desktop. This, perhaps more than any other example, demonstrates the power of a trope as a learning tool.

Writing and Editorial Obligations

Before closing this chapter, it is imperative to state something obvious that every responsible writer and editor already knows. We'll state it anyway. The creators of user documentation are obligated to (1) use effective terminology; (2) ensure that use of language, graphics, and presentations of information are consistent; and (3) strive for complete accuracy. These obligations should, perhaps, be inscribed on parchment to hang on the walls of those concerned.

The most important of these obligations is, of course, accuracy. The others are also important, for if they are not met, the documentation may fail.

Chapter 8

Documentation Architecture

This chapter discusses the construction of physical documents, with particular emphasis on external (hard-copy) documentation. As in the previous chapter, much of what is presented applies equally to internal (on-line) documentation. Again, most of the recommendations derive from human factors research. The chapter discusses documentation architecture at three different levels: total document, page, and line. Topics covered in "Document Level" are physical structure, size, titles and headings, quick-reference considerations, pagination, and print contrast. "Page Level" discusses paragraphing, justification, headers and footers, margins, marginal callouts, graphic sequences, and figure and table incorporation. "Line Level" discusses all-capital versus mixed-case text, typography, print quality, and typographic cuing. The final section discusses the use of language.

Document-Level Considerations

This section discusses factors to consider in the overall design of a document: physical structure, size, titles and headings, quick-reference considerations, paragraphing, pagination, and print contrast.

Physical Structure

The most appropriate physical structure for a document depends upon its purpose. The user's guide, reference manual, and other lengthy documents are essentially books. One of the prime considerations in creating one is to recognize the user's requirements for easy access while seated before a computer. Ring binding is usually the best design choice, as it allows the document to be opened and have its pages lie flat. Ring binders have the additional advantage that they can be easily updated—a matter of no small concern when a software product is first introduced or later updated.

Shorter quick-reference documents—quick reference cards or guides—are usually best prepared in more compact form. Since they are short, they can be reprinted in entirety if necessary; ring binders are unnecessary. This applies also to short job performance aids. However, if a JPA is lengthy—more than, say, 40 pages or so—a ring binder may be more appropriate. JPAs, like user's guides, will be used while seated before a computer; hence, they must be designed for easy access. The ring binder is the best construction for this purpose.

The foregoing are guidelines for selecting physical structure. The main considerations, as these thoughts suggest, is that the choice be based on (1) how the document will be used and (2) the updating requirement. The paragraphs following discuss the physical structure issue in greater depth.

Ring binding. Ring binders are expensive and take up considerable shelf space. Alternatively, they can hold a large amount of information, lie flat when opened, and can readily be updated. They are the preferred—and standard—form for delivering user documentation. Moreover, the small ring binder has become the de facto standard for most lengthy user documentation for desktop computers.

Spiral binding. Spiral binding, of either metal or plastic, meets the same storage and access requirements as ring binding, but cannot be readily updated. Although ring binders are best for many programs, the spiral binding is acceptable for documents that are unlikely to be modified. Whether they will need updating depends upon the quality of the initial document and the state of evolution of the program. Apple Computer, Inc., has traditionally provided user documentation with metal spiral bindings that defy easy updating. Equally impressive is the almost universally high quality of the end products. This suggests that, though it may work for Apple, it may not be a particularly good choice for the small firm that cannot expend the resources Apple does to prepare its documentation. (It is noteworthy that *Inside Macintosh*,1984), the two-volume programmer's manual for the Macintosh computer, was initially prepared in full-size three-ring binders to handle the inevitable updates and corrections, of which there were many. Only after it had been around for a year or so was it published in hard-cover form.)

Nonflexible binding. Nonflexible bindings are undesirable for user documentation because they are difficult to open and have the pages lie flat. Anyone who has used a tightly bound document while working before a computer understands the inconvenience. The binding must be bent using two hands, something must be laid on top to keep it open, the pages curl, and so forth. Some users solve the problem with brute force: They take the document apart, drill holes, and put everything into a folder or ring binder.

Size

The practice of putting user documentation into small binders (usually about 8 by 9 inches) appears to have gathered momentum following the introduction of the IBM PC, the documentation for which was prepared in this form. It is also quite common to deliver the binder in a box, which reserves space on a bookshelf or allows the binder to be stored in the upright position without bookends. The small binder also fits conveniently on most standard bookshelves.

Documentation for larger systems is often provided in full-size ring binders. Larger binders can store more information, naturally, and have this advantage over smaller binders.

In general, a larger binder is preferable to a smaller one. However, the user's operating environment must be considered. Desktop computer users are not usually dedicated computer users. They use software as a productivity tool in the course of their jobs. They may have dozens of application programs and limited storage space; hence, size is an important consideration, and they will usually prefer a smaller document. Users of minicomputers and mainframes are often full-time, dedicated computer users to whom storage is not as important a consideration. Hence, a larger binder is more appropriate.

How large should a user document be? Limanowski (1983) contends that standard full-size binders for storing 8½- by 11-inch pages are much too clumsy, do not fit well on bookshelves, and are difficult to use while seated before a computer. More compact documents (e.g., of IBM PC "standard" size) are easier to work with yet are still large enough to contain adequate information.

Page orientation should conform to that of a bound book: pages bound along the left side, not top or bottom. Flip-up pages are awkward to use on a reading stand and, when placed on a flat surface, result in a considerable distance difference from the viewer to the top and bottom pages.

There has been a trend toward the production of documents that are wider than they are high. Such documents are often difficult to use and may not fit conveniently in bookshelves. Odd document sizes, though interesting from an appearance or marketing standpoint, do not well accommodate the needs of most users.

Clearly, there is no simple answer to the "ideal size" question. The key decision criteria are the user's operating environment, the amount of information being presented, and the existence of certain standards, i.e., small binders for desktop applications and full-size binders for mini-computer and mainframe applications.

What is clear is that certain sizes and document structures should be avoided. Odd-sized documents—very large, very small, wider than high—are inconvenient to use. So are documents affixed to other structures. For example, the user's guide for one of the spelling checkers reviewed during the preparation of this book is contained in a small spiral binding with a rod through the back affixing it to a plastic storage box. The point, it seems, is to keep the guide from getting lost. It may serve that purpose, but it also has the effect of increasing the effective volume of the guide about 10 times. That level of "user friendliness" is going overboard.

Titles and Headings

Titles and headings are of major importance in a document, as discussed in Chapter 7. They perform two basic functions: (1) support the user's understanding of document organization and (2) provide locational cues.

Titles and headings are hierarchical in nature. The document has a title, its major divisions (e.g., chapters) have titles, and each major division has headings and subheadings. It is desirable to have no more than three levels of subordination— headings and subheadings—within each major division. Having more makes it difficult for many readers to maintain orientation.

The various levels of titles and headings can be represented in many different ways, but must appear sufficiently different physically that they clearly indicate their level of subordination. Figure 8.1 shows the scheme used in this and many other published works. This scheme is not necessarily universally applicable but does have the quality just stated: Each title and heading is sufficiently different from others that confusion is unlikely. Confusion is possible when the levels resemble one another, as for example, when the difference between two levels is the use of only bold versus nonbold lettering.

The military and government entities sometimes use decimal numbering to indicate subordination, alone or in support of physical differences among various levels (Figure 8.2). Use of this scheme throughout a document makes it possible to cross-reference information

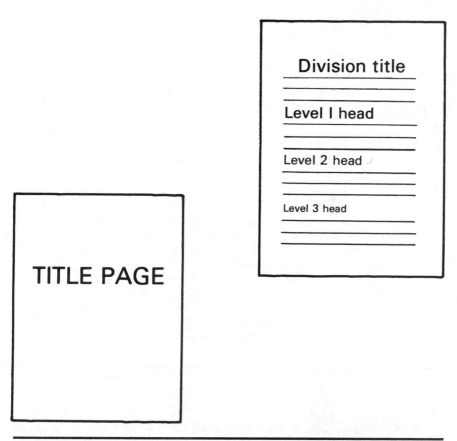

Figure 8.1 A scheme for representing titles and headings popular in books. Subordination is shown by the use of capital versus lower case, title location (centered or left margin), and type size.

down to the lowest level and is quite useful for this purpose. However, as a scheme for indicating subordination, it is cumbersome and can be confusing.

Quick-Reference Considerations

The document must be easy to use. The epitome of inconvenience is to have to wade through a document, page by page, trying to find what is being sought. This is like looking through a novel read 10 years earlier in search of a particular quotation. The key to making the documentation easy to use is to provide a map of the document (table of contents, index) and signposts marking its separate parts (titles, headings, quick-reference tabs). The map and signpost metaphor is appropriate; the document user should be able to find the information sought just as easily as the traveler using a roadmap.

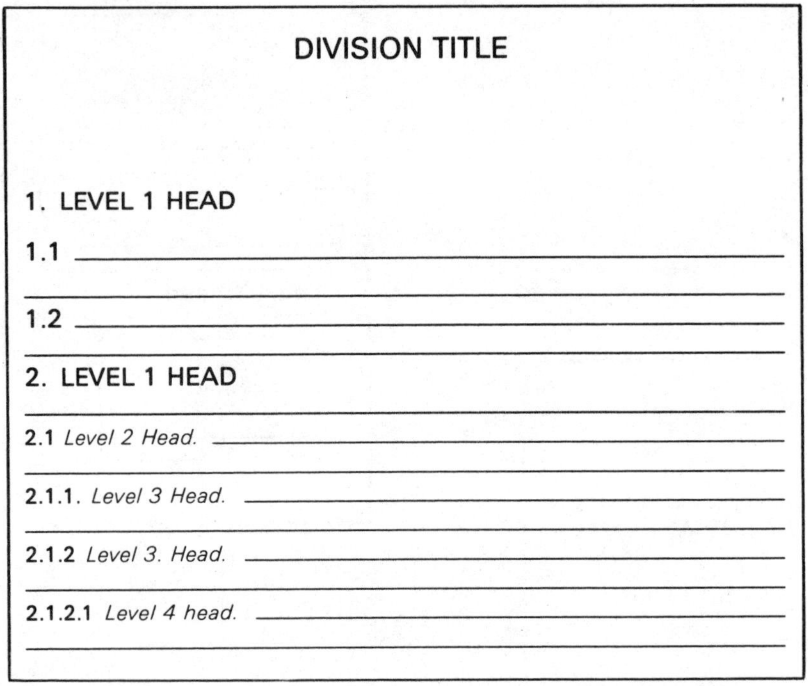

DIVISION TITLE

1. LEVEL 1 HEAD

1.1 _____

_____

1.2 _____

_____

2. LEVEL 1 HEAD

_____

2.1 *Level 2 Head.* _____

_____

2.1.1. *Level 3 Head.* _____

_____

2.1.2 *Level 3. Head.* _____

_____

2.1.2.1 *Level 4 head.* _____

_____

Figure 8.2 Use of decimal numbering to indicate subordination is common in the publications of military and government entities.

Table of contents.   Every document more than a few pages long needs a table of contents. Users refer to this to determine the overall structure and organization of the document, as well as to find the topic they seek. It is of particular importance to the user who is unfamiliar with the document. As experience is gained, dependence on the table of contents will decrease and reliance on the index will increase. The new user will refer to the table of contents to see how the document is organized and may use it in developing a strategy for using the document. Moreover, the table of contents serves as an advance organizer to the document as a whole (see Chapter 7).

A table of contents must contain sufficient detail to be useful. Though one consisting of chapter headings alone is better than nothing, it is often inadequate in providing insight into the contents of the document. Hence, it is better to provide a table of contents that gives the first- and second-level headings contained within each chapter; going beyond this (i.e., to third- or fourth-level headings, if present) is probably not necessary.

Clearly, a precondition for preparing an adequate table of contents is the existence of sufficient titles, headings, and subheadings within the document itself. The importance of these and guidelines for employing them will be discussed in greater detail; also see Chapter 7.

Index. Experienced users of an item of documentation usually rely heavily on its index. If prepared properly, the index provides faster access to the information in the document. Creating an index is an exercise in drudge work. In published books, this task normally falls to the author or, if he or she is willing to pay, to an editor. Indexes vary wildly in adequacy but are a good benchmark test of the overall consideration the author has given to readers. Naturally, this observation applies equally in the publication of computer user documentation. The index should provide a greater level of detail in its coverage of topics than the table of contents. If it is simply an alphabetically sorted version of the former, then it is of limited use. A well-designed and complete index can save the user many hours of wasted time. To develop such an index, the developer must simply invest the time and work needed—do the drudge work.

It is most cost-effective to develop an index after the document has reached the final proof stage, when final page numbers have been assigned. Doing it at an earlier stage means that page numbers will change, and increases the work.

There are a number of aids for developing indexes. The most effective manual method is a six-step content analysis and card sort (Figure 8.3).

The first step is to read through the document and identify topics to be referenced. It is helpful to highlight items and make marginal notes identifying possible key words.

The second step is to scan the marked pages and list the topics on the top of 3- by 5-inch index cards. Write the subject and page number of each item to be referenced on a separate card.

The third step is to lay out the cards on a large flat surface and organize them. Begin by identifying the primary topics (e.g., "keyboard") and place these cards in alphabetic order along the top of the set. Next, place each card with a subtopic under the appropriate primary topic

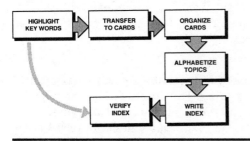

Figure 8.3 Six-step content analysis and card sort procedure for developing an index.

(e.g., for "keyboard," the subtopics might be "attaching," "caring for," "commands," "optional character set," "problems with," "repeat rate," and so forth). If a subtopic is included under more than one major topic, create duplicate cards and place them under the major topic.

The fourth step is to alphabetize subtopics within each major topic.

The fifth step is to transfer the information concerning major topics, subtopics, and page numbers to generate a draft of the index. Indent subtopics from major topics, and separate words beginning with different letters of the alphabet with space as well as a large capital letter to help the reader find the word of interest (Figure 8.2).

The sixth step is to verify the draft index by looking up the entries in the document. The final index is then prepared.

A way of streamlining the manual approach just described is to employ a word processor, outline processor, or database (see Chapter 5). The first and last steps remain the same, i.e., the document must be scanned and the draft index verified. But instead of relying on cards, the major topics and subtopics are compiled using the program. The risk of this procedure is that the indexer does not have access to all of the entries simultaneously but must peer through the screen window at only those entries currently displayed. Hence, the procedure makes it more difficult to keep track.

In addition to using a general-purpose program (word processor, outline processor, database) to support index development, one can use a special-purpose indexing program. Such programs are available for many desktop computers. For example, *MacIndexer* will go through a body of text and create a list of key words which can later be reviewed and organized into an index. Most indexers require much interaction with the developer, and there is some danger in letting a computer decide what words are important enough to be included in an index. Moreover, if the document is contained in several different files, problems arise in integrating the index elements from the various files. However, used prudently, such programs can save time and produce adequate indexes. Before investing in one, make sure it is able to produce an index of the quality and in the format needed in your document. Many indexers lack important features. An indexer should, for example, provide for two columns of text, and automatically indent subtopics and insert page numbers.

Tabs.   Tabs are handy and especially important if a document contains many major divisions or has many pages. The authors reviewed approximately 100 user's guides and reference manuals in preparing the present book. Of these documents, approximately one-fourth used tabs; these were mainly documents for expensive programs. Many of the remaining documents could have benefited from tabs—particularly thick documents with sequentially numbered pages. Finding a particular chapter required use of the table of contents.

Of those documents with tabs, many used them poorly. Some had too many tabs—20, 30, even more. Some used tabs to separate sections one page in length. Some used too few tabs, with tabs marking sections 100 pages or more in length. Then there were those documents with two or three tabs.

What is an appropriate number of tabs for a document? This depends on the nature of the document and how it is to be used. If a reference document consists of 10 chapters, then it makes sense to have one tab for each chapter. For a document with more divisions—for example, a 30-chapter manual—the use of a separate one-word tab for each chapter requires that the tabs overlap in layers and reduces the utility of any single tab. If one-word labels are printed on each tab, it is difficult to use more than about seven tabs without creating multiple layers. Our experience is that documents with more than about seven tabs become awkward. If the document has more than seven major divisions, the solution is to base tabs on higher-level divisions of the document, such as groups of related chapters.

Not everything needs tabs, of course. Tabs will be used for quick-reference purposes by the experienced document user. There is little point in putting tabs in a tutorial, for example. What needs tabs is what the user will want to check frequently. If some things must be left untabbed, the decision can be based on probable frequency of use.

Pagination

There are two main ways to paginate: (1) number pages within each major division or (2) number pages sequentially throughout the document. Numbering pages within divisions has the advantage of providing the reader with an immediate locational cue, e.g., page 3-45 is obviously in Chapter 3. Moreover, it tells how far into the particular division the document has been opened. This information is partially redundant if a page header announces the title of each division, but the page header does not indicate how far into the division the document has been opened. Numbering within divisions also makes it easier to update a document; i.e., one can avoid such abominations as pages 23, 23A, 23B, and so forth and simply replace the relevant pages with new ones.

Although the usual practice is to number pages sequentially within a document, there are rather obvious advantages to numbering within divisions. Howard (1981) recommends that this be standard practice. It is particularly important with longer documents, i.e., those containing more than about 50 pages or having five or more major divisions.

Print Contrast

Print contrast is the brightness difference between the background and characters (or other printed information). Adequate contrast is necessary for effective use and to avoid eyestrain. Professionally printed documents usually have adequate contrast for effective viewing, but those printed under less-than-professional conditions sometimes fall short.

In technical terms, print contrast is defined by this formula:

$$\frac{B1 - B2}{B1}$$

$B1$ is the most bright and $B2$ the least bright of two brightness measurements. Burgess (1984) contends that "readability is best when light reflected from the print differs in intensity up to 100 percent from that of the background, as is the case of black on white."

Print contrast problems occur when the paper on which the text is printed is thin and the material under the page shows through. This can be corrected by using heavier paper. Print contrast can also be a problem when colored paper is used, particularly if colored ink is used on colored paper. It is usually unnecessary to use colored ink on colored paper in user documents. If it is, the paper should be selected carefully so that acceptable contrast between the paper and ink is maintained. Bailey (1982) recommends that colored paper should have a reflectance of 70 percent or greater, and that type no smaller than *10 points* ever be printed on colored paper.

Page-Level Considerations

This section discusses paragraphing, justification, headers and footers, margins, marginal callouts, graphic sequences, and figure and table incorporation.

Paragraphing

Paragraphs serve several purposes. They cue the reader that a thought transition has occurred. They physically divide the page into parts. They give the reader "breathing room" in a long discussion. Of these properties, the first is probably the most important from a design standpoint, for the paragraphs support the reader's interpretation of the material. Reaching the end of a paragraph, a skilled, attentive reader—consciously or not—asks whether the material just read was understood. If not, the paragraph may be reviewed. The longer the paragraphs, the less frequently this opportunity is presented.

Though there are no research-based guidelines for optimum paragraph size (what is presented above is a common-sense analysis), the best practice is to avoid very long paragraphs, e.g., one-half page or more.

One-sentence paragraphs are perfectly acceptable—and in fact quite effective in making a succinct point.

Justification

Text can be justified in several different ways (Figures 8.4*a*, *b*, *c*, and *d*). Left-justified text is aligned on a common left margin, and the right margin is ragged. Right-justified text is aligned on a common right margin, and the left margin is ragged. Center-justified text is aligned on the center of the page, and both margins are ragged. Fully justified text (sometimes referred to as "fill justified") is aligned on both left and right margins; this is accomplished by inserting spaces between and within words to make all lines of equal length.

The human factors recommendations concerning justification are clear on some points but mixed on others. First, right, and center justification are undesirable for extended presentations (Simpson, 1986). Both present text in an unnatural form (though center justification is

A graphic does not necessarily have the same meaning to all users. Its meaning will be governed by the user's culture, ability, training, and experience. As reviewed in an excellent book on ethnic variables in human factors engineering (Chapanis, 1975), Wyndham (1975) provides examples of graphics which are interpreted differently by different groups. Winter (1963) uncovered several interesting examples illustrative of problems with safety posters used in different cultural settings.
(a) LEFT JUSTIFIED

A graphic does not necessarily have the same meaning to all users. Its meaning will be governed by the user's culture, ability, training, and experience. As reviewed in an excellent book on ethnic variables in human factors engineering (Chapanis, 1975), Wyndham (1975) provides examples of graphics which are interpreted differently by different groups. Winter (1963) uncovered several interesting examples illustrative of problems with safety posters used in different cultural settings.
(b) RIGHT JUSTIFIED

A graphic does not necessarily have the same meaning to all users. Its meaning will be governed by the user's culture, ability, training, and experience. As reviewed in an excellent book on ethnic variables in human factors engineering (Chapanis, 1975), Wyndham (1975) provides examples of graphics which are interpreted differently by different groups. Winter (1963) uncovered several interesting examples illustrative of problems with safety posters used in different cultural settings.
(c) CENTERED

A graphic does not necessarily have the same meaning to all users. Its meaning will be governed by the user's culture, ability, training, and experience. As reviewed in an excellent book on ethnic variables in human factors engineering (Chapanis, 1975), Wyndham (1975) provides examples of graphics which are interpreted differently by different groups. Winter (1963) uncovered several interesting examples illustrative of problems with safety posters used in different cultural settings.
(d) FULLY JUSTIFIED

Figure 8.4 Examples of text justification: (*a*) left ("ragged right") (*b*) right, (*c*) center, and (*d*) fully justified.

good for titles and may suit poetry). Right justification is primarily of value for short titles, such as headers or footers.

For extended text, the choice therefore reduces to left- or fully justified text. Walker (1986) and Simpson (1986) both recommend the use of left-justified ("ragged right") text. The objection to fully justified text is that the inserted spaces result in variable interletter and interword spacing from line to line which must be "read through." The more spaces inserted, the more effort required. With left-justified text, this is not a problem—when the eyes reach the end of a line they move automatically down to the start of the next line.

Trollip and Sales (1986) compared the reading time and comprehension of subjects reading left-justified and fully justified versions of the same material. Subjects reading the left-justified version read the material more quickly, but there were no differences in comprehension between the two text presentations. These findings support the notion that text should be left-justified.

Alternatively, Bobker (1986) recommends the use of fully justified text, although this recommendation is not based on empirical evidence. With good typesetting or printing equipment (such as used to reproduce this book, for example), fully justified text is quite acceptable. However, there are some obvious cases in which it is not. For example, with a desktop word-processing system, the inserted spaces may make lines look very uneven—a situation reaching unacceptable proportions with short lines (Figure 8.5).

A reasonable conclusion is that full justification is sometimes acceptable and sometimes not, i.e., acceptable with full-page-width lines and when the equipment can produce decent-looking, fully justified text, unacceptable otherwise.

A graphic does not necessarily have the same meaning to all users. Its meaning will be governed by the user's culture, ability, training, and experience. As reviewed in an excellent book on ethnic variables in human factors engineering (Chapanis, 1975), Wyndham (1975) provides examples of graphics which are interpreted differently by different groups. Winter (1963) uncovered several interesting examples illustrative of problems with safety posters used in different cultural settings.

Figure 8.5 Serious problems occur with fully justified text when column width is narrow.

Headers and Footers

Headers and footers, respectively, are blank space above and below the text of a page. They are commonly used to present page numbers, division titles, document titles, and other information.

Page numbers are obviously important, and the logical place to put them is in a header or footer. Likewise, it is helpful to the reader if the division title is shown on the page. From an information standpoint, there is not much point in putting a document's title in a header or footer; the reader presumably knows the name of the document. However, division titles are informative and useful.

Headers are the best place to put such information, as you can expect the reader's or browser's eyes to begin at the top of the page. It is undesirable to present information in both headers and footers, i.e.; use one or the other—preferably the header.

Margins

Margin width, when its effects are separated from those of line width, does not affect readability or comprehension (Bailey, 1982). (Very short or very long lines should be avoided, as discussed under the next section, "Line-Level Considerations".)

Margin width does affect the utility of a document. Bailey contends that readers prefer ample margins and believes wider margins improve legibility. (The same argument could be extended to headers and footers.) Wide margins provide room for the reader's notes and can be used for marginal callouts, headings, or other support information.

Houghton-Alico (1985) offers several recommendations concerning margins with standard-sized pages (8½ by 11 inches) contained in three-ring binders. The left margin (for a right-hand page) should be 1½ inches. The other borders (right, top, bottom) should be at least 1 inch. If pages are to be perfect bound or spiral bound, the margins should result in a centered page following binding. If margins are inadequate, part of the information content may disappear into the binding or become more difficult to read—a fairly common problem. The type of binding and associated margin requirements must be determined when camera-ready text is being prepared, not after the pages of the document have been sent to the printer.

Although universally applicable rules concerning margin width do not exist, common sense suggests that margins should be sufficient to ensure that (1) all text can be seen when the document is open; (2) the reader has room for notes; (3) icons, headings, and callouts placed in the margin have ample room; and (4) the margins are not so wide as to look like empty "padding."

Marginal Callouts

Marginal callouts are special headings, short paragraphs, or graphics located in the margin. Their purpose is to help the user locate or identify something in the body of the page. Callouts are separate from the text but refer to it. The information, either text or graphics, is located in the margin to indicate the region of relevant text.

A marginal callout should not be used to present in the margin a heading or figure that is essentially part of the text. Rather, a marginal callout is a brief reference to the information on the page. The reader of the text can ignore the callouts, as they are redundant to the text itself. However, the browser or searcher can use them as cues in locating information within the text.

Some documents contain headings and unnumbered figures in the margin. This makes for an interesting format but is inconsistent with the usual practice. The use of simple figures that relate only to the text on the page directly across can be quite effective, since text and figure are co-located. However, this technique should not be used for more complicated figures; such figures should have reference numbers and be placed within the body of the presentation.

Our opinion is that headings belong in their usual place within the text, not in the margins.

Documents with marginal callouts usually have fairly wide margins, which make their contents stand out. Marginal callouts can be made more distinct by using color or a different type font. Doing one or more is desirable.

Graphic Sequences

A graphic sequence is a sequence of illustrations showing changes in a display resulting from an associated sequence of user actions. For example, in a tutorial the text directs the reader to make certain keyboard inputs and then illustrates the effects by showing pictures of the computer screen. The user can follow the directions and check the figures to ensure that he or she is on track, rather than attempting to visualize things based on words alone.

Graphic sequences are one of the best ways to convey information relating to a sequence of user-computer interactions. (It is difficult to envision an effective manual without them, yet there are an enormous number of manuals with very few illustrations. One of the author's favorite word processors has exactly two.)

Graphic sequences can be developed fairly easily. Write the text, then use the computer to dump appropriate screens to a printer for use as illustrations. (This is much easier, in fact, than having an artist draw the screens.)

Figure and Table Incorporation

There are several conventions for incorporating figures and tables into documents so that they will be of greatest benefit to the user:

1. Every figure and table should be labeled with a title and reference number. The single exception to this rule is a marginal figure that is self-labeling and that relates exclusively to the text across from it.
2. Figures and tables should be numbered sequentially and separately.
3. The document should contain a separate list of figures and tables. These are usually located following the table of contents.
4. All figures and tables should be referenced in the text, by number. If the item does not support a discussion point and is not referenced, it does not belong in the document. Sometimes the item is referenced descriptively (e.g., "Figure 8.16 shows a graphic sequence...") and sometimes parenthetically, as is often done in this book. It is redundant to duplicate the figure caption in the text; it is assumed that the reader will read both and needn't encounter the same information in both places.
5. The figure or table should follow closely the point in text at which referenced. Ideally, it should follow the relevant paragraph. If doing this would put blank space at the bottom of a page, it is reasonable to place the figure on the following page.
6. Keep in mind the guidelines concerning routing in the first section of this chapter. Avoid routing, if possible. If different parts of the book use duplicate figures, reproduce them in each required location or use foldouts. It is reasonable to route the reader to another part of the book if it is done infrequently and the figure is noncritical.

Line-Level Considerations

This section discusses all-capital versus mixed-case text, typography, and typographic cuing.

All-Capital Versus Mixed-Case Text

It is quite unusual these days to find any computer documentation produced in all-capital letters. Certainly this is true of printed documentation. On-line documentation is sometimes produced this way, however. It is clear from research that mixed-case text (both upper- and lower-case) is preferable both aesthetically and for improved legibility.

Tinker's (1963) research on typography indicates that all-capital text is read an average of 14 percent slower than lower-case text, and sometimes as much as 20 percent slower. Evidently, the reduction in reading speed is due to loss of word-shape information with all-capital text (see the discussion of pattern recognition in Chapter 2).

Logically, it can be argued that all text—including titles, headings, headers, and footers—should be in mixed-case text to improve legibility. This is going overboard, but certainly all extended text should be in mixed case. Moreover, capitalization of key words can improve reading comprehension, if the the capitalized words are carefully chosen (Dearborne, Johnston, & Carmichael, 1951). Using capitalization for emphasis is much like using underlining, boldface, or italics; the marked words stand out from the background and therefore assume a special significance. The problem arises when all words are in capital letters.

Typography

The subject of typography includes such characteristics of print as type fonts, type size, styles, and layout. The legibility of print governs, in part, how easy a document is to read. By employing type properly, the document minimizes fatigue, maximizes information transmission, and helps the reader find the information desired. Type used improperly has the opposite effect. The following discusses the essentials of typography and gives recommendations for effective use.

Terminology.   "Points" refers to type size, or height (Figure 8.6). A point is a unit of measure equal to $1/72$ inch. For example, 9-point type is $1/8$ inch high, and 72-point type is 1 inch high. Most printed text uses 8- to 12-point type.

Points can also be used as a measure of blank space. The space between the bottom of one line and the top of the line below is measured in points. This distance is referred to as "leading" (pronounced like the heavy metal, a term derived from the metal alloy used in typesetting machines). Historically, leading refers to the metal strips used to widen the space between lines of type. Two points of leading is, for example, $2/72$ inch. Leading significantly affects print legibility.

"Picas," another measure, correspond to $1/6$ inch, and are used to specify the length of a line of text (Figure 8.7). For example, a 30-pica line is about 5 inches long. Excessive line length can create problems for the reader. If an appropriate type size and leading are not selected, the eye can easily jump to the wrong next line after completing a line. Lines that are too short slow reading down because of the excessive number of eye movements required.

Letter "aspect ratio" is the ratio of letter height to width (Figure 8.8). The higher the ratio, the taller and narrower the character. The lower the ratio, the shorter and broader the character. Burgess (1984) recommends that characters have an aspect ratio of 70; character width should be about $7/10$ of character height. Other sources recommend a

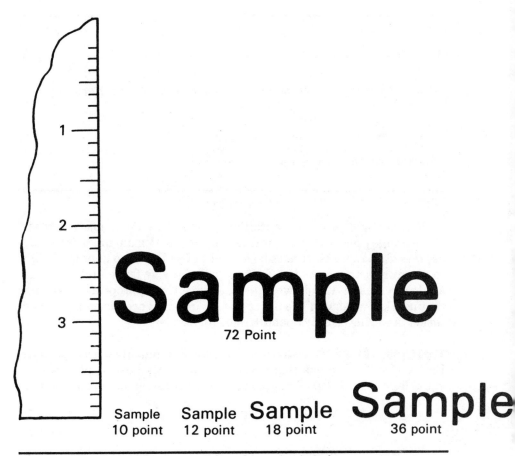

Figure 8.6 The relationship of type points and type size, in inches.

character aspect ratio of about 60, which translates to a width about ⅗ of height. Characters with aspect ratios within the range of these two values should be quite acceptable. Most common type fonts meet this requirement.

"Stroke width" refers to the width of the individual lines that make up each character. Stroke width should be about ⅛ that of character height.

"Kerning" refers to the practice of adjusting the lateral space between letters based on the physical properties of the letters. For example, it is possible to position the letters V and A closer to one another than B and A. Kerning serves to close up blank space within words by moving selected combinations of letters closer together. Most inexpensive word processing systems do not kern either on the screen or on the printed page. The same is true of low-end desktop publishing systems.

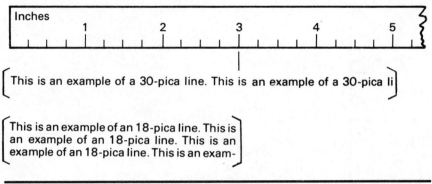

Figure 8.7   The relationship of line length and picas.

"Visual angle" is used to describe the size of a viewed object in terms of the image projected on the retina (Figure 8.9). Visual angle is usually expressed in radians. It may be thought of as the ratio of letter height to viewing distance. As the observer moves away from a letter, visual angle decreases. It follows that selecting the appropriate type size requires knowledge of the average viewing distance, document orientation, and the visual capabilities of the reader.

Type fonts.   Figure 8.10 shows a selection of commonly used type fonts. Bailey (1982) contends that most common fonts have approximately equal legibility. Times Roman, perhaps the most widely used, is said to

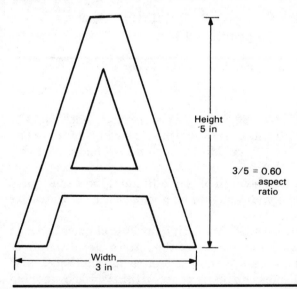

Figure 8.8   *Aspect ratio* is the ratio of letter height to letter width.

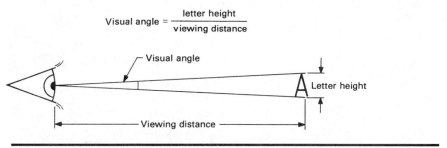

Figure 8.9 *Visual angle*, measured in radians, may be thought of as the ratio of letter height to viewing distance.

be the least fatiguing to proofreaders. Helvetica is perhaps the most common font without serifs and is often used in advertisting copy. Helvetica, which lacks the embellishments or serifs of Times Roman, can be used for extended text, but may not be as easily read as Times Roman. Helvetica is particularly suitable for headlines or for extended text blocks which must be highly legible but different from the standard text used in a document.

The guidelines just given apply to typeset copy but must be followed with common sense when producing text with a dot matrix printer. For example, with the Macintosh, Times Roman type produced by a dot matrix printer is considerably inferior in legibility to such fonts as Geneva, New York, or Helvetica. When produced on a laser printer, its legibility is much improved. It would not be a good type to use for extended text unless produced via typesetting or laser printer.

It is desirable to use a common font, and to use it consistently throughout the document. Bailey believes that using an assortment of fonts can retard readability. Hence, the number of different fonts used in a document should be kept to a minimum.

Designing the line.   The relationships among type size, line length, and leading must be considered in designing the line (Figure 8.11). The most detailed discussion and analysis of these relationships—and the most

Times
Helvetia
Chicago
Geneva
Monaco

Figure 8.10   A selection of several commonly used type fonts.

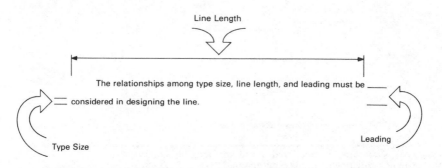

Figure 8.11 The relationships among type size, line length, and leading must be considered in designing the line.

referenced text on the subject of type legibility—is that of Tinker (1963). Tinker suggests that type size be selected after considering (1) viewing distance and (2) the conditions of viewing, i.e., the user's operating environment.

Considering that most documents will be placed flat on a desk while the user is operating a keyboard, we feel that type size should be on the order of 11 to 12 points. Tinker has found that type of 9, 10, 11, and 12 points is equally legible "when set with an appropriate line width and interline spacing (leading)." Burgess (1984) has concluded that the minimum type size for easy reading is 8 points, but this is adequate only under ideal conditions, i.e., those in which the reader controls reading distance, text angle, and lighting. The varied and often nonideal conditions under which user documentation is read argue for larger type size.

Two-column pages usually have columns between 17 and 18 picas (about 3 inches) wide (Tinker, 1963; Bailey, 1982). Single-column text is usually between 21 and 26 picas (about 4 inches) wide. Most readers prefer moderate width (14 to 36 picas) with two-point lead. Lines with lengths within this range are of the same legibility.

When smaller type is used, line length and leading must be adjusted to maintain legibility. Tinker's guidelines for combining the three variables to maintain legibility are shown in Table 8.1.

TABLE 8-1. Point Size, Line Width, and Leading Combinations Required to Maintain Legibility

Point size	Line width range (picas)	Leading (points)
6	14-28	2-4
8	14-36	2-4
9	14-30	1-4
10	14-31	2-4
11	16-34	1-2
12	17-33	1-4

Source: Tinker (1963)

With 6-point type, line width should be limited to 14 to 28 picas, and leading should be 2 to 4 points. Reading difficulty increases with increased line length, reduced leading, and smaller type size. In combination, these factors make it difficult for the reader to find the correct line on which to focus. As type size increases, line width becomes somewhat less critical.

Print Quality

Print quality is governed by how the type is generated and reproduced. Typesetting and competent offset printing produce print of adequate quality. Modern laser printers can produce type of adequate quality, fully formed in nature, and are being used increasingly for reproducing documents in limited quantity. Mechanical or ink-jet dot matrix printer output—though they have improved dramatically in recent years—are of poorer quality and should not be used for generating user documents. Certainly no user document should ever be generated with the usual 5 by 7 or 7 by 9 single-pass dot matrix printer.

Typographic Cuing

Typographic cuing ("patterning") refers to type modification made to make characters stand out from the body of the text. Common cuing techniques to use are underlining, boldface, color, capitalization, or italics—alone, or in various combinations (Figure 8.12). Cuing is normally used to stress certain words. It may also be used to distinguish certain classes of information from others, such as for marginal callouts, as described in the previous section. Sensible use of cuing has been shown to help people find reference information (i.e., as a search aid). It also improves retention of selected portions of text. Overdone, it loses it potency, since its uniqueness is dissipated.

Capitalized words.   Reading comprehension of extended text is best if both upper and lower case are used. However, research indicates that single words are recognized better if in all upper case (Moses & Ehrenreich,

This is an example of <u>underlining</u> used as a typographic cue
This is an example of **boldface type** used as a typographic cue
This is an example of CAPITALIZATION used as a typographic cue
This is an example of *italics* used as a typographic cue
This is an example of <u>**underlining and boldface type**</u> used as a typographic cue

Figure 8-12   Examples of several types of cuing: underlining, boldface, capitalization, italics, and various combinations. Color can also be used.

1981). This is not surprising, considering that a capitalized word stands out within a mixed-case line. Research has also shown that capitalizing the most important words in text improves reading comprehension (Dearborne, Johnston, & Carmichael, 1951). These findings have an obvious practical application. Used sparingly and wisely, capitalization can be used to signal (i.e., "cue") readers that the word has special significance and to raise their attentiveness to it. The use of capitalized words is one type of cuing. As noted earlier, there are others, and similar guidelines apply to all.

Other forms of cuing. Cuing may be done in several different ways: capitalization, underlining, italics, using a negative image (white on black), using color, and by combining the individual cuing methods. When cuing is done on a video display, the additional dimension of blinking may be added. Simpson (1985) recommends the use of blinking as an attention-getting device to alert the operator to something that should be attended to immediately but to limit the number of blinking messages displayed on a screen to one or two.

Simpson characterizes the other cuing methods available with computers—underlining, reverse video, high intensity (equivalent to boldface)—as "highlighting." Within the context of computer programs, he recommends the use of high intensity to focus the user's attention on the current action in an interactive sequence, but the use of the remaining highlighting methods to emphasize important words, much as they would be emphasized in standard written text.

Cuing and individual differences. The effects of cuing vary with the individual. First, its effectiveness appears to be related to reader sophistication. Klare, Mabry, and Gustafson (1955) assessed the impact of underlining on reading speed and retention and found that reading speed was unaffected, but that the effects of underlining varied with the subject's technical sophistication—the more able, the greater the benefit. Fowler and Barker (1974) obtained similar results with highlighted text; however, they also found the effect to depend on the reader's confidence in the importance of the highlighted words. Thus, it appears that cuing is most effective when the reader (1) is aware of the intent of the cuing and (2) knows enough about the task to judge the importance of the cued words. It follows that readers should be informed how and why cuing will be used in a document.

Second, evidence suggests that cuing effectiveness depends on reading skill. Klare, et al. found that underlining increases reading speed of people with high reading aptitude but decreases reading speed of those with low aptitude. Apparently, reading skill affects the time required to process the cued information; skilled readers do it more efficiently than unskilled readers.

Comparison of cuing methods. Of the types of cuing available, which types are recommended? Foster and Coles (1977) conducted a comparative study in which they used three pretest conditions and three cuing conditions. Pretest conditions were (1) a pretest on cued material, (2) a pretest on noncued material, and (3) no pretest. Cuing conditions were no cue, all capitals, and boldface. Boldface resulted in higher test scores than unbolded when the subjects had been pretested on cued material. This was not the case for capitalized text. With no pretest, all-capitals and bolding were both superior to no cuing. The researchers concluded that when a reader has an idea of what is to be found, bolding is superior to all-capitals.

The reader's ability to gain from cuing depends on knowledge of why cuing is being used, as previously noted. Given this, it appears that boldface is superior to all-capitals for cuing purposes. The use of all-capitals retards reading and appears to hinder retention of noncued material; these problems do not exist with boldfaced text.

Amount of cuing. How much cuing is appropriate? Evidence suggests that it should be used sparingly. Hershberger and Terry (1965) examined instructional effectiveness of simple and complex forms of typographical cuing using eighth-grade students. Simple cuing consisted of all-capital passages. Complex cuing consisted of a hierarchical system of cuing consisting of capitalization, red underlining, and black underlining. The researchers found that simple cuing improved learning, but complex cuing did not. These subjects, at least, were unable to profit from the importance information embedded in the cuing system.

While the performance of eighth graders cannot be used as the basis for making decisions on amount of cuing, their inability to benefit from complex cuing makes an important point. Cuing is essentially a code, and it is used to signal importance. The more different types of cuing used, the more difficult it is to decipher the code (Simpson, 1985). Hence, there is always the risk of making the coding system so complex that it cannot be figured out and has no effect. In offering display design recommendations for computer programmers, Simpson observes that the IBM PC offers programmers approximately a dozen different ways of displaying text but suggests that most programs can be written nicely with four or fewer of the possibilities; the use of more is characterized as "overkill."

The Use of Language

This book is not intended to be a text on language. Its coverage of the subject is brief, limited to this section of this chapter. The focus here is on what might be called "language human factors." In a nutshell, it amounts to saying what you mean as simply, directly, and unambiguously as possible. There are many books on writing— technical writing in particular—that may help those seeking it. (The best all-around book on writing in the "plain style" remains, for our money, Strunk and White's *The Elements of Style*—short, pithy, full of simple rules that can readily be followed to improve anyone's writing.)

The Three Principles of Communication

Wickens (1984) suggests that instructors follow three principles in conveying information. These principles, which apply equally to document developers, are to (1) state directly what is meant, without adding excess words; (2) use familiar words; and (3) ensure that all information to be communicated is explicitly stated, leaving nothing to be inferred.

Principle one directs you to communicate concisely and efficiently. Most users are short on time, are impatient, and are trying to obtain information as quickly as possible. Excess verbiage and information not directly related to their interests will only slow them down.

The main concern of principle two is to choose words that convey the desired meaning to the intended user. The language of computer scientists, programmers, and other technical types is usually different from that of users. Use of the technical vocabulary in user documentation is undesirable—unless the intended audience consists of technical types. Common, everyday language is more suited to the average user. If possible, use words that already have meaning for the users. These can be words commonly used in other application programs or words that the user should readily understand. Avoid the use of jargon and unique words that the user will have to memorize.

Principle three has as much to do with being thorough as with appropriate language. People come to documentation with different backgrounds and expectations and do not always obtain the meanings the author intended. The only way to be sure the message has gotten across is to test it with actual users or a close facsimile thereof.

One of the authors of this book recently visited the clean room of a minicomputer manufacturer and observed a sign, posted outside the door, containing the information shown in Figure 8.13. The sign does not really say what it means. Taken literally, it says that it is acceptable

```
┌─────────────────────┐
│ BEFORE YOU ENTER    │
│  ·  No smoking      │
│  ·  No eating       │
│  ·  No drinking     │
└─────────────────────┘
```

Figure 8.13 A sign which does not say what it means.

to smoke, eat, or carry drinks into the room, providing that you do not smoke, eat, or drink before entering. This is a rather gross—but not particularly uncommon—example of how the writer may misstate what is meant. Fortunately, the informed readers of the sign are aware of the restrictions and can read past the misstatement of the sign to its intent. However, not all readers are so well informed.

Consistent Use of Terms

Use terms consistently throughout the text and avoid using multiple terms for the same thing. If a file is "opened" on one page, "activated" on another, and elsewhere "put into service" or "mobilized," the implication is that different things are happening. Figuring out that they are not takes work, and failing to figure it out will result in confusion and errors. The most appropriate word or phrase for an activity or topic should be selected and used consistently (and compulsively) throughout the document. Changes in words made through carelessness or for stylistic reasons will only confuse the reader.

Consistent Use of Phrasing

As well as using terms consistently, it is important to describe identical procedures identically. For example, if, in each section, you are going to describe how to select an item from a menu, say it exactly the same way each time. This eliminates the user's feeling that procedures are arbitrary and simplifies grasping the fundamental operations of the program.

Use of Abbreviations and Acronyms

Abbreviations and acronyms are both information codes in the sense that they stand for something else. Codes must be learned and later recalled. We know that "St. Paul" refers to the saint or city of that name, and that IBM is a computer company. These examples—the first an abbreviation, the second an acronym—are familiar enough that they have gone past being codes and are recognized as having meaning in their own right. This is not the case with unfamiliar abbreviations and acronyms. For example, do you recall from Chapter 3 what ISD means?

Abbreviations and acronyms are used mainly to save space; they are shorter, more compact versions of the words or phrases they represent. In some cases, this space saving can be considerable. However, using them has costs: reduced comprehensibility and additional work for the the reader. The effect of using such terms (A&As?) is a reduction in reading speed and comprehension. The best practice is *not* to use them.

The exceptions are the use of familiar abbreviations or acronyms or the creation of new ones that will become familiar through frequent use. For example, if you are writing documentation for a product called the "Graphics Manager and Scrap Heap Handler" and will refer to it in every chapter, you might be justified in referring to it as the GMSHH after first defining it.

Moses and Ehrenreich (1981) suggest that, if abbreviations must be used, certain rules should be followed. First, abbreviate consistently. Don't use different abbreviations in different places. Second, keep the first few letters of the word and truncate the remainder, e.g., abbreviate documentation to "doc," not "dcm." The "dcm" type of abbreviation is called a "contracted abbreviation," and is formed by deleting selected, noncontiguous letters.

Four Rules for Effective Writing

Use of the "active" rather than the "passive" voice, avoiding compound questions or statements, using short sentences, and using positive rather than negative constructions have all been shown to improve comprehension (Bailey, 1982; Burgess, 1984; Simpson, 1985).

The preceding paragraph commits most of the sins it warns against. It is passive, compound, and long. Let's state it another way to make the same points.

Bailey (1982), Burgess (1984), and Simpson (1985) contend that you can improve reading comprehension by following certain rules. First, use the "active" rather than "passive" voice. Second, avoid compound questions or statements. Third, use short sentences. Fourth, use positive rather than negative constructions.

Active versus passive voice.   Research has clearly shown that the active voice—subject before predicate—is easier to understand than the passive voice. Miller (1962) compared reading performance of people reading active versus passive sentences of the same information content. Examples of active sentences are "The father warned the boy" and "The son liked the old woman." Passive versions of these sentences are "The small child was warned by his father" and "The old woman was liked by the son." Miller concluded that people require 25 percent more time to understand simple passive than simple active sentences.

Bailey used the following example to show how the active voice gets right to the point:

Active voice: *"Flip the switch up to start the motor."*

Passive voice: *"To start the motor, the switch must flipped up."*

Compound versus short sentences. Compound sentences are more difficult to understand. Short sentences are preferable. Simpson (1985) recommends that writers attempt to write short, simple sentences, use commonplace words, and use concrete rather than abstract language. Further, he suggests that when listing multiple items or giving a set of directions, each point should be listed on a separate line. For example, a procedure might be described in sentence form as follows: "To load a file, call the file directory, select a file, type in the file number, and press the Enter key." Here is the list form of the same information:

> To load a file:
> 1. Call file directory.
> 2. Select file.
> 3. Type in file number.
> 4. Press the Enter key.

Positive versus negative constructions. Research has demonstrated that negative constructions take longer to verify than positive constructions (Clark & Chase, 1972; Boomer, 1975). The reason is fairly obvious: negative constructions include an additional operation (logical NOT) that must be performed in order to extract meaning. The reader must translate the negative form of the statement into its positive form to figure out what is meant. Comprehension suffers when the reader must make a logical reversal (Wickens, 1984), such as when translating the statement "the switch is not off" to get the meaning "the switch is on." This effect is due to the increased difficulty in human information processing (see Chapter 2), not to increased sentence length when the negative form is used.

Research on positive versus negative wording of signs indicates that positive wording is more effective than negative (Dewer, 1976; Whitaker & Stacey, 1981). The latter authors, for example, found that a *no left* turn signal consisting of a left arrow with a slash through the symbol is more difficult to comprehend than a *right turn only* sign. This is a simple but clear example of the "no negative" rule.

Research by Greene (1970) relates the positive versus negative rule to reader expectancy. Comprehension appears to be best when sentence structure—and particularly the use of positives and negatives— conforms to the receiver's expectancy. Readers anticipate words as they read; it is undesirable to reverse the negative-positive nature of a statement when the user has been "set up" for expecting one or the other (Chase & Clark, 1972; Boomer, 1975).

Wickens (1984) recommends that writers avoid order reversals, just as they should avoid logical reversals. For example, if step A is to precede step B, and step B is to precede step C, the order of presentation should be A-B-C, not B-C-A or another inappropriate order. For example, say, "Clear the memory and turn off the calculator," not "Before turning off the calculator, clear the memory" (Bailey, 1982).

Revoking the Artistic License

Is it really necessary to write and edit according to these recommendations? Most competent readers can understand long, compound sentences, passive constructions, and so forth. Using the banned techniques might result in a more varied and interesting writing style. It might get very monotonous, for example, to write everything in short sentences. (This point is, of course, debatable; more people continue to read Hemingway than Faulkner).

However, user documentation is not the appropriate forum for demonstrating stylistic virtuosity. The idea is to convey information as simply and as reliably as possible. You would not write a novel this way, but you are not writing a novel.

9

Graphics

This chapter presents techniques for developing readable graphics and tables. These techniques will make your graphics and tables both attractive and effective. Topics covered are graphic functions, the speed-accuracy trade-off, types of graphics, graphic design rules, and table design rules.

Graphic Functions

"One picture is worth more than ten thousand words" (Chinese proverb).

Graphics serve two main purposes: They provide (1) design elements and (2) information (Bobker, 1986). As design elements, graphics attract attention to specific areas of the page or screen and provide "controlled emphasis" to the document. As information providers, graphics provide many types of information more effectively than text. The well-designed graphic does both: It draws the reader's attention to appropriate areas and provides relevant information that is easy to obtain.

The most important function of well-designed graphics is to convey information in the most effective way possible. Graphics, if used properly, can reduce the information load in text and, in many cases, provide more information in less space. Graphic elements can be structured to the immediate task of the user, and they can also be designed to minimize information processing for certain cognitive tasks.

As an example, consider how a keyboard might be described with text and with graphics. Without graphics, the writer must describe the location and function of each key. The user must already know where keys are located, or the writer must describe these locations in text. The user would have to scan and study text or tables to acquire relatively small units of information. Each time the user required information on an additional key or function, the list might have to be reviewed. On the other hand, if a clear illustration of the keyboard is provided along with related information on the function of each key, the user has a clear match between the physical input device—the keyboard—and related information. There are no lists to check or pages to thumb through. Demands on the user's memory are relaxed and the information is transmitted more efficiently.

The physical arrangement of a visual display terminal, a keyboard, a user documentation book, a box of disks, a printer, a telephone, and assorted other items on the top of a desk could not be described in much detail in less than a few pages. A single small illustration or photograph can convey the same information in far greater detail than is possible with text. Whenever the intent is to convey what something looks like, it is almost always best to provide a picture or illustration of it rather than to attempt to describe it with words. This is not to say that a picture can replace words in every situation. It is to say that expediency, succinctness, and the tasks of the system user must be of primary importance when preparing a document for computer use. Graphics should, therefore, be used liberally and with purpose.

The document developer should determine if each topic in a document can be presented most effectively through text, graphics, tables, or a combination of one or more of these methods. It is usually most effective to combine text with graphics and, in a supporting role, text with tables. Text is clearly effective in expressing the context and in providing procedures and details. Tabular approaches are clearly most appropriate when simple data elements must be related to one another, as in the case of a matrix or a decision table. Graphic presentations convey information quickly and simply. Effective graphics can place far fewer demands on the user, particularly when language comprehension is a problem.

Graphics can also be very effective as a visual stimulus for the operator (Weidman, 1965). Primary reference information can be contained in either text, graphics, or tables, but can be keyed to the graphic. When the user can associate a particular type of graphic or table with a particular type of information, the information can be obtained more quickly than would otherwise be possible. Through the consistent use of graphic forms, the document developer can provide numerous keys for retrieving information.

Information presentations are most effective when their format supports the immediate needs of the user. According to Kammann

(1975), text-based instructions are understood about two-thirds of the time. Presenting the same information graphically in the form of a process chart or a list of actions or events increases the reader's understanding. Kammann has found that process flowcharts are far more effective than text alone in conveying information. Moreover, the advantages of flowcharts sustain for users of all types—from novice through expert. Proceduralized behavior is best supported by proceduralized instructions. The best way to present such information is with a flow diagram or a listing.

The Speed-Accuracy Trade-Off

Several research studies have shown that the speed of the user's response is improved with graphic versus text-based presentations. Conversely, in situations in which accuracy is more important than speed, text should take precedence over graphic presentation. Total comprehension is best, as one might expect, when text and graphics are *combined*.

In a straightforward demonstration of the relative merits of text and graphic presentation of equivalent information, Boomer (1975) conducted a study of enlisted Navy personnel and their ability to learn the operation of a specialized control panel. In one situation, instructions concerning the operation of the control panel were provided by pictures. In a second situation, the information was provided by text. In a third situation, the information was provided by pictures supported by text. Response speed was superior in the graphics-only condition, and response accuracy was superior in the text-only condition. Most important was the finding that redundant text did not facilitate performance of the task, but that text that *elaborated* on the steps illustrated in the graphics resulted in the best all-around performance. In sum, the results show that text and graphic information should support one another. Text should not only restate what is shown in the graphics but, in addition, should elaborate on the information provided in the graphics.

The results of research conducted by Haney (1969) provide what may be even more convincing evidence that tabular presentation of information should be used whenever possible. Haney compared test technician performance in a study using both narrative instructions and tabular instructions. Narrative instructions resulted in three times as many errors as tabular instructions, although testing times were practically identical. All subjects preferred the tabular format. Haney contends that when information is "action-sequenced," as in the case of procedural information, the information is obtained most easily and most accurately when it is presented in tabular form.

Types of Graphics

The first type of graphic is the *picture*—a photograph or illustration. Unlike the icon, which is intended to represent a single object, a picture usually provides information on the location and appearance of several objects. There are few, if any, substitutes for a good picture.

The second type of graphic is the *icon*. Icons are typically symbolic and convey a single idea (Figure 9.1). A common example of an icon is an image of a file folder such as would be displayed on the Macintosh "desktop." The symbolic value is based on user expectations for the object represented by the icon. For example, most literate individuals expect a picture of a file folder to represent a collection of related items. Icons are particularly useful when users have different language backgrounds, for the icon is a graphic representation of a concept.

The third type of graphic is the *procedure*. Such graphics include flowcharts, flow process charts, and other types of illustrations intended to present the order of events that occur over a period of time (Figure 9.2). Sometimes charts of this type are tied to specific time lines or quantitative data, but usually they simply represent a sequence of events, without a specific scale.

The fourth type of graphic is any figure intended to convey *quantitative information*. Examples are graphs and charts (Figure 9.3). Such graphics show the relationships among two or more variables. [Two excellent books on designing such graphics are Cleveland's *The Elements of Graphic Data* (1985) and Tufte's *The Visual Display of Quantitative Information* (1983). Both books provide rules for developing effective presentations of data and should be consulted by the document developer who recognizes a need for quantitative data in the user document.]

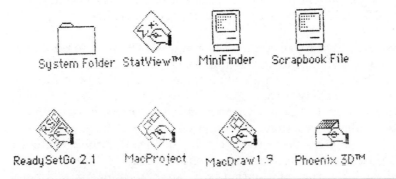

System Folder   StatView™   MiniFinder   Scrapbook File

ReadySetGo 2.1   MacProject   MacDraw1.9   Phoenix 3D™

Figure 9.1   Different types of icons.

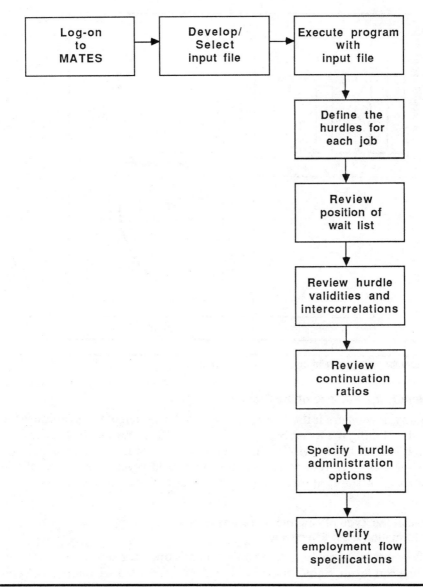

Figure 9.2 A sequential flowchart of user activities.

Graphic Design Rules

The following pages present a set of basic rules for graphic design. We have provided examples of each of the points, as well as a few examples of how graphics should *not* be designed. The discussion focuses mainly on the last three types of graphics mentioned previously, but the first category—pictures—can also be improved by applying many of the principles.

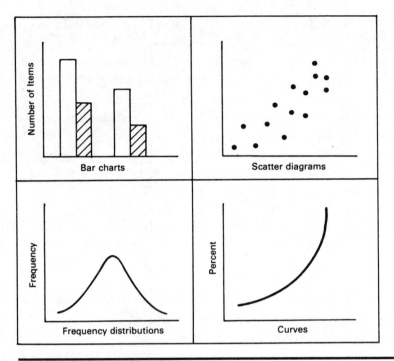

Figure 9.3 A mixture of quantitative data charts.

Identify the Purpose of the Graphic

Many developers fail to state the intended function of the graphic prior
to developing it. Paller, Szoka, and Nelson (1981) maintain that the first
step should be to write a short sentence that states exactly what the
graphic is to convey to the reader. You need a very clear idea of the
purpose of the graphic before it can be developed properly.

Select the Type of Graphic that Conveys the
Information Most Effectively

The most effective type of graphic depends upon the type of information
to be conveyed. Some information is best presented with a photograph
or a detailed drawing, which can provide important information to the
reader simply and quickly.

Pictures of computer screens are an essential part of most user documents but in practice are seldom used to the extent they should be.
Pictures of screens presented in sequence can be particularly effective
in communicating the capabilities of a program or illustrating a
sequence of events. In preparing these illustrations, the developer
should work through the sample problem and obtain a "screen dump"

at each important step along the way. Figure 9.4 illustrates a series of screen dumps intended to describe the capabilities of a graphic database for managing marine shipping facilities. The graphic sequence illustrates a series of interactions between user and computer in simple, explicit form; the user can study the screens with or without being on line.

Some types of information are best presented with a schematic drawing. The flow or process chart is particularly effective for showing a sequence of events. Although such charts do not provide the detail and fidelity of screen pictures, they do show the sequence of operations in a procedure.

A schematic drawing can be combined with pictures. For example, this might be done to show the computer inputs required within a procedure. Figure 9.5 shows an example which portrays how to copy a file from one disk to another using the mouse input device with the Macintosh computer. The sequence could also be shown with a series of screen dumps, but this would require many more illustrations.

A major concern in designing this type of graphic is to select or create symbols that reliably convey the appropriate information to the reader. The symbols and graphics must convey their meanings accurately to all types of users. The novice user must be able to look at the graphic and, in a reasonable period of time or perhaps with the assistance of some text instruction, determine what is being said. The experienced user, however, should be able to recall what the symbols mean when he or she has not looked at the supporting documentation for a period of time.

Guidelines for presenting quantitative information are provided by Paller, Szoka, and Nelson (1981); Tufte (1983); and Cleveland (1985). The guidelines are valuable to anyone presenting such information. A few of these guidelines are summarized in the following paragraphs.

Whenever time-dependent data are to be presented, there are at least three choices of presentation: (1) curve chart, (2) step or surface chart, and (3) bar or column chart. The curve chart (Figure 9.6) is the preferred method to present changes in a variable across time. Readers typically associate such lines with changes over time.

The step or surface chart can be used to present time-dependent data and is commonly used to present financial history, often averaged over a period of a week, a month, or perhaps a quarter. Stepped displays help to improve the usability of data which are extremely variable in the short term; values are averaged over a suitable time interval and presented in step or surface format.

Bar or column charts are not particularly suitable for presenting time-dependent data, but some data—particularly if noncontinuous in nature—lend themselves to the bar or column format.

Parts of a whole can be presented in several ways. Most common are

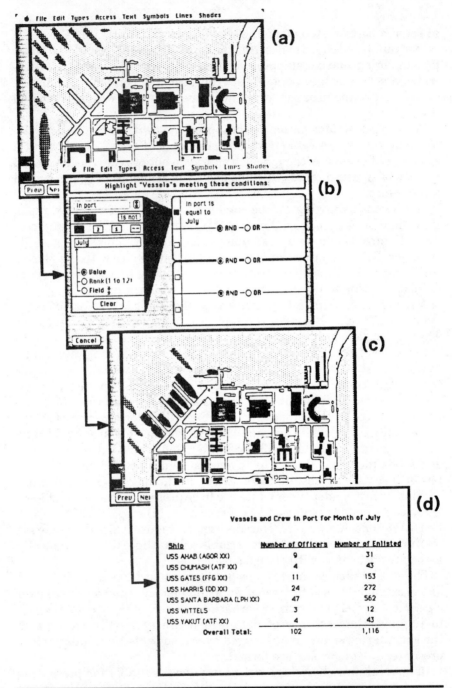

Figure 9.4 Sequential "screen dumps" from a graphic relational database.

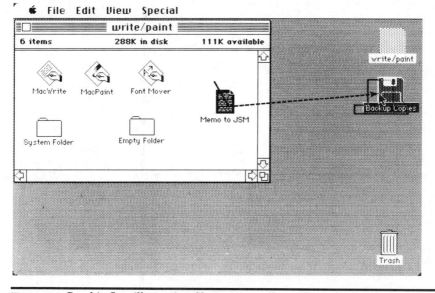

Figure 9.5 Graphic flow illustrating file copy procedures. (*From* Macintosh user's manual *Apple Computer, 1984.*)

the pie chart or bar chart (Figure 9.7). Pie charts are effective for presenting simple information on the parts comprising a whole, though they are often abused and overused. [Tufte (1983) takes the extreme position of recommending that pie charts *never* be used.] In using a pie chart, it is advisable to limit the number of categories to a maximum of five; having more than five categories can make them all the more difficult to interpret. Labels should be shown in or adjacent to the pie wedges rather than on a separate key that requires the reader to match the key code with the pie. When bar charts are used to provide information on the parts of a whole, it is a good idea to provide the reader with any additional information that might be required, such as the percentage of the whole that each part comprises. Do not require the reader to examine the axis on the graph and subtract values in order to find out this information.

Comparisons of several items are best made with vertical or horizontal bar charts. There are really no strict rules as to whether bar charts should be vertical or horizontal; it is best to determine this by examining the data and the presentation that best fits the specific requirements at hand. The books mentioned earlier provide many examples and useful design guidelines and should be consulted by the reader interested in using such charts; the same holds for graphs showing the relationships among variables.

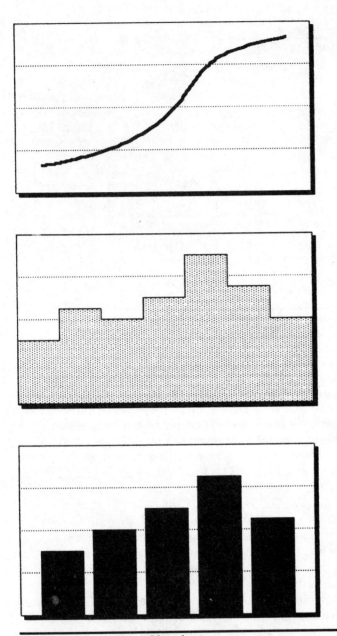

Figure 9.6 Curve, step, and bar charts.

Verify That Users Can Interpret the Graphic

A graphic does not necessarily have the same meaning to all users. Its meaning will be governed by the user's culture, ability, training, and experience. As reviewed in an excellent book on ethnic variables in

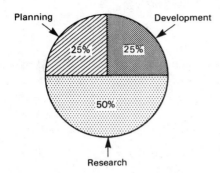

Pie Chart

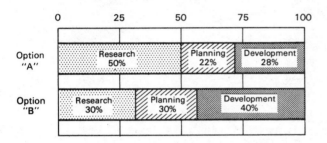

Bar Chart

Figure 9.7 Pie and bar charts for showing parts of a whole.

human factors engineering (Chapanis, 1975), Wyndham (1975) provides examples of graphics which are interpreted differently by different groups. Winter (1963) uncovered several interesting examples illustrative of problems with safety posters used in different cultural settings. For example, South African workers had little understanding of before and after concepts presented in successive pictures on posters. There were other problems associated with the use of red on the posters and confusion regarding blood and fire. Perspective drawings were not viewed in perspective, so that objects were perceived as being located inappropriately. A distant, small figure in one poster, for example, was viewed as being a small child. Figure 9.8 illustrates one type of test used by Hudson (1960, 1968) to investigate perceptual differences such as this. African, American, and Vietnamese viewers perceive these pictures differently. The intended messages of these posters were lost because the designers failed to take into account the cultural variables and customs of the users.

Another interesting example is that of the skull and crossbones

Figure 9.8 Symbols that can be interpreted differently by different user groups. (*From Hudson W., "Pictorial Depth Perception in Sub-cultural Groups in Africa,"* Journal of Social Psychology, *1960, no. 52, pp. 83–208.* Reprinted with permission of the Helen Dwight Reid Educational Foundation. Published by Heldref Publications, 4000 Albermarle St., N.W., Washington, DC 20016. Copyright © 1960.)

symbol; it signifies danger to most North Americans and Europeans, but some other cultures interpret it quite differently. It has also been shown to be relatively ineffective as a warning to children on poisonous substances. The lesson is that in designing symbols and graphics, you must consider all members of the potential audience and the meanings different members will ascribe to what you design.

Although the graphics designer does not usually have to be concerned with user variation in the cultural extreme, it is certainly important to take into account the user's ability, background, and experience. To this end, it is highly desirable to conduct an objective assessment of the interpretability of different symbols and graphics. Chapter 12 presents an overview of some of the methods that may be applied to documentation testing and evaluation and are applicable in such evaluations. Groups of naive users should be presented with and asked to specify the meaning of candidate symbols and graphics. It is important *not* to rely on the judgments of graphic designers, writers, programmers, or other members of the development team; valid measures of graphic interpretability can only be obtained from representatives of the potential audience for the graphic.

Display Concepts and Data Appropriately

Tufte (1983) has provided a number of excellent examples of what he terms "lying graphics," graphics that convey what the author intends—but not necessarily the truth. Tufte provides six principles for maintaining integrity in graphics. These principles pertain to the display of data but can be applied to any variables that might be presented in documentation:

1. The representation of numbers, as physically measured on the surface of the graphic itself, should be directly proportional to the numerical quantities represented.

2. Clear, detailed, and thorough labeling should be used to defeat graphical distortion and ambiguity. Write out explanations of the data on the graphic itself. Label important events in the data.

3. Show data variation, not design variation.

4. In time-series displays of money, deflated and standardized units of monetary measurement are nearly always better than nominal units.

5. The number of information-carrying (variable) dimensions depicted should not exceed the number of dimensions in the data.

6. Graphics must not quote data out of context.

Graphics Should Tend Toward the Horizontal

In terms of aesthetic qualities, practical considerations of labeling, and page layout, there are many arguments for developing graphics that are greater in length than in height. Tufte (1983) contends that the visual system is "naturally practiced" in viewing things on the horizontal, and that graphic design should take advantage of this tendency. The second argument for horizontal presentation is ease of labeling. English is written on the horizontal plane. Whenever a graphic is presented in the vertical plane, there can be problems finding acceptable places for text labels. The third argument—one that pertains specifically to plots of data—is that most readers find it easier to conceptualize cause and effect when a graph is horizontal, with the causal variable along the horizontal axis and the variable being measured along the vertical axis. The fourth argument is that the eye may have an easier time moving horizontally than vertically. The horizontal field of view is wider than the vertical field of view, and Westerners may find that horizontal eye movements—like those required in reading—require less effort than vertical movements.

It has been proposed that graphics be designed with due consideration of the so-called "Golden Section" or, as it sometimes called, the "Golden Ratio" or the "Golden Rectangle." This rule of aesthetic proportion was developed around the fifth century B.C. and is the basis for much classical architecture and art. The Golden Section, as defined by Tufte (1983), is as follows: "a length is divided such that the smaller is to the greater part as the greater is to the whole." It can be expressed mathematically with this formula:

$$\frac{a}{b} = \frac{b}{a + b}$$

(a is the smaller dimension and b the larger dimension.)

The ratio is 1.618, thus producing the Golden Rectangle, as shown in Figure 9.9. The Golden Rectangle presents what can best be called "pleasing" geometry, although it is by no means the most appropriate form for all designs. It is simply a form that has, over the course of time, been accepted as being aesthetically pleasing. There are certainly other forms and ratios that are also aesthetically pleasing.

Avoid Content-Free Decoration

Unless the graphic is being provided to add aesthetic interest to the document, it is advisable to minimize decoration. Content-free decoration is decoration that does not add to the information content of the graphic. Although embellishments can make many graphics more

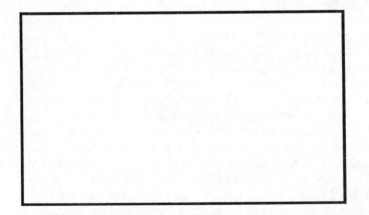

Figure 9.9 The Golden Rectangle.

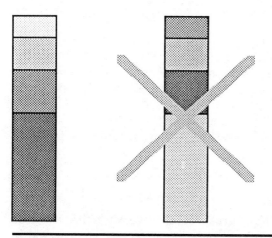

Figure 9.10   Acceptable and unacceptable shade patterns.

interesting and draw the reader to an area of the page, excessive embellishments often clutter the page. Most users of computer documents are interested primarily in solving their particular problems so they can continue with their work at hand. They are not interested in superfluous artistic embellishments.

Avoid Garish Shades and Fill Patterns

With the proliferation of computer graphics applications, many users find the variety of shades and fill patterns irresistible, regardless of their final appearance on the graphic and their impact on legibility. Availability of such shades and patterns is no justification for their use. Simple gradients in shades of gray are usually best for distinguishing different items, and lines and fills should be selected for the purpose of conveying information to the viewer. Garish patterns can create moire (wavy) patterns that make them difficult to view. Select shade patterns that are simple and are chosen to convey the necessary information required by the user.

The designer should also seek to organize shade patterns in such a way that the shades convey meaningful information—information beyond identifying a particular space as unique from other spaces. When categories of information are scaled, as in the case of a series of bars, for example, shades should be organized in gradients to convey the continuous nature of the variable (Figure 9.10). For example, when preparing a vertical bar chart with multiple areas inside the bar, place the darkest shade on the bottom and the lightest shade on the top.

Direct the Reader's Attention

The attention of the reader should always be directed to the portion of the graphic that is of greatest relevance to the point being made. This can be done with arrows or with a combination of arrows, shading, color, or other techniques. The important point is that it should not be left to the viewer to figure out what specific part of the graphic is relevant to a discussion and what is not. Adding a focusing cue reduces the time required to obtain the relevant information from the graphic.

Use Graphics and Text Together

Tufte (1983) argues that graphics are most effective when they are used in conjunction with text. Graphics that simply repeat what is said in text are not particularly useful to the reader unless the information is somehow summarized by the graphic and expressed more succinctly. A graphic that shows the movement and manipulation of icons with a pointing device, for example, can effectively convey much information to the user. In this instance, there is certainly nothing wrong with providing a graphic that explains an operation for the user who is familiar with the graphic symbology. The less experienced user can refer to the text if necessary to obtain the information detail needed to perform the task.

Anyone who has assembled a swing set, bicycle, or most any other large consumer product that is delivered unassembled has encountered illustrated instructions—some far worse than others. (One of the authors recently assembled a large swing set for his daughters. About 50 large metal parts, a single 8½-by 11-inch exploded illustration, and a plastic bag containing no fewer than 500 nuts, bolts, screws, washers, and associated components were delivered to the doorstep. These instructions should have been proceduralized, and step-by-step descriptions should have accompanied the overview and individual illustrations.)

Place Graphics Near Their Points of Reference

Graphics will be most effective for the reader if placed close to the point in the text at which first mentioned—most preferably on the same page. The reader should not have to turn pages to reference a figure related to a passage of text or, worse yet, turn to a separate section of a document containing illustrations. Graphics should be integrated with supporting text so that the reader can quickly and effortlessly view one and then the other.

Maintain Style Across Graphics

A single style for graphics should be developed at the outset of a document and carried through to the end of the document. By having the same basic layout, shades, line widths, type styles, and graphic style, the user does not have to spend time adjusting to new features each time a new graphic is introduced.

Maintain Style Within a Graphic

It is very important to maintain consistency within an individual illustration as well as across different illustrations. For example, do not mix type styles simply because the desktop publishing system you use enables you to print 15 different type fonts. Select a readable font and use it consistently throughout the graphic.

Verify That Graphics Are Friendly

If the document developer and graphic artist have done a good job designing the graphics and illustrations in a document, they should convey the intended information to the user with the least amount of effort and error. There is no substitute for having a group of individuals view the graphics created for a document to verify that they are understandable and that they present the information the author wants them to present. In addition to having users evaluate graphics, it is very useful to assess the "readability" of graphic presentations through the use of a checklist. The list in Figure 9.11 can be used to help ensure that graphics are readable and understandable. This list is extracted from Tufte (1983).

Rules for Table Design

Many of the rules discussed above apply equally to the design of tables. In addition, the following rules apply to tables.

State the Purpose of the Table

This rule is analogous to the corresponding rule for graphics. The function of a table should be stated prior to putting pencil to paper. Before laying out the table, take a moment and write a single sentence about the intended function of the table. Specifically, describe the information the reader should be able to obtain from the table.

Friendly	Unfriendly
Words are spelled out, mysterious and elaborate encoding avoided.	Abbreviations abound, requiring the viewer to sort through text to decode abbreviations.
Words run from left to right, the usual direction for reading occidental languages.	Words run vertically, particularly along the y axis; words run in several different directions.
Little messages help explain data.	Graphic is cryptic, requires repeated references to scattered text.
Elaborately encoded shadings, cross-hatching, and colors are avoided; instead, labels are placed on the graphic itself; no legend is required.	Obscure codings require going back and forth between legend and graphic.
Graphic attracts viewer, provokes curiosity.	Graphic is repellent, filled with chartjunk.
Colors, if used, are chosen so that the color-deficient and color-blind (5 to 10 percent of viewers) can make sense of the graphic (blue can be distinguished from other colors by most color-deficient people).	Design insensitive to color-deficient viewers; red and green used for essential contrasts.
Type is clear, precise, modest; lettering may be done by hand.	Type is clotted, overbearing.
Type is upper- and lowercase, with serifs.	Type is all capitals, sans serif.

Figure 9.11 Rules for selecting "friendly" graphics. (*From Tufte's* The Visual Display of Quantitative Information, *Graphics Press, 1983.*

Identify the Variables to Be Presented

Before designing table format, consider the variables that will be listed and the nature of each variable. In a research experiment, the variable that is manipulated by the experimenter is called the *independent* variable. The variable that changes as a result is called the *dependent* variable. For example, in a study of the effects of smoking on health, the independent variable might be the amount of smoking, and the dependent variable the incidence of heart disease. In most experiments, there are a number of independent variables as well as a number of dependent variables. In general, a table should be formatted to show independent variables across the horizontal dimension and dependent variables along the vertical dimension.

Thinking about a table in these terms should help the designer identify the information that he or she should be presenting and how it should be formatted. In Figure 9.12, this classification can be thought of in terms of *cause* and *effect*. Across the top are listed various actions the user can perform with a particular operating system on a Macintosh: drag a document, drag a folder, drag an application, or drag a disk. Down the first column on the left are the places to which the user can drag an item. This is analogous to a classification variable. The results

	Drag document	Drag folder	Drag application	Drag disk
To folder on same disk	Moves it there	Moves it there	Moves it there	
To folder on different disk	Copies it there	Copies it and its contents there	Copies it there	
To a different disk	Copies it there	Copies it and its contents there	Copies it there	Copies it there
To trash	Discards it	Discards it and its contents	Discards it	

Figure 9.12   Another table illustrating requirement, action, and result. (*Courtesy of Apple Computer.*) for highlighting differences between columns and rows.

of these possible actions are listed in the cells of the matrix. If a user drags an application icon to the trash can, for example, it will be discarded. If a folder icon is dragged to the trash can, the folder and its contents will be discarded. The user can see the differences among the different actions and quickly find the desired information once the basic layout of this table has been determined.

Distinguish Columns and Rows

Columns and rows can be distinguished with space, lines, or by alternate shading. There are no strict rules for determining which should be used, but it is probably true that readers are less likely to lose their place in a large table when inadequate space is placed between different rows or columns. Alternate shading, as long as it reproduces well in the final document (and text is readable when it is placed on top of the shading) can be an effective method for distinguishing between different rows or columns.

Combine Tables When Appropriate

Considering how the user will use the table in a document, it is usually far more appropriate to combine a number of smaller tables into a single, large table. Tufte (1983) has coined the term "supertable" to describe a large table that combines a large number of smaller tables. As long as the rows and columns are clear, a single, large table can reduce access time because the user does not have to thumb through a large number of separate pages. It is also easier to compare information across these "smaller" tables when they have been combined into a larger table.

Place Procedural Information in Tables

As reviewed in the early part of this chapter, comprehension of procedural information is poorest when it is presented in text and the best when presented graphically or in a well-organized table. If there is a dynamic aspect to a procedure or it might vary depending on the outcome of selected events, it may be advisable to use a flow process chart with loops and decision points to present procedures. If the procedures tend not to vary, however, and there are no actions that are repeated or contingent upon other events, then these linear procedures are best presented in tabular formats.

Chapter 10

Documentation Models

This chapter presents detailed descriptions of the documentation prepared for two existing programs: (1) *WordPerfect* (SSI Software) and (2) *Microsoft Chart*. Both are concrete examples—models—of good documentation. In each case, the developers analyzed documentation requirements carefully, worked hard, committed the required resources, and produced end products of the highest quality.

The two models differ considerably. *WordPerfect* is a sophisticated, keyboard-intensive word-processing program for IBM PCs and compatibles using the MS-DOS operating system. Its users are professional word-processing operators, writers, and others who can be expected to use the program frequently enough to maintain their skills. It scores high in the power department but takes a fair amount of time to master (see Figure 6.2). To meet the user's documentation requirements, SSI offers a variety of documentation elements: tutorial, user's manual with reference information, keyboard overlays, quick-reference card, and other materials.

Microsoft Chart is a powerful but easy to learn and use graphics program for the Macintosh computer. Most of its users will use it occasionally. Its documentation consists of a single manual containing a tutorial, user's guide, and reference information. The manual is fairly representative of the best documentation currently being prepared for Macintosh applications—typified by those for Microsoft and Apple Computer products.

This chapter is divided into two sections. The first describes the documentation for *WordPerfect* and the second that for *Microsoft Chart*. Each section discusses the documentation in terms of document design (see Chapter 7) and architecture (see Chapter 8).

WordPerfect Documentation

SSI Software, the manufacturer of *WordPerfect*, received two awards during 1986 for the *WordPerfect* documentation package: Award of Distinction from the Society for Technical Communication and Best Computer Software Documentation from the Computer Press Association.

WordPerfect is delivered in a box (9¼ inches high by 8½ inches wide by 2¾ inches deep) which contains an 8- by 9-inch three-ring binder. Within the binder is a plastic three-ring insert containing five 5¼-inch floppy diskettes, a keyboard overlay, and a transparent, stick-on, color-coded keyboard code reminder. One of the diskettes contains an interactive tutorial. Separately bound, but provided within the binder, is a removable guide covering system installation. Provided separately is a 3½ by 8-inch quick reference card which is printed on two sides and which unfolds to a full size of 8½ by 11 inches. The *User's Manual* itself is divided into sections covering system setup, a tutorial, and separate reference sections for the program's various features. The program includes an on-line help feature. The various documentation components are illustrated in Figure 10.1. In sum, the documentation system consists of these components:

- *User's Manual*
  - System setup
  - Tutorial
  - Reference sections
  - *Installation Pamphlet*
  - *Quick-Reference Card*
  - Disk-based tutorial (supports user's manual tutorial)
  - Keyboard overlay
  - Stick-on keyboard code reminder
  - On-line help feature

User's Manual

The *User's Manual*, as noted, is provided in a compact three-ring binder. The binder consists of seven major divisions and a glossary/index, with a plastic tab on each (see Figure 10.1).

Ten-point Helvetica type is used throughout the manual. Text is left-justified with ragged right margin. The manual is printed in two colors: text in black; headings, footers, and screen illustrations in blue. Illustrations are used extensively throughout the manual, particularly in the first two sections, and account for about one-third of all page content.

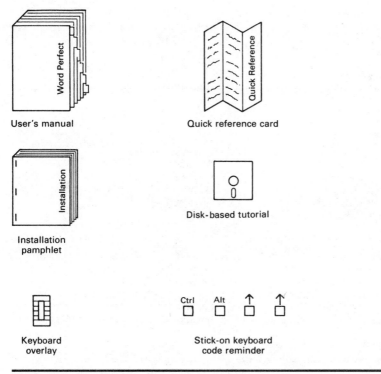

User's manual

Quick reference card

Installation
pamphlet

Disk-based tutorial

Keyboard
overlay

Stick-on keyboard
code reminder

Figure 10.1 *WordPerfect* documentation components. The program also includes an on-line help
feature.

Organization. The *User's Manual* opens to a one-page table of contents
(Figure 10-2). The Contents page is concise and gives a clear indication
of the guide's organization, providing an advance organizer to the user.

The document is structured in modular fashion. Each of the seven
major divisions—GETTING STARTED, LEARNING, REFERENCE, SPELLER/THE-
SAURUS, SPECIAL FEATURES, MERGE, and MATH—is marked by a tab and
can be turned to without referring to page numbers. Pages are
numbered independently within each module.

The document is organized logically and is accessible to the novice
user as well as being suitable for the experienced user. The novice
begins with the first three sections—INTRODUCTION, GETTING STARTED,
LEARNING—and, after gaining experience, will progress to the more technical information in the REFERENCE sections that follow.

The INTRODUCTION contains a one-page guide to the manual itself (Figure 10.3), i.e., a description of the manual's contents and when each
module should be used, depending upon the user's goals. As previously
mentioned, the first action given on this page is to use the *Installation*

Pamphlet—a separate guide—to install the program. In short, the organization of the manual and a general strategy for using it are provided explicitly. This sequence is as follows:

■ Contents

Introduction

Getting Started

Before you start	Exit WordPerfect
The Template	Typing
5 Keys to know	Formats
Conventions	Codes
Start WordPerfect	Printing
Preview WordPerfect	Filing

Learning

Lesson 1 - Typing	Lesson 7 - Footnotes/Page Numbers
Lesson 2 - Editing	Lesson 8 - Text Columns
Lesson 3 - Formatting	Lesson 9 - Mail-Merge
Lesson 4 - Troubleshooting	Lesson 10 - Memo-Merge
Lesson 5 - Moving Text	Lesson 11 - Macros
Lesson 6 - Spell-Checking	Lesson 12 - File Management

Reference

Alphabetical reference of WordPerfect features

Speller/Thesaurus

Special Features

Text Columns	Line Draw
Footnotes/Endnotes	Statistical Typing
Redline/Strikeout	Macros
Paragraph/Outline Numbering	Macro Chaining
Table of Contents/Lists/Index	Sort

Merge

Macros and Merges	Forms Fill-in
Mailing Labels and Envelopes	Math and Merge
Merge to the Printer	Flights of Fancy
Reports and Lists	Merge Code Glossary
Document Assembly	

Math

Subtotals/Totals/Grand Totals
Math Formulas

Glossary/Index

Figure 10-2 *WordPerfect* table of contents. (*From* WordPerfect [user's manual], *SSI Corporation, 1985.*)

- User opens manual to Contents (see Figure 10.2) and obtains overview of document organization.
- User turns page to About the Manual (see Figure 10-3).
- User is routed to *Installation Pamphlet* to install program.
- After installation, user returns to About the Manual and obtains a detailed overview of each module and its function.

About the manual

The Installation Pamphlet should be read first if WordPerfect has not been installed on your machine.

Getting Started   This section acquaints you with WordPerfect. After a brief introduction, the main ideas behind WordPerfect are discussed.

Learning   Twelve lessons take you step-by-step through various word processing tasks.

Reference   Information is included about each WordPerfect feature and how it is used.

Speller/Thesaurus Detailed instructions are included on how to use these two features. There is also a lesson in the Learning section on the Speller.

Special Features   Those features are included which require a little more explanation than what can be covered in the Reference section. See the Table of Contents for a list of those features.

Merge   The acknowledged backbone of office automation, WordPerfect's merge deserves more than a casual glance. You are in for some pleasant surprises.

Math   Anyone who needs to add subtotals, totals and grand totals should read this section on WordPerfect's Math features. Four-function math formulas can also be created.

Glossary/Index   Included is a glossary for those new to computers, a feature summary and, of course, a complete index.

Figure 10.3 *WordPerfect* "About the manual" page. (*From* WordPerfect [user's manual], *SSI Corporation, 1985.*)

- User completes GETTING STARTED module, which provides overview of program and a familiarization exercise.
- User completes LEARNING module, an interactive tutorial supported both by the manual and a separate tutorial diskette.
- User refers to REFERENCE module to obtain detailed information concerning program's word-processing features.
- User refers to special reference sections to obtain detailed information on program features supporting word processing: SPELLER/THESAURUS, SPECIAL FEATURES, MERGE, and MATH.
- User uses GLOSSARY/INDEX to locate information by topic.

The general sequence for using the various parts of the manual at different stages is shown in Figure 10.4.

Installation Pamphlet

The user is routed to the *Installation Pamphlet* at the beginning of the GETTING STARTED module in the *User's Manual*. It is impossible to miss this step unless the user skips the opening module of the manual.

The *Installation Pamphlet* is a 48-page staple-bound document with binder holes that fits into the back of the *User's Manual*, but can be removed for use during program setup. Topics covered are program installation, use of *WordPerfect* with DOS, printer installation, special characters, the Convert program (for translating files from other word processors), a description of program files, and the use of *WordPerfect* with RAM drives.

Once setup has been completed, the pamphlet is no longer needed and

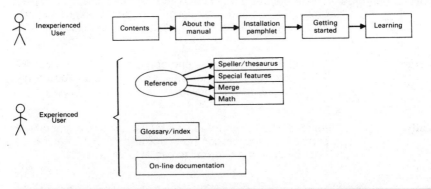

Figure 10.4 Typical sequence for using *WordPerfect* documentation. The sequence at top is completed by the inexperienced user. The experienced user (bottom) relies primarily on the REFERENCE and GLOSSARY/INDEX sections and on-line documentation.

can be returned to the *User's Manual* or placed elsewhere; it will not be used again until another installation must be done. Setting up this particular program is quite involved, and the amount of setup information is greater than that typically found in a *User's Manual*. Hence, providing the information in a separately bound document makes considerable sense. It can be used more conveniently this way during setup, and it can be put out of the way after setup has been accomplished.

Presumably, many of the users of the *Installation Pamphlet* will have limited prior experience with computers. It is designed in cookbook fashion to guide them systematically through the setup procedure. It begins with an equipment and interface checklist (Figure 10.5). Next, it guides the user step by step through setup procedures involved in booting the computer, entering date and time, formatting diskettes, copying the master diskettes, and so forth. A segment of one page of the setup procedure is shown in Figure 10.6.

The user is able to set up the program by following the procedures even if a complete computer novice. Every step of each procedure is explicitly stated. After completing installation, the user returns to the GETTING STARTED module in the *User's Manual* to complete the next phase of program operation.

GETTING STARTED **Module.** The GETTING STARTED module is the first content module the new user of this program will review following program installation. It covers the following topics:

- Before You Start: Reminds the user to use the installation pamphlet, if not done already.

- The Template: Describes the keyboard template (Figure 10.7), defines color codes for book, and the use of function keys.

- 5 Keys to Know: Describes purpose of Num Lock, Help, Backspace, Enter, and Cancel keys.

- Conventions: Defines terms and conventions followed in manual (Figure 10.8).

- Start WordPerfect, Preview WordPerfect, Exit WordPerfect: These three topics, covering about six pages, present some very simple keyboard exercises to familiarize the user with a few basic features of the program (Figure 10.9). The exercises are not so much to train the user as to build confidence.

- Typing, Formats, Codes, Printing, Filing: Each of these topics, covering a single page, describes basic functions of the program.

1 Complete the Check List

The following check list helps you organize information and materials needed to install WordPerfect. Your dealer should be able to help you answer these questions.

What kind of disk system are you using?

☐ Hard disk drive

☐ Two disk drives

What kind of monitor do you have?

☐ Monochrome non-graphics (usually green or amber)

☐ Color graphics

☐ B&W graphics (may be Black and Green, Black and Amber, etc.)

What is the brand name of your printer?_____

If you have more than one printer attached to your computer, which printer will you use most often?_____

Is your printer parallel or serial?

☐ Parallel

☐ Serial

If your printer is serial, gather the following information from your dealer or printer manual:

Baud rate_____
Parity (none, odd, even)_____
Stop bits (1 or 2)_____
Data bits (7 or 8)_____

Figure 10.5 One page of the installation checklist. (*From* WordPerfect [installation pamphlet], *SSI Corporation, 1985.*)

This module does what one expects the introductory material in a user's manual to do: makes sure the user is ready to start (program has been installed), describes the keyboard aid (template), defines the use of special keys, tells the conventions followed in the manual, offers a simple exercise, and provides an overview of the key aspects of the program.

Start WordPerfect

Selection of printers takes place from within WordPerfect. The following steps guide you through starting WordPerfect prior to selecting printers.

Two disk drives

With DOS running,

INSERT The WordPerfect 4.1 diskette into drive A

INSERT The Printer diskette into drive B

ENTER **b:** to change the default drive to B

ENTER **a:wp** to start WordPerfect

Hard disk

With DOS running,

INSERT The Printer diskette into drive A

ENTER **cd\wp** to change to the WP directory

ENTER **wp** to start WordPerfect

A *help* screen appears at startup time until printers are selected. Press any key to display a blank WordPerfect screen.

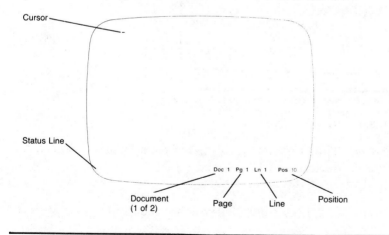

Cursor

Status Line

Doc 1 Pg 1 Ln 1 Pos 10

Document (1 of 2)   Page   Line   Position

Figure 10.6 One page of the setup procedure in *WordPerfect* [Installation Pamphlet]. (*From* WordPerfect installation pamphlet, *SSI Corporation, 1985.*)

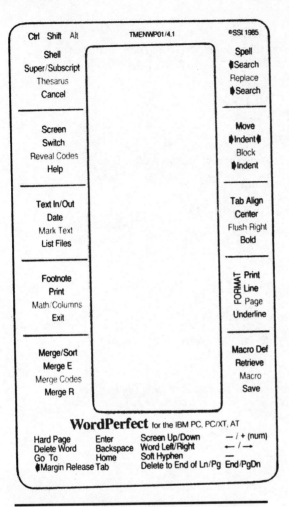

Figure 10.7 *WordPerfect* keyboard template—printed in three colors, but not shown. (*From* WordPerfect, *SSI Corporation, 1985.*)

LEARNING Module.   The LEARNING module is 146 pages long and consists of a five-page introduction and 12 lessons.

The Introduction contains three parts:

- "What You Need": Tells what diskettes are required.

- "The Lessons": Describes lesson structure (see following).

- "Learning Hints": Eight hints relating to keyboard usage and the avoidance of errors commonly made by users.

■ Conventions

These words have specific meanings and are used throughout the lessons and reference material:

CURSOR   move the cursor to the indicated place

TYPE   type the bolded characters

ENTER   type the bolded characters, then press the Enter key

BLOCK   define a block of text

INSERT   insert the given diskette into the specified drive

REPLACE   remove the diskette from the indicated drive and replace it with the given diskette

Keys may appear by themselves, with another key, or as a series of keys to press. Keys not separated by commas mean to hold down the first key while quickly striking the second.

[F8]   press the key

[Alt][F8]   hold down the Alt key then press the F8 key

[Alt][F8] , [1]   hold down the Alt key then press the F8 key, release both keys then type 1

[F7] , [N] , [↵]   press the F7 key, type an "n," then press the Enter key

Figure 10.8 The Getting Started module defines the conventions followed in the *WordPerfect* manual. (*From* WordPerfect [user's manual], *SSI Corporation, 1985.*)

The entire Introduction sets up the learner for the tutorial. The "What You Need" part makes sure the learner is ready to start. "The Lessons" part gives the rules of the game. The "Learning Hints" part anticipates problems and offers hints for avoiding them. Of these three parts, "The Lessons" is the most lengthy and offers a top-down view of lesson organization. The first page illustrates overall lesson organization (Figure 10.10). The second page illustrates page organization, the graphics conventions followed, and shows how the page presentations relate to user keyboard actions (Figure 10.11).

Each of the 12 lessons in the tutorial is about 10 pages long and can be completed in less than an hour. The lessons are cumulative but can be completed separately. The learner can complete one, terminate the session, and continue with the next when convenient. Lessons of this

■ Preview WordPerfect

During the preview you will type, edit, and print a few paragraphs of text. Some of the fundamentals of WordPerfect are introduced here.

Type a paragraph Type the following paragraph without pressing the Enter key. Use the Backspace key to erase mistakes as you type.

Bears have been searching for food in campgrounds since the tourist season started. For this reason, we are increasing patrols for the next few weeks.

Insert a tab Change the format by inserting a tab.

CURSOR To the "B" in the word "Bears"

Use the arrow keys to move the cursor.

Tab Indent the first line of the paragraph

Insert some text Edit the paragraph.

CURSOR To the "f" in the word "food"

TYPE **Chinese take-out**

Space Bar Insert space between "take-out" and "food"

Use the Help key The Help key displays information about each feature.

F3 Read the first Help screen

Insert the Learning diskette in drive B if you are asked to do so.

C Find out where the Center key is located

Shift F6 Read about the Center key

Space Bar Return to your paragraph

Don't forget to replace your data diskette if you had to insert the Learning diskette.

Figure 10.9 Portion of PREVIEW WORDPERFECT familiarization exercise. (*From* Word-Perfect [user's manual], *SSI Corporation, 1985.*)

■ Introduction

The twelve lessons in this section introduce you to many of WordPerfect's features. The first three lessons should be done together. The rest of the lessons can be completed individually as you have time.

If you have not read the Getting Started section, take a moment to glance over the information and become familiar with any new ideas or terms. You should already know how to start and exit WordPerfect properly before beginning the lessons.

What you need

While installing WordPerfect you should have made working copies of the original diskettes that came in your WordPerfect package, or copied the files onto a hard disk.

If you are running WordPerfect from a diskette drive, you will need the following working copies:

- WordPerfect diskette

- Learning diskette

- Speller diskette (lesson 6 only)

- Data diskette (lesson 12 only)

The WordPerfect diskette contains all the files you need to run WordPerfect and your printer. The Learning diskette contains sample WordPerfect documents that are used in the lessons. The Speller diskette contains the dictionary that WordPerfect uses to check your spelling. The Data diskette is a blank, formatted diskette for copying a file.

All these working diskettes are created when you install WordPerfect (see the Installation pamphlet for details).

Figure 10.10   Introduction to LEARNING module. This provides an overview of the tutorial. (*From* WordPerfect [user's manual], *SSI Corporation, 1985.*)

length or somewhat shorter are close to the ideal. Longer lessons—or a single extended session lasting several hours—are undesirable for several reasons: inconvenience to the learner, loss of attention, and fatigue being the most obvious.

Each lesson begins with a "setup" page (Figure 10.12) which (1) defines the task, (2) specifies the features covered by the lesson, and (3) describes applications of what is to be learned. This setup information works as an advance organizer to the lesson that follows.

The lessons use a screen-based, cookbook instructional style with

The lessons   Each lesson begins with an illustration of the finished product and a brief introduction. A series of steps then guide you keystroke-by-keystroke through several word processing tasks. Questions at the end of the lesson help you understand some of the basic ideas presented in the steps.

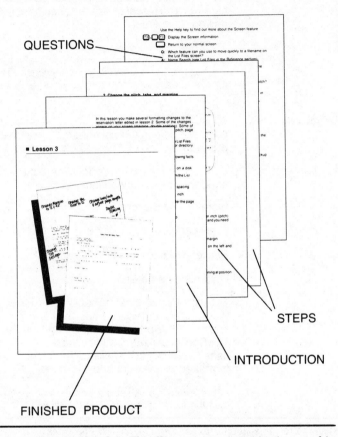

QUESTIONS

STEPS

INTRODUCTION

FINISHED PRODUCT

Figure 10.11   Second page of LEARNING module. This illustrates page organization, graphics conventions, and the relation of the presentation to user keyboard actions. (*From* Word-Perfect [user's manual], *SSI Corporation, 1985.*)

marginal graphics (Figure 10.13). A display screen is shown at the top of the page (in blue), a step-by-step procedure is given below, and the relevant keys are illustrated in the margin beside the text description of the procedural step.

The lesson is followed by a set of questions (Figure 10.14) to permit the learner to test comprehension of the material just covered.

REFERENCE **Modules**.   There are five reference modules in the manual: REFERENCE, SPELLER/THESAURUS, SPECIAL FEATURES, MERGE, and MATH.

In this lesson you type a letter that confirms a reservation at Lone Pine National Park. Several WordPerfect features that help you highlight and emphasize text are used in this letter.

When you are finished, you print the letter, save it on your disk, then clear the screen.

Features

While working through the lesson, you learn the following facts about WordPerfect's features:

- Backspace deletes to the left
- Center centers a line of text
- Bold and Underline highlight text
- Caps Lock shifts the letters on your keyboard to uppercase
- Word Wrap automatically returns the cursor to the left margin
- Print lets you print the document on the screen
- Exit clears your screen

Applications

The skills you learn in this lesson can be used for

- Business letters
- Letters of introduction
- Letters to friends
- Most correspondence

Figure 10.12   Setup page of Learning module. This works as an advance organizer to the lesson that follows. (*From* WordPerfect [user's manual], *SSI Corporation, 1985.*)

The "Reference" module is 152 pages long, organized alphabetically, and covers the general features of the program. The remaining Reference modules, varying in length from about 10 to 100 pages, cover advanced features or utilities available with *WordPerfect*. All of these modules, like the tutorial, make extensive use of illustrations and support text descriptions with marginal illustrations of the relevant keys (Figure 10.15).

The reference modules covering advanced features (e.g., Math) are stand-alone modules. They provide the only coverage in the *User's Manual* of their particular features. In addition to providing reference information, they also present an overview of the particular feature and describe how to initiate its operation.

1 Center, bold, and underline the heading

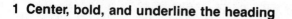

```
                    Lone Pine National Park




                                          Doc 1   Pg 1   Ln 3   Pos   10
```

Shift F6	Begin centering
F6	Begin bolding
F8	Begin underlining
TYPE	**Lone Pine National Park**
	Use the Backspace key to erase mistakes.
	If you have a color or graphics monitor, underlined text is displayed as a separate color or in reverse video.
F6	End bolding
F8	End underlining

Figure 10.13 Lesson page of Learning module. The screen is shown at the top of the page and the procedure is given below, with marginal illustrations of relevant keys. (*From* WordPerfect [user's manual], *SSI Corporation, 1985.*)

Glossary/Index.   The manual contains a separate glossary and index. The glossary is an alphabetic listing and short definition of technical terms. Figure 10.16 shows one page of the glossary.

The index is, well, an index. However, it has two slightly unusual features. First, in addition to listing topics by name, it also lists some topics by keyboard command (e.g., ^ for Control-C key combination); the index uses symbols as well as words to reference topics.

Use the Help key to find out more about the Cursor Conrol feature:

F3 , →   Display Cursor Control information

Space Bar   Return to your normal screen

Q: Where are the Caps Lock, Escape, Tab, and Arrow keys on your keyboard?
A: Use the keyboard illustration on the Quick Reference card.

Q: When can you use the Tab key?
A: To indent the first line of a paragraph.

Q: Do you need to press the Enter key at the end of each line of text in a paragraph?
A: No, word wrap moves the cursor down to the next line.

Q: What happens to the position number (**Pos**) at the bottom of your screen when you turn Bold or Underline on?
A: The number is bolded and/or underlined when the features are on.

Q: What happens to the "Pos" at the bottom of your screen when Caps Lock is on?
A: The "Pos" changes to "POS."

Q: Which key is used to clear the screen?
A: The Exit key.

Figure 10.14 Questions following a lesson in the Learning module. (*From* WordPerfect [user's manual], *SSI Corporation, 1985.*)

Second, the index references topics by both major division (e.g., Learning, Reference) and page number. As noted earlier, pages are numbered independently within each major division of the manual. Hence, there are several pages in the manual with the same page numbers, and the only way to identify a page uniquely is by specifying both page number and major division. (Such page number redundancy is undesirable but often inescapable when a documentation system, consisting of many different parts, is developed.) Figure 10.17 shows one page of the index with both of these features evident.

Quick Reference Card

WordPerfect is a keyboard-intensive program that uses an enormous number of key combinations involving the Alternate, Shift, Control, and function keys, which are combined in various ways to exercise program features. These combinations are so numerous that it is doubtful that any program user without a photographic memory or many months of experience could remember them all.

Three related tools are provided to support the user in this regard: (1)

■ Advance   [Adv▲][Adv▼][AdvLn:]

The Advance feature lets you print text one-half line up or down from your regular text. You can also use it to move the printer to a specific line on the page.

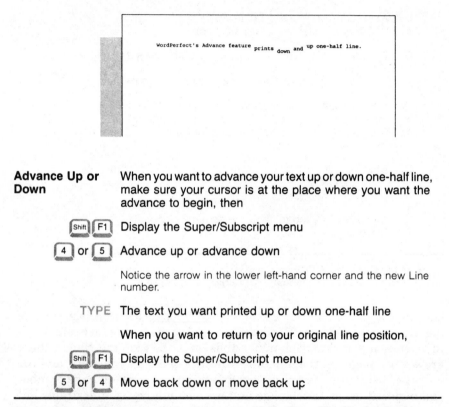

Advance Up or Down   When you want to advance your text up or down one-half line, make sure your cursor is at the place where you want the advance to begin, then

[Shift][F1]   Display the Super/Subscript menu

[4] or [5]   Advance up or advance down

Notice the arrow in the lower left-hand corner and the new Line number.

TYPE   The text you want printed up or down one-half line

When you want to return to your original line position,

[Shift][F1]   Display the Super/Subscript menu

[5] or [4]   Move back down or move back up

Figure 10.15 A sample page in the REFERENCE module. (*From* WordPerfect [user's manual], *SSI Corporation, 1985.*)

Quick Reference Card, (2) keyboard template, and (3) stick-on keyboard code reminder. All use color coding to distinguish among Alternate, Shift, and Control key combinations. The Alternate key is represented by blue, the Shift key by green, and the Control key by red.

The stick-on keyboard code reminder consists of colored labels which are attached to the Alternate, Shift, and Control keys.

The keyboard template (see Figure 10.7) is placed around the function keys.

The *Quick Reference Card* is placed where convenient, and provides a summary of the various key combinations; there are about 200 of

■ Glossary

Alphanumeric
composed of letters and numerals. WordPerfect sorts words alphanumerically or numerically.

ASCII
American Standard Code for Information Interchange is one of the standard formats for representing characters so that files can be shared between programs. A DOS Text File is in ASCII format.

Backspace
a key on your keyboard which deletes the character to the left of the cursor.

Backup
to copy files for safe keeping.

Baud
the rate of speed (referred to as baud rate) at which information is sent between two computer devices. It is used, for example, when sending files to serial printers or across modems.

Bit
a binary digit, the smallest storage unit for data in a computer.

Boot
to start your computer. The Disk Operating System (**DOS**) is loaded into your computer's memory and executed.

Buffer
a temporary data storage area used by computers and some printers.

Byte
the amount of space needed to store a single character (number, letter or code). A byte generally represents eight binary digits (bits). For example, if a character requires one byte of storage space, that one byte is translated to eight bits when processed in the computer. 1024 bytes equals one kilobyte or (**Kb**).

Carriage Return
the return of the printhead (or wheel) to the beginning of the next line. In word processing your cursor returns from the end of one line to the beginning of the next. This can be accomplished manually by pressing the Enter (Return) key, or automatically by allowing WordPerfect to *wrap* the line (see Word Wrap).

Figure 10.16   A sample page of the GLOSSARY. (*From* WordPerfect [user's manual], *SSI Corporation, 1985.*)

them. The card, when fully opened, is 8½ by 11 inches, but folds in two places down to one-third this size. It is printed on two sides. The key combination reference information is contained on one side, and the other side explains the color code, identifies important keys on a photo-

■ Index

Figure 10.17 A sample page of the INDEX. (*From* WordPerfect [user's manual], *SSI Corporation, 1985.*)

graph of the keyboard, and provides a summary of instructions for starting the program, saving documents, clearing the screen, and exiting the program.

The key combination reference information is listed in three columns on the opposite side of the card. Program functions are listed alphabetically by name and followed by the color-coded key combinations required to exercise the function. Figure 10.18 shows one of the three panels of this information (without color).

On-Line Help

WordPerfect has a context-sensitive help feature which can be accessed while using the program by pressing Function key 3 (F3). The help feature offers help tailored to the current operating context (i.e., what the operator is attempting to do) and permits the user to select information.

The Bigger Picture

The authors chose *WordPerfect*'s documentation for several reasons, many of which are probably obvious to the reader. First, the documentation system is just that. It consists of the various components necessary to support the operator during initial learning and later, after considerable skill has been gained. Each module of the *User's Manual* has a mission and fulfills that mission.

Second, the design and architecture of these documents is fully professional and of the highest quality. In terms of documentation design, the material is organized around tasks; orientation cues (advance organizers, headings) are used appropriately; graphics and color are used effectively to support text; the instructional style is appropriate; and so forth. In terms of documentation architecture, the type is readable, the page formats are clean and clear; and quick-reference tools (Contents, tabs, index, quick-reference card, keyboard template) as well as various other features making for an attractive and useful documentation system have been provided.

In simple terms, SSI has met the basic requirement of creating a documentation system that takes the needs of users into account.

Microsoft Chart Documentation

Microsoft Chart documentation consists of a 183-page, 8¼- by 9-inch spiral-bound manual which includes an introduction, a two-stage tutorial, and reference information under one cover. The program also incorporates an on-line help feature. In sum, the documentation system consists of these elements:

Features

Feature	Keystrokes
Advance Line	Shift-F1
Advance Up/Down	Shift-F1
Alignment Character	Shift-F8
Append Block (Block on)	Ctrl-F4
Auto Rewrite	Ctrl-F3
Backspace	←
Binding Width	Shift-F7, 3
Block	Alt-F4
Block, Cut/Copy (Block on)	Ctrl-F4
Block Protect (Block on)	Alt-F8
Bold	F6
Cancel	F1
Cancel Hyphenation	F1
Cancel Print Job(s)	Shift-F7, 4
Case Conversion (Block on)	Shift-F3
Center	Shift-F6
Center Page Top to Bottom	Alt-F8
Change Directory	F5, ↵
Change Print Options	Shift-F7
Colors	Ctrl-F3
Column, Cut/Copy (Block on)	Ctrl-F4
Columns, Text	Alt-F7
Conditional End of Page	Alt-F8
Copy (List Files)	F5, ↵
Create Directory	F5, =
Ctrl/Alt Key Mapping	Ctrl-F3
Date	Shift-F5
Delete	Del
Delete (List Files)	F5, ↵
Delete Directory (List Files)	F5, ↵
Delete to End of Line (EOL)	Ctrl-End
Delete to End of Page (EOP)	Ctrl-PgDn
Delete Word	Ctrl-←
Display All Print Jobs	Shift-F7, 4
Display Printers and Fonts	Shift-F7, 4
DOS Text File	Ctrl-F5
Endnote	Ctrl-F7
Enter (or Return)	↵
Escape	Esc
Exit	F7
Extended Tabs	Shift-F8
Flush Right	Alt-F6
Font	Ctrl-F8
Footnote	Ctrl-F7
Full Text (Print)	Shift-F7
Generate	Alt-F5
"Go" (Resume Printing)	Shift-F7, 4
Go to DOS	Ctrl-F1
Hard Page	Ctrl-↵
Hard Return	↵
Hard Space	Home, Space Bar
Headers or Footers	Alt-F8
Help	F3
Home	Home
Hyphen	−
Hyphenation On/Off	Shift-F8, 5
H-Zone	Shift-F8, 5
♦Indent	F4

Figure 10.18   One panel of the *WordPerfect Quick Reference Card* (printed in three colors). (*From* WordPerfect, *SSI Corporation, 1985.*)

- *User's Manual*
  - Introduction
  - Tutorial
- Reference
- On-line help feature

This documentation is much simpler than that of *WordPerfect*, but adequate for its purpose. The differences between the two programs are that *WordPerfect* is keyboard-based, uses the MS DOS operating system, provides little prompting, and requires the user to memorize approximately 200 key combinations; whereas *Chart* is menu-based, operates on the Macintosh, and provides extensive prompting.

User's Manual

The *User's Manual*, as noted, is provided with spiral binding. It lacks tabs, but page numbers are printed in black boxes at the right edge of the pages, and the level of these boxes changes from chapter to chapter. Thus, it is possible to locate a major division by the level of the page numbers.

Ten-point Times type is used throughout the manual. Text is left-justified with ragged right margin. The manual is printed in a single color. Illustrations are used extensively, particularly in the first two sections, and account for about one-half of all page content.

Organization. The *User's Manual* opens to a one-page Table of Contents (Figure 10.19). The Contents page is concise and gives a clear indication of the guide's organization, providing an advance organizer to the user.

The document is structured in modular fashion and divided into four parts—INTRODUCTION, LEARNING MICROSOFT CHART, HOW TO MAKE A CHART, CHART REFERENCE—plus a GLOSSARY and INDEX.

The document is organized logically and is accessible to the novice as well as being suitable for the experienced user. The novice begins with the first three sections and, after gaining experience, progresses to the reference module that follows.

The INTRODUCTION provides a general description of the program, a figure illustrating how charts are created (Figure 10.20), and a description of the manual and its contents and how each module should be used. The INTRODUCTION contains two advance organizers: (1) chart creation (see Figure 10.20) and (2) manual organization. Figure 10.20 is an excellent example of an advance organizer for the operation of a program. It summarizes in one simple graphic how the program works.

Table of Contents

Figure 10.19   Table of Contents of *Microsoft Chart* user's manual. (*From* Microsoft Chart, *Microsoft Corporation, 1984.*)

The organization of the manual and a general strategy for using it are provided explicitly. This sequence is as follows:

- User opens manual to Table of Contents (see Figure 10.19) and obtains overview of document organization.

- User completes "LEARNING MICROSOFT CHART" module.

- User completes "HOW TO MAKE A CHART" module.

- User refers to "CHART REFERENCE" module to obtain detailed information concerning program's features.

- User uses INDEX to locate information by topic.

The general sequence for using the various parts of the manual at different stages is shown in Figure 10.21.

Introduction

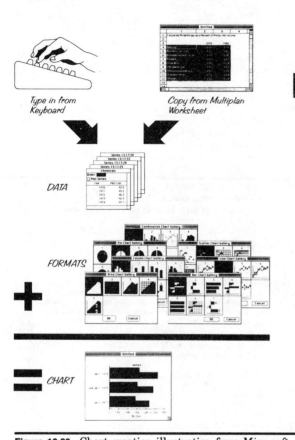

Figure 10.20 Chart creation illustration from *Microsoft Chart* user's manual, which neatly summarizes the chart creation process and serves as an advance organizer. (*From* Microsoft Chart, *Microsoft Corporation, 1984.*)

LEARNING MICROSOFT CHART **module**. The LEARNING MICROSOFT CHART module combines program setup information with a familiarization exercise. Setting up this program is almost comically simple when compared to most programs, as shown on the first page of the module (Figure 10.22). Note the page format, with marginal text callouts referring to the text on the main part of the page. This format is used throughout much of the manual. Note also the amount of white space on the page. In the main, this manual restricts a particular page to a single topic, which may be covered in a short paragraph, often with a supporting illustration. Thus, the information is readily separable by the reader.

The familiarization exercise walks the learner through data input,

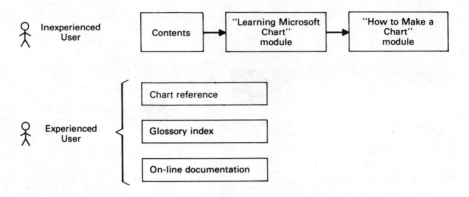

Figure 10.21 Typical sequence for using *Chart* documentation. The sequence at top is completed by the inexperienced user. The experienced user (bottom) relies primarily on the Reference and Glossary/Index sections and on-line documentation.

Learning Microsoft Chart

"Learning Chart" will take you through the process of entering data on projected sales, making a chart of that data, adding data on actual sales, using the chart to compare projected and actual sales, and revising graphic details. After you work through these lessons, you will understand the basic features of Microsoft Chart.

We assume you are already familiar with the fundamental concepts of using Macintosh. If you've never used Macintosh before, read the owner's guide, *Macintosh*, before continuing.

To use Microsoft Chart you need:

■ An Apple Macintosh™ computer
■ The Microsoft Chart disk
■ A printer (optional)

To start Microsoft Chart:

► Turn on the Macintosh power switch.
► Put the Microsoft Chart disk into the disk drive.
► Double click the Chart icon to start Microsoft Chart.

Figure 10.22 Program "setup" page from Learning Microsoft Chart module of user's manual. (*From* Microsoft Chart, *Microsoft Corporation, 1984.*)

chart generation, display formatting, adding titles and legends, and saving and printing a chart. Each step in the exercise is covered on two or three pages. Figures 10.23*a* and *b* are two facing pages in the presentation chart that explain the data-input process. Note that the cookbook instructional style is used; the learner is directed to perform certain operations, without extensive explanation of "why." Text is supported by accompanying graphics which are embedded in the page but not called out by figure number.

Microsoft Chart

When the New Series window is in front, Chart is ready for you to create a new series. No matter where the pointer is, if you start typing, a new series window will appear and what you type becomes data in that window.

► Type *300*
► Press the Enter key.

8

When you begin to type, Chart opens a new window to receive the data. Its name is the word "Series" followed by the current time.

► Type the rest of these values and press the Enter key after each one:

400
490
580

If you make a mistake while typing, use the Backspace key to erase the error and retype.

You have just entered four data points in your new series. To plot the data on the chart:

► Click the Plot Series box in the series window.
► Bring the chart to the front by clicking anywhere in the chart window.

(a)

Figure 10.23 Two facing pages from familiarization exercise in LEARNING MICROSOFT CHART module of user's manual: (*a*) a procedure and (*b*) results. (*From* Microsoft Chart, *Microsoft Corporation, 1984.*)

The familiarization exercise, though similar to a tutorial, is not really tutorial in nature. Mainly what it does is direct the learner to perform certain operations that illustrate different facets of the program. It does not explain what is going on in much detail, and its coverage of program features is quite global. At the conclusion of the exercise, the learner will have been exposed to certain key aspects of the program and will have gained some general knowledge of how it works; more importantly, perhaps, is that the learner will have gained some confidence in using the program. The operation of the program is covered in greater detail in the tutorial contained in the HOW TO MAKE A CHART module (see next section).

Providing a familiarization exercise such as this raises an interesting educational issue. Instruction traditionally progresses in a top-down fashion—from principles to application. The familiarization exercise just described jumps right into applications—but ones so simple that the

Learning Microsoft Chart

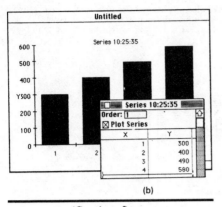

(b)

Figure 10.23 (*Continued*)

Learning Microsoft Chart

Review and Going Further

In these lessons, you've learned the basic functions of Microsoft Chart:

- How to create a new series by typing values.
- How to plot the data on the chart.
- Where the labels come from.
- How to change the name of a series.
- How to change the categories of a series.
- How to format data.
- How to get data from a file on the disk.
- How to add a new series to the chart.
- How to add a legend.
- How to change the chart type with the Gallery commands.
- How to delete a label.
- How to add text to a chart.
- How to add a border around text.
- How to save a document.
- How to print a chart.
- How to end a charting session.

Now that you understand the basics, you can use the rest of this manual to learn more about Chart. Part II, "Using Chart," is organized according to what you want to do. Part III, "Reference to Chart," gives details on each command as well as other information. There is both a glossary and an index to aid you in producing the charts you need.

Figure 10.24 Summary at end of familiarization exercise in Learning Microsoft Chart module of user's manual. (*From* Microsoft Chart, *Microsoft Corporation, 1984.*)

How to Make a Chart

To plot the data:

► Click the Plot Series Box

► Click anywhere in the chart window to bring it to the front.

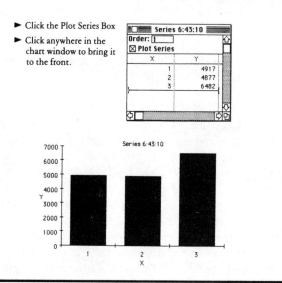

Figure 10.25 Sample page from overview in How To Make a Chart module of user's manual. (*From* Microsoft Chart, *Microsoft Corporation,1984.*)

underlying principles are obvious. When does such an approach make sense? When (1) it is easier to demonstrate something than to explain it *and* (2) what is being demonstrated is simple. In other cases, it is pref-

How to Make a Chart

You now know the fundamentals of Microsoft Chart: how to enter data, how to plot the data, and how to change the basic chart type. The remaining chapters in "Using Chart" explain more about data and how to customize a chart for your needs.

Data tells more about series, including how to create a series, change its name, and edit and format values (which appear in the right column of a series window) and categories (which appear in the left column).

Charts explains about Microsoft Chart's built-in chart formats.

Creative Formatting describes the legend, axes, and text in more detail, tells how to draw arrows and lines wherever you want them, and explains how to overlay one chart on another to produce a more complex chart.

Data Power shows you how to copy data directly from Microsoft Multiplan worksheets into a series window—and establish a permanent link if you wish. It also explains how to analyze data with built-in formulas to calculate trends, percentages, and more.

Chart Documents explains how to open, save, and print chart documents.

In addition, there is a directory of every command and other useful information in Part III, "Chart Reference."

Figure 10.26 Overview of five lessons contained in How to Make a Chart module of user's manual. (*From* Microsoft Chart, *Microsoft Corporation, 1984.*)

erable to take the traditional approach. For simple Macintosh applications, which have much similarity to one another, such a familiarization exercise is often feasible. For more varied and complex applications, it is usually not.

The final page of the LEARNING MICROSOFT CHART module summarizes the points covered (Figure 10.24).

HOW TO MAKE A CHART MODULE.   The HOW TO MAKE A CHART module is 68 pages long and consists of a six-page introduction and five lessons covering the topics Data, Charts, Creative Formatting, Data Power, and Chart Documents.

The introduction contains a four-page "how-to" section which explains the main steps in creating a chart (enter data, plot data, add data, change chart type) and an overview of the five lessons following. Figure 10.25 shows a page illustrating one of these steps (plot data); note that the procedure is described quite generally and that the user is not being directed to perform it. Rather, it offers a framework for understanding how the step is performed in many situations. The overview (Figure 10.26) follows the procedural description and precedes the first lesson. Thus, the introduction works as both a procedural and structural advance organizer for the lessons.

Each lesson in the tutorial is about 10 pages long and can be completed in less than an hour. The lessons are cumulative but can be completed separately. The learner can complete one, terminate the session, and continue with the next when convenient. Each lesson begins with a setup page, which provides a description of the principles underlying the subject area. The pages following present step-by-step procedures for using the program in that subject area.

Figure 10.27 shows the setup page for the Data area; this explains how data are organized and used by the program, display limitations, data presentation, and terminology (series, data points, categories, etc.).

The lesson is broken down into the subsections required to work in the particular domain. For example, the Data area is divided into subsections for "Creating a Series," "Entering Data," "Editing Data," "Changing How Data Looks," and "Plotting Data on the Chart." Each of these subsections describes relevant procedures. Figure 10.28 is one page from the "Entering Data" section. Instructional style is screen-based. Each step of the procedure is described and accompanied by an illustration of the screen display. Note that this is not cookbook style, as the procedure is described in general terms and the reader is not directed to perform specific steps. The procedure can be followed in performing a wide range of data-entry tasks.

Data

In Microsoft Chart, the numeric data that provide the basis for a chart is organized into tables called *series*. There may be many series in a Chart document. Each series may contain as many as 64 data points. You can have around 100 data points total to begin with (if you do elaborate formatting or, for example, have a Text series with a lot of very long categories, there may not be room for that many). Each series can be viewed in its own window.

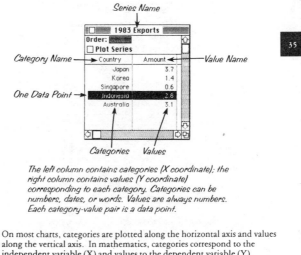

Series Name

Category Name — Country   Amount ← — *Value Name*

One Data Point → Indonesia

Categories   Values

The left column contains categories (X coordinate); the right column contains values (Y coordinate) corresponding to each category. Categories can be numbers, dates, or words. Values are always numbers. Each category-value pair is a data point.

X and Y

On most charts, categories are plotted along the horizontal axis and values along the vertical axis. In mathematics, categories correspond to the independent variable (X) and values to the dependent variable (Y).

Figure 10.27   First page of first lesson in How to Make a Chart module of user's manual. (*From* Microsoft Chart, *Microsoft Corporation, 1984.*)

CHART REFERENCE **module.** Most of the reference module deals with commands. Commands are issued with menus, and the contents of the reference module shows the menus with a page number following each menu option (Figure 10.29). Figure 10.30 shows a single page of the reference module which covers the Unlink command. This way of organizing a reference section is unconventional; reference sections are usually organized alphabetically. However, since the user of this program is menu-oriented, organizing the reference section around those menus makes sense.

GLOSSARY AND INDEX.   The manual contains a separate glossary and index. The glossary is an alphabetic listing and short definition of technical terms. The index contains what an index usually contains.

Data

Entering Data
in a Text or
Number Series

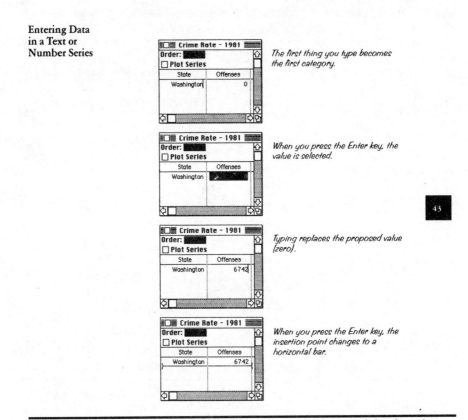

The first thing you type becomes the first category.

When you press the Enter key, the value is selected.

Typing replaces the proposed value (zero).

When you press the Enter key, the insertion point changes to a horizontal bar.

Figure 10.28 Sample page from lesson in How to Make a Chartmodule of user's manual. (*From* Microsoft Chart, *Microsoft Corporation, 1984.*)

On-Line Help

Chart has a series of help menus which may be used to access help information either separately or from within the program. The user obtains help information within the program by selecting the About Microsoft Chart option from a menu. This causes a dialog box to appear, permitting the user to select the type of help information desired. When a selection is made, a series of help screens may be paged through to obtain help information. This type of help information is not context-sensitive; it leaves it up to the user to decide what type of information to seek. However, the program is fairly simple to use, and this type of help information is adequate. *Chart* on-line help is illustrated and discussed in greater detail in Chapter 11.

Microsoft Chart

Contents

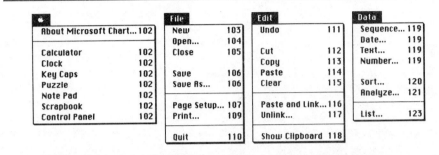

Figure 10.29 One page of the Contents page of the Reference module of *Microsoft Chart* user's manual. Note that page numbers are given opposite commands in pull-down menus. (*From* Microsoft Chart, *Microsoft Corporation, 1984.*)

Commands

Unlink

Edit	
Undo Clear	⌘Z
Cut	⌘H
Copy	⌘C
Paste	⌘U
Clear	⌘B
Paste and Link...	
Unlink...	
Show Clipboard	

The Unlink command dissolves a link between a series and the source of the data. The source may be a different document or it may be another series in the same document (see Analyze from the Data menu).

This command is only available if a series window containing a linked series is active. The dialog box tells the source of the data.

Only the link is dissolved. The copied data remains in the current document and can now be modified. The document or series from which the information was linked is not affected.

Figure 10.30 One page in Reference module of *Microsoft Chart* user's manual. (*From* Microsoft Chart, *Microsoft Corporation, 1984.*)

On-Line Documentation

The term "on-line documentation" was defined quite broadly in Chapter 1 as any computer-based documentation that might be used to support the learning and use of a computer program. This broad definition encompasses many different things, e.g., help screens, help menus, prompts—and even tutorials and guided tours. The term is commonly used more narrowly, in reference to information provided within a running program. People usually think of help screens and help menus as on-line documentation. Most probably do not regard a separate tutorial—or even a prompt within a program—as such. Our definition is admittedly broad—because we want to address this topic conceptually. The goal is to put forth some ideas to stimulate your thinking about the topic, rather than to perpetuate the myopia that traditionally surrounds it.

The chapter is divided into three sections. Section one describes several different ways to implement on-line documentation at a conceptual level. Section two presents some on-line documentation models— actual programs that illustrate some of the features discussed in the first section. As on-line documentation becomes increasingly sophisticated, the link between it and system design increases; there comes a point where documentation and program are indistinguishable. Thus, the final section discusses the connection between documentation development and system design.

Ways to Implement On-Line Documentation

On-line documentation can be implemented in many different ways but has a common objective: to help the computer operator learn and use a program. In some implementations, the emphasis is on learning; in others, on use. We need to keep in mind this objective—perhaps with an emphasis on either learning or use— for it is what we are attempting to achieve in using such documentation. On-line documentation is not a thing—e.g., a help screen—but a technique that can take many different forms.

Three Unique Properties of On-Line Documentation

The objective just stated applies equally to paper documentation. Given this, one might reasonably ask how, beyond their obvious physical differences, the two types of documentation differ. There are at least three potential ways: (1) speed, (2) intelligence, and (3) adaptation.

First, if designed properly, on-line documentation provides faster information access than paper documentation.

Second, on-line documentation can show intelligence. For example, the program can track program state and appropriately tailor the type of help information it provides.

On-line documentation can be adaptive. For example, it can change the amount of help information it provides based on the operator's success rate in performing certain program operations.

The speed factor is quite self-evident, but the intelligence and adaptive factors are not. Moreover, these two factors may be totally absent or present in various degrees, may be implemented in several different ways, and are not entirely independent.

One way to think about the three factors and their interrelationships is to use the traveler-roadmap metaphor. Learning and using a computer program are analogous to traveling through unfamiliar territory. The computer operator travels the geography of the program, moving from program state to program state, to accomplish the desired goal. The starting point is with the program inactive; thus, the first thing the operator must do is activate it, i.e., get on the road. Next in his or her "travels," the operator may open a new file or load an existing file. Various types of work are then performed on the contents of the file. Usually, new objects are created, existing objects are edited, and some objects are deleted. Output may be produced on a printer. The working file is saved. The session is terminated, i.e., the destination is reached.

A traveler moving through physical geography must take similar actions: get on the road and perform certain on-the-road tasks (e.g., identify landmarks, maintain proper speed, make turns, etc.) before reaching the destination. The computer operator uses on-line documentation to help with navigation; the traveler uses a roadmap. Now, let us consider some alternative ways of providing the map information to the traveler and how these vary in terms of the three variables just mentioned: speed, intelligence, adaptation.

The most common way for a traveler to obtain geographic information is from a physical roadmap. To use this map properly and safely, the driver must stop the car and locate the information needed. The driver then sets the map aside, puts the car back on the road, and continues driving. The physical roadmap is slow, has no intelligence, and is nonadaptive. Its use relies entirely on the operator.

Now, suppose that the automobile is equipped with an electronic map display, such as ETAK, that provides a continuously updated display of the automobile's location on an electronically generated map. To determine current location, routes, location of starting point and destination, and other pertinent information, the driver examines the electronic map instead of a paper map. The electronic map is fast; the driver does not have to stop to use it. It is also intelligent; it keeps track of current location and displays the type of information useful to the driver automatically. It is not adaptive. It knows nothing about the driver; all it knows is geography and current location.

For the program just described to be adaptive, it must know something about the driver and alter on that basis the type or amount of information it provides. An *automatically* adaptive program does this automatically. A *manually* adaptive program adapts based on user request. We might imagine the electronic map display just described working in either way. For example, a manually adaptive version of the map display might permit the driver to select the level of detail presented on the display screen. An automatically adaptive version would have to decide what to display based on what it knew about the driver in terms of such factors as route experience, driving skill, goals, and so forth. An automatically adaptive program is obviously much more difficult to create, since it must gather data and make decisions. A manually adaptive program is simple by comparison.

Now, let us extend this analogy over to on-line documentation. Use of a paper roadmap—slow, unintelligent, nonadaptive—is comparable to providing a manual on disk, help menus separate from the program, or providing other forms of on-line documentation that rely upon the user to locate and select the information needed. Use of an electronic map display—fast, intelligent, nonadaptive—is comparable to providing context-sensitive help within a program. Use of an electronic map display that tailors navigational information to the individual user— fast, intelligent, adaptive—is comparable to providing individually tailored, context-sensitive help information.

The best way to show how the three factors may come into play in on-line documentation is by example. Let us consider how speed, intelligence, and adaptation are exhibited in some hypothetical on-line documentation systems.

Unintelligent, Nonadaptive Documentation

Let us suppose that we provide on-line documentation in the form of a computer-based manual. To use this documentation, the user calls up a screen containing the table of contents, then views various pages of the manual on the screen. The manual is simply a computerized version of a paper manual. It is slow because the user must access information in the traditional way. It is unintelligent because it has no knowledge of what the operator is attempting to do. It is nonadaptive because it consists of fixed pages of information that are in no way tailored to the user.

We may be able to make such documentation faster. It will be slowest if it is contained in a separate program that requires the operator to discontinue work on the main program to use it. In this case, the operator must terminate work on the ongoing program, access the electronic manual, and then return to the main program. By providing access to the manual within the main program, we make it possible for the operator to use it without terminating that program.

However, this form of documentation is inherently unintelligent and nonadaptive. You may recognize that it is quite common. Such documentation is provided to support the operating systems of some minicomputers and mainframes, where large manuals are made available for on-line use. It is also quite common with desktop applications, particularly those for the Macintosh. Most Macintosh applications offer a help option on the Apple menu which, when selected, offers a list of help topics which may be read. Arguably, this approach is reasonable for simple desktop applications for which documentation requirements are limited. The same cannot be said for more complex desktop applications or for complex applications on minicomputers or mainframes. What is absolutely awful and inexcusable is to provide documentation in this form exclusively, without hard-copy documentation.

The obvious advantage of such documentation from the developer's viewpoint is the ease with which it can be created. It is based on a paper manual and may be nothing more than an electronic copy. It is usually organized in the same way. The computer code required to implement such on-line documentation is relatively simple, since the documentation requires few, if any, "hooks" into the main program. It can be created separately from the program. Even if the help information is to be accessible within the program, the documentation still exists entirely in a single, separate module.

Intelligent, Nonadaptive Documentation

Intelligent documentation, by its nature, is fast. Its intelligence is part of what gives it speed. This "intelligence" may vary in degree, from marginal to considerable, as noted in Chapter 1. "Intelligence," as used here, does not necessarily imply artificial intelligence, although it may.

The foundation of this intelligence is a mapping between what the user is doing with the program (the task) and relevant information in the documentation, i.e., the "task-information mapping" (Figure 11.1). The more finely this mapping is made, the more "intelligent" the documentation.

Let us consider some of the levels of "fineness" in making this mapping. Assume that we want to develop on-line documentation for a word-processing program and that the program performs three broad classes of operations:

- File handling
- Text entry and editing
- Printing

Each class uses a different operating mode, and we can "map" between the program and help information on this basis (Figure 11.2). We design

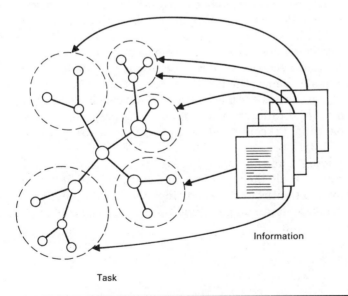

Information

Task

Figure 11.1   The foundation of intelligent documentation is a mapping between what the user is doing in the program (the task) and relevant information in the documentation.

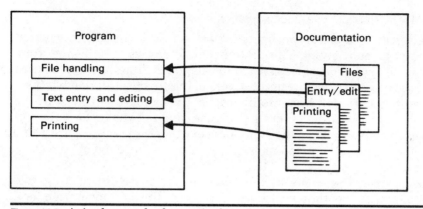

Figure 11.2 A simple example of a mapping between program modes and relevant parts of user documentation.

the program so that it takes mode into account when responding to a user help request. For example, if the user is in the file-handling mode and requests help information, information on that topic is presented. Likewise for the other two operating modes. This is a crude mapping, but illustrates the basic idea.

In actual practice, the mapping would be made much more finely than as just described. For example, in the word-processing program, we would break down each of the three classes of operations into subclasses and attempt to map at that level. The mapping might include dozens or hundreds of cross-links between the program and help information. In mapping at finer levels, modes are less effective as an indicator of the type of help information needed. The operator might need help while operating within a mode. Hence, the intelligence must be able to interpret the help request on the basis of more refined criteria. These criteria can be obtained in several different ways; among the possibilities are (1) within-mode mapping, (2) command interpretation, or (3) operator definition (Figure 11.3).

Within-mode mapping is an extension of the technique just described. For example, we might divide the text entry and editing mode into two classes of operations, text entry and text editing, and then break down these classes themselves—for example, dividing text editing into such categories as the following:

- Editing keys
- Edit screens
- Cursor movement
- Document scrolling and paging

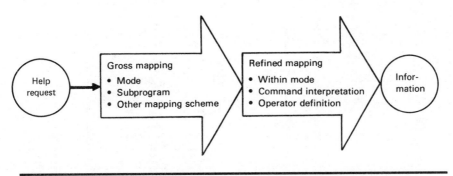

Figure 11.3 The task-information mapping can be refined by mapping within mode, interpreting commands, or having the operator define the type of help information desired.

- Jumping to a page
- Deleting text
- Inserting text
- Overwriting text
- Blocking text
- Moving text
- Selecting type font
- Selecting type style
- Search and replacement
- Within-text commands

Program operations must be broken down at a level of detail that will be useful to the operator. Within a text- or command-based program, this level is the individual command and command statement. To provide information at this level of detail, it must be segmented at this level, and the intelligence must determine what type of information the operator needs (Figure 11.4). Segmenting the information more finely is not usually a problem; however, determining what type of information is needed becomes successively more difficult. The intelligence must look for obvious markers (modes, submodes, etc.), make inferences, or ask the operator what type of information is needed.

Command interpretation. Eventually, as the level of detail becomes finer, a point will be reached where markers are unavailable, and the intelligence must make inferences about what type of help information is needed. One way to do this, if the program is command-based, is to

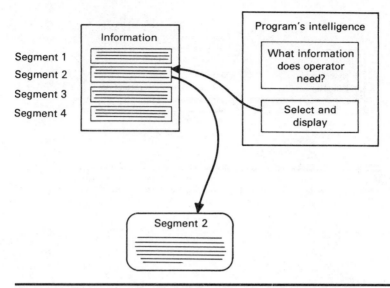

Figure 11.4 To provide refined help information, the information itself must be segmented at a refined level, and the program must have the intelligence to identify the type of help needed at a refined level.

scan the incoming commands to make an assessment of what the operator is attempting. This is like listening to a child speak, judging the adequacy of the communication, attempting to determine the intent, and then offering helpful suggestions for improvement.

Doing this requires true artificial intelligence and is beyond the scope of what is feasible in most applications. However, short of this, cruder inferences can be made. For example, the command interpreter can keep track of the types of errors being made and, when errors with a particular type of command advance beyond a threshold, may offer a particular type of help. A word-processing program might permit the operator to attempt an illegal operation three times and then present a help screen explaining the error and what to do about it.

Operator definition. Another approach to identifying the type of help information is to ask the operator what specific type of help is needed. Help menus rely entirely on the operator to do this and have no intelligence at all. However, the help menu approach can be used with intelligent help to allow the operator to target the specific type of help needed in an area already identified by the machine. For example, suppose that the operator is using the word-processing program just described to perform text editing and wants to move a block of text. The intelligence knows that text editing is being performed based on the operating mode and that certain classes of operations are possible because text has been blocked (i.e., highlighted by the operator). The possible operations at that point are deletion, copying, moving, or storage on disk. If the operator requests help, the program can query the operator to find out the specific operation (deletion, copying, moving, or storage) for which help is needed.

Adaptive Documentation

Adaptive documentation is documentation that takes the needs of the individual user into account. One way to provide such documentation is to offer different levels of help within a program such that the amount of on-line help provided to the user is varied based on user expertise. Suppose, for example, that a program will be used by operators with three experience levels: novice, average, and expert. Help is offered at these three levels. Novices are provided with more help than average operators, and average operators with more help than experts.

There are two basic ways to determine the level of help to offer: (1) operator selection and (2) program determination. The easiest of these is for the operator to select the amount of help provided. Alternatively, if the program is "smart" enough, it may be able to make the determination.

Note that, regardless of how the level of help is determined—by operator or program—the amount of help provided should be reflected in all aspects of help information. This extends beyond help screens, help menus, and so forth, to include such matters as prompts, error and alert messages, descriptions of procedures—to any information relevant to learning and using the program.

Information requirements for automatic adaptation.   What must a program "know" in order to adapt itself to the user? Two general classes of information are required: (1) operator profile and history (operator record) and (2) current system context and task record (Figure 11.5). Both of

```
Operator profile and history:
 • Who is operator?
 • How many hours using program?
 • Types of tasks performed in past?
 • Success rate by task?
 • Current settings of adaptation variables?
 • Record last updated?
Current system context and task track record:
 • Where am I?
 • Where have I been?
 • What is this operator attempting to do?
 • How may I help?
```

Figure 11.5 Some of the information the program must know to be automatically adaptive.

these are historical records, and their compositions vary with the particular program.

The information in the operator record tells the program about the operator, e.g., who he or she is, how many hours have been spent using the program, types of tasks performed in the past, success rate (e.g., type and number of errors, trials to completion, benchmark test scores), how long since last using the program, and the current settings of adaptation variables (e.g., type and amount of prompting and help information to provide). The operator record is constantly updated as the operator uses the program based on the current performance level.

The task record is generated in real time based on the operator's current and recent interactions with the program. In simple terms, this record provides the information required for the program to answer or infer the answers to such questions as the following:

- Where am I?

- Where have I been?

- What is this operator attempting to do?

- How can I help?

The answer to the last question is governed by the particular operator, as defined by the operator record.

Ideally, enough intelligence is built into the program so that it can determine the type and amount of help information to provide for a particular operator within a given operating context. Writing software that can do this sort of thing may require techniques taken from artificial intelligence and be quite costly. Moreover, this degree of helpfulness is probably not necessary in most programs; it marks the limit.

Voluntary Versus Involuntary Help

Voluntary help is help provided by the program at operator request; all of the types of help information discussed above are voluntary. Typically, the operator requests such help by making an overt request. Some of the ways such help is requested are as follows:

- Issuing a standard help command through the keyboard

- Pressing a help key

- Pressing the Control-? or Control-H key combination

- Selecting a help option from a menu

- Moving the cursor over an object and issuing a help command

- Opening a help file

Involuntary help is offered by the program without request. To offer appropriate help, the program must be intelligent enough to know precisely what the user's problem is. This may be possible if the operator consistently makes certain obvious errors, such as using incorrect command words or command syntax. It may also be possible, when the operator begins, to set up the program to issue a command; for example, when the program is in a particular mode and the operator enters part of a complex command, the program "reads" the command and uses its intelligence to present an extended prompt providing details on the command—without waiting for a help request. In essence, help is built into the program itself in the form of context-dependent, extended prompts.

Interpreted broadly, on-line help is any information the program provides to the user to support learning and use of the program. Thus, a prompt itself is help information, and so are other types of information presented within the program that are not ordinarily thought of as help, per se. For example, all of the following may be regarded as on-line help:

- A list of menu options
- An error message
- An alert message
- A warning
- A list of steps in a procedure

Each of these elements should be built into the program, as appropriate, to support the user. In other words, help information should not be compartmentalized but should be built into the program itself.

On-Line Documentation Models

This section describes some of the on-line documentation features of actual programs to illustrate the conceptual discussion of the previous section. The discussion is organized in three parts: Unintelligent, Nonadaptive Documentation; Intelligent, Adaptive Documentation; and Adaptive Documentation.

Unintelligent, Nonadaptive Documentation

Common forms of unintelligent, nonadaptive documentation are help files and help menus—on-line documents in which the user must locate the desired information without the aid of computer intelligence. In general, such documentation is not as desirable as intelligent documentation. (Adaptive documentation, while desirable in principle, remains, at present, a remote ideal for most applications.) However, unintelligent, nonadaptive documentation can be quite effective if the program it supports is relatively simple, the information is organized logically, and the implementation permits information to be located easily and quickly.

The best examples of such documentation are found in Macintosh applications. This is for two reasons. First, the developers of Macintosh applications—in particular, Apple Computer and Microsoft—have taken great care to provide high-quality documentation for all of their products. Second, the Macintosh operating system incorporates many documentation elements inherently. Some of the built-in documentation properties of such applications are its graphic, iconic user interfaces, which make the various program objects and functions highly visible (see Figures 2.1a, b, and c); the extensive use of pull-down menus, which list available commands and their keyboard equivalents (see Figure 6.9); dialog boxes, which are small windows containing text-entry fields and symbolic control devices (such as "radio buttons"); alert boxes, which are used to warn the operator of problems or to obtain an operator okay before a far-reaching operation (such as leaving an application without saving a file).

On-line documentation for most Macintosh applications is obtained by selecting the About [program name]... option from the Apple menu (see Figure 1.13). After making this selection, the help information may be reviewed without interrupting or terminating the work being conducted with the program; after reviewing the help information, the user returns to the program where it was left off.

Microsoft Chart, which was discussed in Chapter 10, is a fairly representative example of a Macintosh application. It incorporates a wide range of Macintosh-type involuntary, on-line documentation (pull-down menus, dialog and alert boxes, detailed prompts, etc.) and voluntary on-line documentation based on a help menu. The user can access the help information independently of or within the main program. It is accessed outside the program by activating the help file in the Finder or within the program by selecting the About Microsoft Chart... option on the Apple menu. In either case, selecting help causes a dialog box to appear listing the subjects covered in the help file (Figure 11.6).

The user can scroll through the subjects to find the one desired. The mouse pointer is then used to select the option and then to "click" on the Show button on the lower left of the dialog box. Doing this causes a help window to appear on the screen (Figure 11.7). The user may page forward and backward through the help windows to obtain the desired information. When the user is through, help is deactivated and the program returns to its state prior to the help request.

The help menu approach is quite effective in Macintosh applications

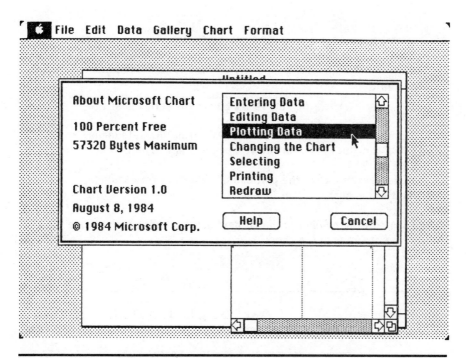

File Edit Data Gallery Chart Format

Untitled

About Microsoft Chart

100 Percent Free

57320 Bytes Maximum

Chart Version 1.0

August 8, 1984

© 1984 Microsoft Corp.

Entering Data
Editing Data
Plotting Data
Changing the Chart
Selecting
Printing
Redraw

Help   Cancel

Figure 11.6 *Microsoft Chart* help menu, which is presented when the About Microsoft Chart option is selected from the Apple menu. (*From* Microsoft Chart, *Microsoft Corporation, 1984.*)

for a number of reasons: they are largely self-documenting already, help information can be obtained without interrupting the main application, and the amount of help information that must be provided is usually quite limited. In non-Macintosh applications this approach may not be as desirable—particularly if the amount of involuntary help (menus, prompts, etc.) is limited, the main application must be interrupted to access the help menus, and a large amount of documentation must be provided.

Intelligent, Nonadaptive Documentation

Common forms of intelligent, nonadaptive documentation are context-dependent help screens and prompts—on-line documents in which the relevant content is located by the computer.

EinsteinWriter (Perceptronics, Inc.) is an MS-DOS word-processing program for IBM PCs and compatibles that rates high in both usability and power (see Figure 6.2). Like most such programs, it makes extensive use of keyboard commands. However, unlike the majority, it provides extensive on-screen prompts and menus to help the user recall

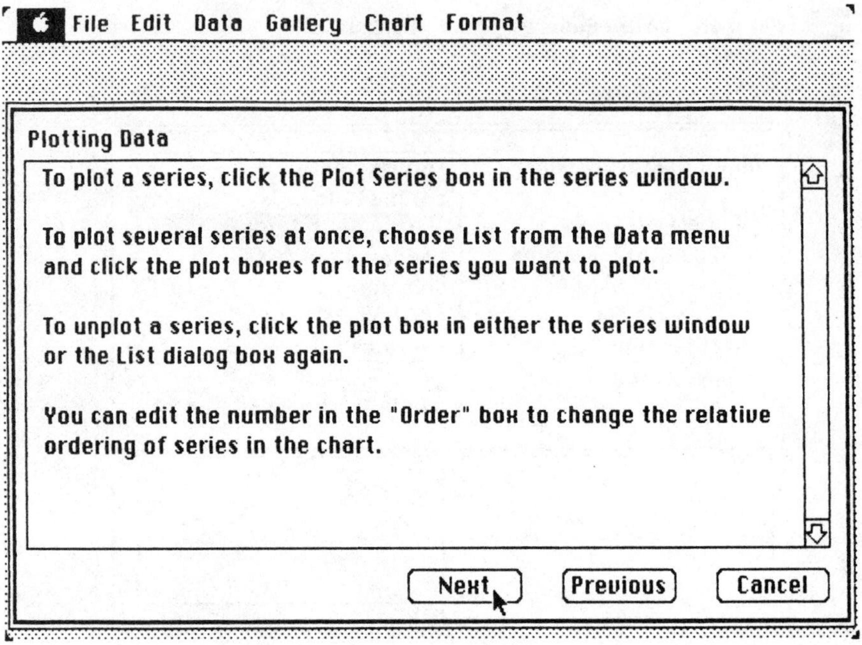

Figure 11.7 A help screen obtained via the help menu in *Microsoft Chart*. *(From* Microsoft Chart, *Microsoft Corporation, 1984.)*

the relevant commands within the particular operating context. In addition to such involuntary forms of on-line documentation, the program incorporates an intelligent on-line help feature.

Involuntary on-line help. *EinsteinWriter* is activated from DOS with the W command. Doing this causes the main command menu to appear. This menu defines the assignments of the function keys, tells how to obtain on-line help (with the Alternate-H key combination), and how to quit the program. In addition, information at the top of the screen tells program state, text file name, date, and time; and information at the bottom of the screen tells how to use the menu, get to it from elsewhere in the program (with Escape key), and obtain help information. Regardless of where the user is within the program, this menu can always be reached with the Escape key. The information contained in the screen is a form of on-line help that does not have to be requested by the user; it is always readily available.

Text is normally created in the Edit mode, which is activated with Function key 1 (F1). Making this selection causes the Edit screen to appear. The same status information appears at the top of the screen.

The bottom lists several keyboard commands commonly used during editing. Pressing the Alternate-I key combination causes several additional commands to be shown . Pressing Alternate-I a third time causes the commands to disappear, making additional screen space available.

EinsteinWriter makes use of commands embedded within the text for defining page breaks, adding lines to pages, defining headers and footers, selecting layout template, and providing printer commands. These commands do not print but are used by the program for one of the purposes just stated. Each command is marked by a dot (.) at the left margin followed by the particular command and argument; for example, the command .L4 tells the program to use layout template number four. The commands are quite involved and difficult to recall. The program provides context-sensitive prompting at the bottom of the screen to help the operator construct proper commands.

To illustrate, when the operator decides to use one of the "dot" commands, a dot is typed at the left margin; the program responds immediately by displaying a set of dot command prompts at the bottom of the screen. Each prompt identifies one of the six classes of dot command indicators (the letters P, A, H, F, L, or D), which must follow the dot. The operator then types one of these letters; doing so causes a new set of prompts, tailored to the particular command, to appear in the prompting area. This type of prompting amounts to command interpretation; as the command is constructed, the program interprets it and provides succesively more refined information to support the user. The same technique can be extended to command-based systems employing longer command statements consisting of command words and various arguments constructed according to syntactical rules.

Context-sensitive prompts, such as just described, are a type of involuntary help quite uncommon in computer programs, but they can be very effective. They are certainly more convenient than using a separate help feature. This particular program uses similar techniques on most of its display screens and is an excellent example of a program that goes out of its way to provide the user with the type of information needed to operate the program effectively. Contrast this approach, for example, with that of *WordPerfect*, which requires its users to memorize nearly 200 commands and rely on memory while using the program.

Voluntary on-line help. *EinsteinWriter* offers voluntary on-line help via a universal help command: the Alternate-H key combination. Pressing this key combination will provide help information based on the current operating mode (Edit, Compose, Layout, Print, File). For example, if Alternate-H is selected while in Edit mode, the first of a series of Edit help screens will be presented; the operator may page forward and backward through these screens, and exit them by pressing the Escape key.

The same help technique is available in other modes; in each case, the help information is tailored to the particular mode.

EinsteinWriter is a fast and capable program. The fact that it uses menus, provides extensive on-screen prompting, and offers context-sensitive prompting and help information in no way makes it less than a first-rate word processing program. Notably, the program was designed by human factors professionals who have found that power and friendliness are not incompatible.

Adaptive Documentation

Adaptive documentation may adapt, as noted above, based on operator selection or program determination. When the operator sets the adaptation level, the program is "manually" adaptive; a program which decides for itself how to adapt is "automatically" adaptive.

Currently, automatically adaptive systems of any type—not just in the area of on-line documentation—are quite rare. To our knowledge, none has become commercially available. Work on such systems is progressing, particularly in artificial intelligence laboratories and within government laboratories. Such systems will probably become much more common in the next few years.

Manually adaptive systems are fairly common. In general, the ways in which they adapt are broader than in the manner in which they provide on-line documentation. However, what they do is relevant in addressing this question. What follows is a brief description of some manually adaptive systems which are in commercial use and which have been studied in the laboratory.

University library system.   The University of California employs a mainframe-based system in its libraries to permit the user to locate books and other publications via terminals. At the beginning of a session, the user is prompted to specify whether the search program will be used in "command" or "lookup" mode. Command mode requires typed-in commands. Lookup mode uses a network of menus and provides much more detailed prompting to the user. The search program provides the same capabilities in both modes, although command mode is faster for expert operators. Lookup mode is obviously designed for the novice or occasional user. As the user gains experience, the mode of interaction may be changed; most users transit from menus to commands after experience on the system.

UNIX and EIES.   The archetypal command-based operating system is probably UNIX, the proponents and detractors of which have waged a running battle concerning its "user friendliness" (Norman, 1981;

DeLeon, Harris, & Evans, 1983). Interestingly, it appears that even experts have serious problems using it. In a broad study of UNIX, Kraut, Hanson, and Farber (1983) analyzed 9 days worth of data generated by 186 UNIX users, ranging in experience from novice to expert, to investigate patterns of command usage. Among their findings were that users relied on a small subset of the available UNIX commands; 20 percent of commands accounted for 70 percent of usage. These findings suggest that UNIX users at all levels of skill have serious problems; this observation probably extends to users of many other command-based systems.

Findings such as those just described have led some investigators to consider the use of menus as learning tools for a command language; i.e., have the system adapt by permitting the user to transit from menus to command language as learning progresses, as with the university library system just described. Hiltz and Turoff (1981) report survey data obtained from a variety of users following the introduction of the Electronic Information Exchange System (EIES), which allows users to access data using either menus or commands. Following the introduction of EIES, data concerning use and preferences for mode of access during learning were collected at intervals from about 200 users. Usage data revealed that nearly 90 percent of users began with menus, but the majority made the transition to commands after 50 hours on the system. These results suggest that complex systems should be adaptable and designed so that they incorporate different features for different classes of users.

"Training wheels" systems.   Another way to permit a system to adapt is to limit the number of features novices can access based on their current levels of skill and to lock out potentially failure-prone or dangerous features until a certain level of competence has been reached. This is the idea behind so-called "training wheels" systems. Folley and Williges (1982) developed models of user performance in text editing and found that the models used by novices and experts overlap, but that novices used smaller models. It follows that limiting the available commands during early learning, if done properly, may reduce error possibilities without having a negative effect on performance and, by consequence, may increase learning efficiency.

Carroll and Carrithers (1984) describe research with a training wheels system for a commercial word processor in which error-prone features were disabled during early learning. Subjects using the training wheels system reached criterion more rapidly, had lower error rates and reduced error recovery times on all errors (not just those blocked), showed better comprehension on posttests, and had better attitudes about the program than those using the standard program.

Documentation Development and System Design

Developing on-line documentation requires the skills of system designers and programmers, as well as documentation developers. We have no data on this matter but suspect that the majority of such documentation is written and implemented by programmers rather than documentation developers. However, professional documentation developers can play a very useful role in organizing and writing the material to be provided on line.

The importance of the system designer and programmer increases with the sophistication of the on-line documentation provided. Unintelligent, nonadaptive documentation, since it exists outside the main program, can in theory be written by a nonprogrammer. The programmer's job is to incorporate the material into the program by transferring it from paper or text files into files accessible by the program. Such documentation can also be written after the program has been written.

Intelligent or adaptive documentation are different matters. Including intelligent or adaptive features requires decisions during the early part of design. If context-sensitive prompts or help screens are to be included in the program, the time to do so is as the program is being created, not afterwards. Clearly, making the system adaptive requires even more far-reaching decisions.

Thus, as on-line documentation becomes more sophisticated, the role of the system designer and programmer increases, and that of the documentation developer diminishes. There comes a point at which the documentation developer's role becomes one of advising the system designer and recommending that certain features be provided within the program. The very best on-line documentation, such as that provided in a program such as *EinsteinWriter*, was designed by people having an understanding of both programming and user documentation requirements. If program designers and programmers have such skills, then the on-line documentation they produce will reflect it. If not—and this may be in the majority of cases—then documentation developers are obliged to step out of their traditional role to make suggestions and recommendations to the software folks.

Chapter 12

Test and Evaluation

User documentation is tested to ensure its quality. The objectives of testing are to identify any defects, areas of omission, errors, or other shortcomings that reduce documentation effectiveness. The importance of such testing is obvious; without it, the documentation may be less effective than possible or, in the worst case, unusable.

Defects are inevitable in all but the most trivial documentation. As the documentation grows larger and more complex, the probability of errors and the effort required to find them increase proportionately. If documentation developers do not make a sufficient effort to test and evaluate their products, defects will remain.

Defects vary in significance. Some, such as a few misspellings, do not significantly affect documentation utility and are not serious. Others, such as factual errors in the descriptions of program features or commands, are very serious, for they will affect the user's ability to operate the program. Minor errors are tolerable, but serious errors are not. However you test and evaluate the documentation, you must identify and correct the serious defects which may cause the user problems.

There are many different techniques for testing and evaluating user documentation. User documentation undergoes continuous testing, evaluation, and refinement throughout development. Much of this is done informally: an editor reviews a writer's draft, a subject-matter expert reviews a document for accuracy and completeness, preliminary documents are circulated among the members of the development team. In addition to such informal efforts, it is highly desirable to test and evaluate documentation in more formal ways; that the members of a development team and subject-matter experts are satisfied is no guarantee that the end user will find the documentation usable or effective.

This chapter describes several ways such testing and evaluation may be done.

Though there is more than one way to test and evaluate documentation, some testing principles are universal. The first of these is the "divide-and-conquer" principle. This principle requires you to view your documentation system in terms of its individual components and to test each separately. Only then can you determine whether each is meeting its objectives.

The second universal principle is "human myopia." This principle (first introduced in Chapter 1 in another context) holds that every individual involved in a documentation development project has blind spots that make it impossible for him or her to discover certain types of defects. Individuals develop habitual, stereotyped ways of perceiving things that limit their ability to view things with complete objectivity. Other individuals, with other biases, will see things differently. This is why it is so important for testing and evaluation to involve a team of individuals with different backgrounds and experience.

The chapter consists of two sections. The first provides a test and evaluation overview. The second describes the steps in the test and evaluation process.

Test and Evaluation Overview

Documentation test and evaluation is part of the larger test and evaluation that occurs during program development. It is useful to consider this larger test and evaluation process to see how documentation test and evaluation fits in.

Program test and evaluation is often described as having three phases: (1) module testing, (2) integration testing, and (3) acceptance testing (Simpson, 1985). Module testing focuses on individual program modules. During integration testing, program modules are combined and tested together.

Module and integration testing are usually performed by programmers, who uncover routine programming errors, design errors, and shortcomings in the design specifications. By the end of integration testing, all of the technical problems in the program should be uncovered and corrected.

During acceptance testing, the program is put through its paces by representatives of its target audience. The objective is to determine the program's shortcomings from the user's viewpoint and to correct these shortcomings. The concern is not so much with technical errors as with program usability.

While these three phases concern program test and evaluation, they have implications for documentation test and evaluation. Documentation may undergo informal evaluation before an operating program is available, but cannot be tested fully until the user has both documentation and program. Having an operating program is even more critical if on-line documentation is used. Thus, the availability of an operating program governs when documentation testing and evaluation can commence. As there is usually considerable incentive to complete a program and get it to the marketplace, documentation test and evaluation cannot extend unreasonably beyond the completion of acceptance testing; this period usually defines the time at which documentation test and evaluation must end. In short, program test and evaluation govern the start and end points of documentation test and evaluation.

Module Testing

During module testing, programmers will test program modules as they create them. Eventually, these modules will be tested by other programmers, assigned testers, and others on the programming staff involved in wringing out the program. Such testing often proceeds iteratively: a module is created and tested, errors are found, it is revised, tested again, and so forth. Eventually, it will be in good enough shape to put on the shelf, allowing the programmer to begin work on the next module. The programmer and others then go through the same process for the next module, the next, and so on, until enough modules have been completed to begin module integration.

At this early stage of program development, formal documentation test and evaluation is usually impractical. However, considerable informal work can be done. First, documentation developers can use working modules to support documentation development and to verify the accuracy of documentation concerning particular modules. Each item of factual information in an item of documentation should be tested against the program itself. Nothing should be presented in documentation *unless* it has been verified to be complete and accurate.

Thus, the documentation developer can use the preliminary version of a module both to support documentation development and to verify the accuracy of the part of the document devoted to the module.

Integration Testing

In practical terms, integration testing is indistinguishable from module testing. The tester will continue to work on the program and attempt to identify defects, and the program will undergo further refinement. As modules are combined, the program resembles, increasingly, the final product. It therefore becomes more useful to the document developer in support both of document development and verification.

Documentation test and evaluation during both module and integration testing is informal, performed by documentation developers themselves. It is not until acceptance testing commences that actual operators get into the act.

Acceptance Testing

The purpose of acceptance testing is to determine how well typical operators can use the program. Usability is governed not only by the program itself but by several other factors, one of which is user documentation. Acceptance testing focuses primarily on the program and its usability. Testers are concerned with such matters as operator errors, how long it takes to complete tasks, areas of difficulty, and anything that reflects on the program. Such testing often leads to the discovery of design defects that have nothing to do with the program's usability. However, acceptance testing is not primarily intended to uncover such defects. Rather, its concern is program usability.

Acceptance tests are most effective when conducted on a complete program. The realities of program development are such that this will often be impossible, and acceptance testing must occur concurrently with module and integration testing. If so, whatever modules are tested should be complete and have complete documentation.

The Test and Evaluation Process

Documentation user testing usually occurs during acceptance testing, although it may occur earlier or later, depending on circumstances. What is required of such tests is that a formal testing process be followed. The main components of this process are a test plan, subjects, subject training, tasks, data collection methods, stimulus materials, an operating program, and user documentation. The testing process specifies the content of each component and the relationships among the components.

The steps and components in the process follow.

Step 1. Select Tasks

User documentation is intended to help the user operate the program to accomplish certain tasks. Thus, user testing must assess the degree to which a sample of users can perform all or a representative selection of these tasks. The first step in the testing process is to select the tasks to be covered during testing. The list of tasks to be tested should be extensive and should address all major phases of software use. Do not assume that certain tasks are so simple that users will have no problems performing them. At the very least, select a variety of tasks from different functional areas of the product.

Step 2. Determine Data-Collection Methods

Documentation may be tested in several different ways, ranging from the informal to the highly formal. Among the methods commonly used are the following:

- Indirect methods
  - Interviews
  - Subject logs
  - Questionnaires
  - Rating scales
- Direct methods
  - Observations
  - Written tests
  - Performance tests

None of these methods is the "best" method, in the comparative sense. Each is suitable for obtaining a different type of information. The indirect methods do not directly reflect subject performance with the program or the documentation; the direct methods do.

The indirect methods provide less hard data, are less expensive to apply, and are more open-ended. By "open-ended" it is meant that subjects (participants in the tests) can volunteer thoughts on shortcomings in program and documentation. It is desirable to obtain at least some open-ended data, i.e., to let subjects make observations and suggestions. Alternatively, the direct methods are more conclusive in what they tell. Thus, test and evaluation should involve a combination of indirect and direct methods.

Indirect methods. Interviews may be unstructured or structured. Unstructured interviews usually focus on a few general questions, and the person being interviewed is able to respond quite broadly, make comments, and offer insights. Structured interviews are based on a detailed set of questions and allow less leeway in responses. While interviews are useful for gaining general information on a subject's reactions, attitudes, or opinions concerning a program and its documentation, they do not reflect actual performance and are inconclusive.

A subject's log is a log written by the subject while operating a program. Its primary value is as a memory aid to the subject during interviews or while completing written questionnaires. It is particularly important during user testing as a way of identifying errors encountered while operating the program or in program documentation. This log is a sort of diary that is completed as each task assignment is performed. It is a record of both objective information concerning program and documentation defects and the operator's subjective experiences in using program and documentation.

Questionnaires are the written equivalent of the interview. Like interviews, they may be unstructured or structured. Unstructured (open-ended) questionnaires focus on a few general questions and permit broad responses. Structured questionnaires contain a detailed set of questions and require specific responses. Like interviews, questionnaires are helpful for gaining general information but are inconclusive.

Rating scales require the subject to rate something on a numeric scale. For example, the subject might be asked to rate the ease of access of reference information in a manual on a scale from 1 to 5. It is crucially important in using this technique to provide "anchoring points," i.e., labels that define the meaning of the end points of the scale. If this is not done, raters will use their own internal, and differing, rating criteria. In the example just given, a scale value of 1 might be assigned the label "very easy to use" and a value of 5 the label "very difficult to use." Another effective approach is to anchor a number of different scales, each for a different aspect of documentation, as having "high effectiveness" or "low effectiveness." In this way, relative assessments can be made of different features of the documentation, and priorities can be established for addressing problem areas. Rating scales can be used to "objectify" subjective data and are an extension of the questionnaire and interview techniques; they may be administered as part of a questionnaire or during an interview.

With either an interview or a questionnaire, it is important to verify that the users have had considerable exposure to the program and are thoroughly familiar with the features under examination. It is only when a user becomes very familiar with a product that many of the problems with the documentation surface. The more experience subjects have with a product, the more information they can provide. Individuals with limited exposure to the product will have the least to say, and what they say will often be obvious to system and documentation developers. This concept was verified by Harris, Casey, and Brubaker (1986) in a study of human factors issues in a computer-aided design system. Based on over 30 extensive interviews and 300 surveys returned by users, the researchers concluded that there was a direct relationship between experience with the system and the user's ability to critique system capabilities and documentation. In summary, it is important to test the naive user but equally important to test the user who is familiar with all aspects of the product.

An alternative to the written log, which can slow the subject as he or she records notes (perhaps on the document itself), is the use of a tape recorder. When using documentation for the first time, subjects can be given a dictating machine on which to record any comments as they attempt to use the documentation. Set procedures for making voice records can be provided for the subject, e.g., stating the page and paragraph number, the problem they are trying to solve, what is it they do not understand, and so forth. Videotaping also falls into this category, but with any record of this type, retrieving the data off of the record can be very time-consuming. An audiotape approach can be designed to work around some of these potential problems if recording procedures are established for the subjects.

Direct methods.   The direct methods are direct in the sense that they reflect actual performance by the subject. The subject may be observed while using the program and supporting documentation, tested to determine recall of facts and procedures, or put through a performance test requiring the use of the program and documentation. These methods can demonstrate conclusively that a program can be operated or that an item of documentation is able to do its job.

The observational technique, like interviews and questionnaires, may be used formally or informally. Informal observations of subjects are quite common. As the subject attempts to use the program, a trainer or subject-matter expert will usually be in attendance, answering questions, identifying problems, and overseeing the session. The observer may make notes concerning problems encountered, possible solutions, and anything else that seems to be of importance to the successful operation of the program.

Formal observation involves watching the subject and keeping records according to a detailed protocol. The observer will record such information as keystrokes, errors, times to complete operations, and other actions. The protocols may require various levels of detail, depending upon their objectives.

Written tests assess the subject's knowledge of information concerning the program. Part of this knowledge is gained from documentation, and part from previous interactions with the program. While such tests can be useful in assessing the subject's knowledge about facts and procedures, they do not actually require the subject to operate the program or use the documentation. Hence, they have less face validity than performance tests. They are one technique for assessing documentation in isolation. For example, if two alternative forms of documentation have been prepared, these can be provided to different groups of subjects, and the two forms of documentation can later be compared on the basis of written test scores.

Performance tests require the subject to perform a task to demonstrate a level of competence. Like written tests, they can focus on the program, the documentation, or both. Such tests are the most powerful way of evaluating the program and documentation, since they require the subject to perform.

A performance test concerning the operation of a computer program will consist of a task to perform under certain conditions. The subject is then put before the computer and asked to produce certain results. Subject performance is measured during the task and afterward. Such measures usually reflect accuracy and speed in performing the intermediate steps and in producing an acceptable end result. A similar technique can be used to test an item of documentation in isolation. For example, the subject might be provided with documentation and directed to obtain certain information and record it.

Making the choice of methods. The appropriate choice of methods depends very much on the goals of and resources available during test and evaluation. If the goals are to establish, conclusively, that program or documentation are adequate for a broad range of representative users, then both indirect and direct methods must be used. If the goals are more limited—and the developer has other evidence that the documentation is adequate—then indirect methods can be used alone.

Some combination of all of these methods is desirable. Virtually every test and evaluation should use posttest interviews with subjects, and these interviews should include both structured and a few open-ended questions. Every subject should be required to maintain a log. If many detailed questions must be asked and interviews cannot cover the ground, questionnaires should be used. Rating scales are also optional.

Every evaluation should involve some observations of subjects; if procedures are tricky, then a protocol should be developed and formal observations should be made.

Written and performance tests are the most conclusive methods to assess the effectiveness of program, documentation, or both; they are also the most expensive and time-consuming. Of these two methods, the performance test is the most valid indicator of the subject's ability to operate the program or use the documentation. The written test is primarily of value in comparative studies of alternative forms of documentation or program features. However, comparative studies are relatively rare during documentation test and evaluation; the primary goal is to evaluate a single existing program or documentation system. If the program and documentation being developed have many untried features and if resources are available, then a fairly wide range of performance tests should be used. Where untried features are fewer or resources are more limited, performance tests should be used selectively on representative and potentially error-prone features.

Step 3. Select Subjects

Select subjects who are typical of the eventual users of the program and documentation. They should have the background, technical knowledge, and skills you expect in the target audience. Unless this audience includes programmers, do not include programmers in testing. Programmers are not typical users—they can overcome many obstacles that nonprogrammers cannot.

If the program and documentation will be used by a range of users of different backgrounds, technical knowledge, and skills, then it is necessary to select representatives of this range. Ideally, a sufficient number of subjects in each user category is used, and data are obtained from each group separately. An alternative approach is to select subjects from the least able group and to base the test and evaluation on the data obtained from that group. There is some danger in doing this; what serves computer novices is not always acceptable to experts, as discussed previously. However, if most program and documentation users belong to the least able category, it is reasonable to focus on them during user testing.

The number of subjects to use is problematical. If statistical methods are to be employed, the number of subjects is governed by the requirements of statistical significance. User testing is usually less formal and does not have such requirements. However, a sufficient number of subjects must be used to obtain a consensus on interviews, questionnaires, and ratings, as well as to get convincing results on written and performance tests. In all but the most informal tests, a reasonable minimum number of subjects to use is about a dozen; this number will not usually support statistical evaluation. Using more subjects is desirable. Using fewer compromises data generalizability.

Step 4. Write Test and Evaluation Plan

A test and evaluation plan is important as a guide in implementing the test and evaluation process. Like most plans, it specifies the who, what, where, when, and how of the process it covers. The who are subjects and test administrators. The what are the objects of evaluation—program, documentation, or both. The where is the location of the test and evaluation. The when are the times at which test and evaluation events are to occur. The how are the methods to be used for data collection and analysis.

Step 5. Develop Stimulus Materials

The term "stimulus materials" is used broadly here to refer to the various materials required during training, task performance, and data collection. This includes such training materials as lesson plans and tests; task performance materials, such as task assignments to be performed at the computer; and such data collection materials as interview protocols, questionnaires, rating forms, observation protocols, written and performance tests, schedules, and anything else required to implement the test and evaluation. These must be developed before test and evaluation commence.

Step 6. Train Subjects

Subjects must be trained appropriately for the test and evaluation. "Appropriate" means suitable for the types of users and the conditions under which the program will be used in practice. If the program is of the desktop variety and most users will learn to operate it on their own, then no training is required; in fact, such training compromises the evaluation, as it supports learning by other means than will be provided when the program is delivered to the user. Alternatively, if the program is complex and will require some formal training, then subjects should be trained in the manner they will be in practice.

Step 7. Collect Data

Data collection occurs during and after the subjects perform task assignments at the computer. These task assignments must be specific and require the subjects to exercise all or most of the major facets of the program, using the documentation in support. The nature of the task assignments depends on the program. Ideally, these assignments are comprehensive. If this is impractical due to resource limitations or program complexity, then task assignments should cover, as a minimum, key tasks in each representative area of the program and the most difficult or error-prone tasks.

The subjects perform the task assignments and data are collected.

Step 8. Analyze Data

The data collected during step 7 are analyzed formally. Conclusions are reached concerning the causes of performance deficiencies, and these are related back to the program and supporting documentation. A set of recommendations is then prepared for making revisions to program, documentation, or both.

Step 9. Revise Program and Documentation

The recommendations prepared during step 8 are provided to the program design and documentation staff. Program and documentation are revised accordingly.

If serious problems are encountered during step 8, it may be necessary to retest the program and collect additional data to ensure that the changes made to program and documentation have had their desired effects. In principle, test and evaluation continue until the data indicate that program and documentation are satisfactory.

Bibliography

Adams, D.: *The Hitchhiker's Guide to the Galaxy*, Pocket Books, New York, 1979.

Aristotle: "The Poetics," in F. Ferguson (ed.), *Aristotle's Poetics*, Hill and Wang, New York, 1961.

Bailey, R.W.: *Human Performance Engineering: A Guide for System Designers*, Prentice-Hall, Englewood Cliffs, N.J., 1983.

Bannon, L.J.: "Helping Users Help Each Other," in D.A. Norman and S.W. Draper (eds.), *User Centered System Design*, Erlbaum, Hillsdale, N.J., 1986.

Bethke, F.: "Measuring the Usability of Software Manuals," *Technical Communication*, vol. 29, no. 2, 1983, pp. 13–16.

Biedny, D., and Berman, I.: "The Business of Desktop Publishing," *MacUser, Special Supplement on Desktop Publishing*, June 1986, pp. 13–17.

Bobker, S.: "The ABC's of Desktop Publishing," *MacUser, Special Supplement on Desktop Publishing*, June 1986, pp. 1–5.

Boomer, H.R.: "Relative Comprehensibility of Pictorial Information and Printed Words in Proceduralized Instructions," *Human Factors*, vol. 17, no. 3, 1975, pp. 266–267.

Boucher, D.A.: "Electronic Publishing Taking Off in Business Sector," *Computer Graphics Today*, May 1986, pp. 17–45.

Bransford, J.D., and Johnson, M.K.: "Contextual Prerequisites for Understanding: Some Investigations of Comprehension and Scale," *Journal of Verbal Learning and Verbal Behavior*, vol. 11, no. 6, 1972, pp. 717–726.

Burgess, J.H.: *Human Factors in Form Design*, Nelson-Hall, Chicago, 1984.

Card, S.K., W.K. English, and B.J. Burr: "Evaluation of Mouse, Rate-Controlled Isometric Joystick, Step Keys, and Text Keys for Text Selection on a CRT," *Ergonomics*, vol. 21, no. 8, 1978, pp. 601–613.

Card, W.K., T.P. Moran, and A. Newell: *The Psychology of Human-Computer Interaction*, Erlbaum, Hillsdale, N.J., 1983.

Carroll, J.M., and J.C. Thomas: "Metaphor and the Cognitive Representation of Computing Systems," *Human Factors*, vol. 12, no. 26, no. 4, 1984, pp. 377–389.

Carroll, J.M., and J.C. Thomas: "Metaphor and the Cognitive Representation of Computing Systems," *IEEE Transactions on Systems, Man, and Cybernetics*, vol. 12, no. 2, 1982, pp. 107–116.

Casey, S.M., and D.H. Harris: *Results of Interviews with CADD Users: TN-650-1*, Anacapa Sciences, Santa Barbara, Calif., 1986.

Chapanis, A.: *Ethnic Variables in Human Factors Engineering*, Johns Hopkins University, Baltimore, 1975.

Chase, W.G., and H.H. Clark: "Mental Operations in the Comparison of Sentences and Pictures," in L. Gregg (ed.), *Cognition in Learning and Memory*, Wiley, New York, 1972.

Clark, H.H. and Chase, W.G.: "On the Process of Comparing Sentences Against Pictures," *Cognitive Psychology*, vol. 3, pp. 472–517.

Cleveland, W.S.: *The Elements of Graphing Data*, Wadsworth, Monterey, Calif., 1985.

Cohill, A., and L. Folley: "Document Design for an Interactive System," *Proceedings of the Human Factors Society 27th Annual Meeting*, Human Factors Society, Santa Monica, Calif., 1983, pp. 1039–1042.

Davis, D.B.: "Business Turns to In-House Publishing," *High Technology*, April 1986, pp. 18–26.

Dearborne, W.F., P.W. Johnson, and L. Carmichael: "Improving the Readability of Typewritten Manuscripts," *Proceedings of the National Academy of Sciences*, vol. 37, 1951, pp. 670–672.

DeLeon, L., W.G. Harris, and M. Evans: "Is There Really Trouble with UNIX?" *Proceedings, Human Factors in Computing Systems*, Association for Computing Machinery, Baltimore, Md., 1983, pp. 125–129.

Dewer, R.E.: "The Slash Obscures the Symbol on Prohibitive Traffic Signs," *Human Factors*, vol. 18, no. 3, 1976, pp. 253–258.

Dickinson, J.: "The Business of Words," *PC Magazine*, January 28, 1986, pp. 93–200.

Dooling, D. and Lachman, R.: "Effects of Comprehension on Retention of Prose," *Journal of Experimental Psychology*, vol. 88, 1971, 216–222.

Duffy, T.M., T.E. Curran, and D. Sass: "Document Design for Technical Job Tasks: An Evaluation," *Human Factors*, vol. 25, no. 2, 1985, pp. 143–160.

Felici, J., and E. Spire: "A Face for All Seasons," *MacWorld*, February 1985, pp. 44–50.

Folley, L.J., and R.C. Williges: "User Models of Text and Editing Command Languages," *Proceedings, Human Factors in Computer Systems*, Human Factors Society, Santa Monica, Calif., 1982, pp. 326–331.

Foster, J., and P. Coles: "An Experimental Study of Topographic Cueing in Printed Text," *Ergonomics*, vol. 20, no. 1, 1977, pp. 57–66.

Fowler, R.L., and A.S. Barker: "Effectiveness of Highlighting for Retention of Text Material," *Journal of Applied Psychology*, vol. 59, no. 2, 1974, pp. 358–364.

Goodman, D.: "Publishing Turns into an Electric Leaf," *MacWorld*, July 1985, pp. 70–79.

Green, Casey: "Micro Planner for Macintosh Is Expensive, Hard to Learn," *InfoWorld*, November 11, 1985, pp. 36–39.

Greene, J.: "The Semantic Function of Negatives and Passives," *British Journal of Psychology*, vol. 61, no. 1, 1970, pp. 17–22.

Haney, R.: "The Effects of Format on Functional Testing Performance," *Human Factors*, vol. 11, no. 2, 1969, pp. 181–188.

Harris, D.H., S.M. Casey, and C. Brubaker: *Factors in User-Computer Effectiveness: Study of the CADD System* (TR 650-3), Anacapa Sciences, Santa Barbara, Calif., 1986.

Hendricks, D., R. Kilduff, P. Brooks, R. Marshak, and B. Doyle: *Human Engineering Guidelines for Management Information Systems*, U.S. Army Material Development and Readiness Command and Management Information Systems Directorate, Human Engineering Laboratory, Aberdeen, Md., 1982.

Hershberger, W.A., and D.F. Terry: "Typographic Cueing in Conventional and Programmed Text," *Journal of Applied Psychology*, vol. 49, no. 1, 1965, pp. 55–60.

Hiltz, S.R., and M. Turoff: "Human Diversity abd the Choice of Interface: A Design Challenge," *Proceedings, Human Interaction and the User Interface*, Association for Computing Machinery, Ann Arbor, Mich., 1981, pp. 125–130.

Houghton-Alico, D.: *Creating Computer Software User Guides: From Manuals to Memos*, McGraw-Hill, New York, 1985.

Hudson, W.: "Pictorial Depth Perception in Sub-cultural Groups in Africa," *Journal of Social Psychology*, vol. 52, 1960, pp. 183–208.

Hudson, W.: "The Study of the Problem of Pictorial Perception Among Unaccultured Groups," *International Journal of Psychology*, vol. 2, 1968, pp. 89–107.

Inside Macintosh (2 vols.), Apple Computer, Cupertino, Calif., 1984.

Judisch, J.M., B.A. Rupp, and R.A. Dassinger: "Effects of Manual Style on Performance in Education and Machine Maintenance," *IBM Systems Journal*, vol. 20, no. 2, 1981, pp. 172–183.

Kammann, P.: "The Comprehensibility of Printed Instructions and the Flow Chart Alternative," *Human Factors*, vol. 17, no. 2, 1975, pp. 183–191.

Kernighan, B.W., and D.M. Ritchie: *The C Programming Language*, Prentice-Hall, Englewood Cliffs, N.J., 1978.

Klare, G.R., J.E. Mabry, and L.M. Gustafson: "The Relationship of Patterning (Underlying) to Immediate Retention and to Acceptability of Technical Material," *Journal of Applied Psychology*, vol. 39, no. 1, 1955, pp. 40–42.

Kraut, R.E., S.J. Hanson, and J.M. Farber: "Command Use and Interface Design," *Proceedings, Human Factors in Computing Systems*, Association for Computing Machinery, Baltimore, Md., 1983, pp. 120–124.

Lachman, R., J.L. Lachman, and E.C. Butterfield: *Cognitive Psychology and Information Processing*, Erlbaum, Hillsdale, N.J., 1979.

Limanowski, J.J.: "On-Line Documentation Systems: History and Issues," *Proceedings of the Human Factors Society 27th Annual Meeting*, Human Factors Society, Santa Monica, Calif., 1983, pp. 1027–1030.

Lu, C.: "Page Make-up Programs for Micros," *High Technology*, April 1986, p. 22.

Macintosh Plus, Apple Computer, Cupertino, Calif., 1986.

"Macintosh Provides Elegant Solution," *Computer Graphics Today*, May 1986, p. 4.

Mayer, R.E.: "Can Advance Organizers Influence Meaningful Learning?" *Review of Educational Research*, vol. 37, no. 2, 1979a, pp. 371–383.

Mayer, R.E.: "Twenty Years of Research on Advance Organizers: Assimilation Theory Is Still the Best Predictor of Results," *Instructional Science*, vol. 8, no. 2, 1979b, pp. 133–167.

Maynard, H.B. (ed.): *Industrial Engineering Handbook*, McGraw-Hill, New York, 1971.

Microsoft Chart (program documentation), Microsoft, Bellevue, Wash., 1984.

Meilach, D.Z.: "IBM PC Programs Striving for Macintosh Look," *Computer Graphics Today*, May 1986, pp. 18–22.

Miller, G.A.: "The Magic Number Seven, Plus or Minus Two: Some Limits on Our Capacity to Process Information," *Psychological Review*, vol. 63, no. 1, 1956, pp. 81–97.

Miller, G.A.: "Some Psychological Studies of Grammar," *American Psychologist*, vol. 17, no. 11, 1962, pp. 748–762.

Moses, F.L., and S.L. Ehrenreich: "Abbreviations for Automated Systems," *Proceedings of the Human Factors Society 25th Annual Meeting*, Human Factors Society, Santa Monica, Calif., 1981.

Mosier, J.N.: "Design and Validation of a Checklist to Aid in Choosing Word Processor Software," *Proceedings of the Human Factors Society 28th Annual Meeting*, Human Factors Society, Santa Monica, Calif., 1984, pp.165–169.

Norman, D.A.: "The Trouble with UNIX," *Datamation*, November 1981, pp. 139–150.

Onosko, T.: "You're My Type," *MacUser, Special Supplement on Desktop Publishing*, June 1986, pp. 18–24.

Paller, A., K. Szoka, and N. Nelson: *Choosing the Right Chart*, Integrated Software Systems, San Diego, Calif., 1981.

Poor, A., and B. Brown: "Project Management Software: The Top Sellers," *PC Magazine*, February 11, 1986.

Simpson, H.: *Design of User-Friendly Programs for Small Computers*, McGraw-Hill, New York, 1985a.

Simpson, H.: *Programming the IBM PC User Interface*, McGraw-Hill, New York, 1985b.

Simpson, H.: *Programming the Macintosh User Interface*, McGraw-Hill, New York, 1986.

Smith, S.: "Exploring Compatibility of Words and Pictures," *Human Factors*, vol. 23, no. 3, 1981, pp. 305–315.

Tinker, M.A.: *Legibility of Print*, Iowa State University Press, Ames, Ia., 1963.

Trollip, S.R., and G. Sales: "Readability of Computer-Generated Fill-Justified Text," *Human Factors*, vol. 23, no. 2, 1986, pp. 159–163.

Tufte, E.R.: *The Visual Display of Quantitative Information*, Graphics Press, Cheshire, Conn., 1983.

Walker, J.: "Outline Documentation and Help Systems," *Tutorial 5, CHI'86*, Boston, Mass., April 1986.

Wesley, M.D.: "Pagemaker Then and Now," *MacUser, Special Supplement on Desktop Publishing*, June 1986, pp. 27–28.

Whitaker, L.A., and S. Stacey: "Response Times to Left and Right Directional Signals," *Human Factors*, vol. 23, no. 4, 1981, pp. 447–452.

Wickens, C.D.: *Engineering Psychology and Human Performance*, Charles E. Merrill, Columbus, Ohio, 1984.

Wiedman, T., and F. Ireland: "A New Look at Procedures Manuals," *Human Factors*, vol. 7, no. 4, 1965, pp. 371–377.

Winter, W.: "The Perception of Safety Posters of Bantu Industrial Workers," *Psychological Africana*, vol. 10, no. 1, 1963, pp. 127–135.

"Word Processing Programs for IBM, AT&T, Compaq, and Other Compatible Personal Computers," *Software Digest: Ratings Newsletter*, January 1986, pp. 1–73.

WordPerfect Word Processing Software (program documentation), SSI, Orem, Utah, 1985.

Index

About the Authors

HENRY SIMPSON is a research psychologist with the training technology department for the human factors group at the U.S. Navy Personnel Research and Development Center in San Diego. Previously, he was a senior scientist with Anacapa Sciences, Inc., and a research engineer and project director with Human Factors Research, Inc. He holds a B.S.E.E., an M.A. in English, and a Ph.D. in Educational Psychology from the University of California at Santa Barbara. His areas of special interest are cognitive psychology and human factors. Dr. Simpson has conducted research, designed and developed management information systems and other programs for microcomputers, and is the author of 10 books. His three previous books for McGraw-Hill are *Design of User-Friendly Programs for Small Computers, Programming the IBM PC User Interface,* and *Programming the Macintosh User Interface.* His articles on microcomputers have appeared in such publications as *BYTE, Microcomputing,* and *Digital Design.*

STEVEN M. CASEY is president of Ergonomic Systems Design, Inc., of Santa Barbara, California. He conducts research and provides human factors design services for developers and manufacturers of software and hardware. He has written user documentation for mainframe computer models, PC-based computer models, and process control systems. Previously, he was principal scientist at Anacapa Sciences, Inc. His 80 publications include articles in *Human Factors* and other technical journals and reports. Dr. Casey holds a Ph.D. and M.S. in Psychology/Human Factors from North Carolina State University and a B.S. in Psychology from the University of California at Santa Barbara.